# BETHLEHEM

# BETHLEHEM

## BIOGRAPHY OF A TOWN

## NICHOLAS BLINCOE

CONSTABLE • LONDON

CONSTABLE

First published in the USA in 2017 by Nation Books,
an imprint of Perseus Books, LLC, a subsidiary of Hachette Book Group, Inc.
This edition published in Great Britain in 2017 by Constable

1 3 5 7 9 10 8 6 4 2

A CIP catalogue record for this book
is available from the British Library.

Hardback ISBN: 978-1-4721-2866-9
Trade paperback ISBN: 978-1-4721-2865-2

Printed and bound in Great Britain by Clays Ltd, St Ives plc

Papers used by Constable are from well-managed forests
and other responsible sources.

Constable
An imprint of
Little, Brown Book Group
Carmelite House
50 Victoria Embankment
London EC4Y 0DZ

An Hachette UK Company
www.hachette.co.uk

www.littlebrown.co.uk

*In Loving Memory of*
*Anton and Raissa Sansour*

# Contents

# CONTENTS

# BETHLEHEM

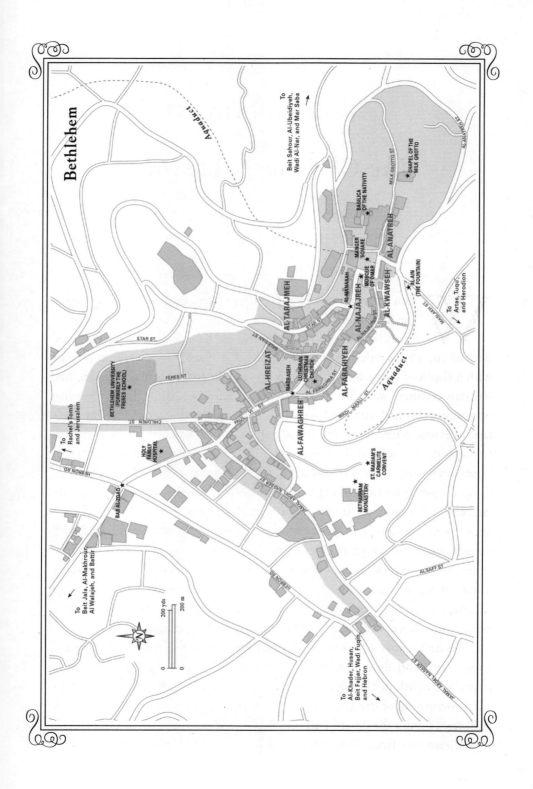

# The Christmas Pudding

When I first visited Bethlehem in December 1994, I came carrying a Christmas pudding. It seemed the ideal gift for my girlfriend's parents—especially at Christmas, especially in Bethlehem. Leila's father, Anton Sansour, was a math professor, a small man with a shock of white hair that stood up straight from his head. Raissa, her Russian mother, was slim and poised and icily beautiful. They were the opposites who had attracted and had been inseparable since the day they met at Radio Moscow in the 1960s, where Anton worked in the evenings to support himself while completing his PhD. Bethlehem was Anton's hometown but oddly, so I thought, he had never seen a Christmas pudding. I wasn't sure how to explain it, so I began reading the list of ingredients aloud. He laughed. It turned out that almost everything in the pudding grew in his garden, and the rest had reached the town on the backs of camels, carried through the desert by Arab traders like the gold, frankincense, and myrrh of the Nativity story. The ingredients on the label, minus a few chemicals, are: sultanas, raisins, almonds, apricots, figs, cinnamon, nutmeg, suet, egg, flour, breadcrumbs, glacé cherries, orange and lemon peel, lemon juice, orange oil, lemon oil, molasses, sugar, and cognac.

This isn't a story of cultural appropriation: the idea of boiling dried fruit, sugar, eggs, and flour until it turns into a dark cannonball is definitely a mark of English genius. Nevertheless, the distinctive gooey Yule taste captures something of the essence of Bethlehem, a place where hills filled with fruit trees border the desert, and the ancient Spice Route carried more exotic ingredients up from the Arabian Peninsula and beyond. This clash of cultures—farmers and nomads—shaped Bethlehem and influenced the course of world history. The ingredients in my Christmas pudding reached Europe's pastry chefs in stages, from the most ancient times, through the Roman era and Islamic age, the Crusades and Ottoman rule, to make my pudding a dough-based relic of East–West trade, and of European relations with the Holy Land. It is a piece of history: it is history made pudding.

THE JORDAN RIFT VALLEY was torn open when the Arabian Peninsula pulled away from Africa in the Miocene period, up to twenty-three million years ago. The desert around Bethlehem once sat deep underwater and the edge of the Mediterranean lapped the borders of modern-day Jordan. The soft-sifting waves gradually laid down millions of years of sediment that turned to limestone, before a fierce earthquake forced the layers upward. Palestine rose out of the sea, pushing the waves back to create the present Mediterranean shoreline. Bethlehem lies toward the southern edge of a chain of mountainous hills known as the Judaean Hills and in Arabic as *Jibal al-Khalil*, the Hebron Mountains or, literally, the Mountains of the Beloved. The hills were formed as the limestone sheets were tilted and concertinaed to create a landscape that is both beautiful and alarming. The entire vista is filled with hills, and hills between hills, until the view looks like the electrocardiogram of a hyperactive heart attack patient.

The Bethlehem *muḥāfaẓat* or governorship ranges between twenty-five hundred and three thousand feet above sea level, though it feels like much more because the Dead Sea is fourteen hundred feet *below* sea level. The line between the Bethlehem wilderness—*El-Bariyah*—and the fertile hills is dramatic: the harsh stone suddenly turns into a rich green landscape filled with terraces of olive groves and orchards, carved from the hills in artificial steps that resemble the sides of Aztec pyramids. The underlying geology of the farmland and desert is much the same; the difference is partly the climate—the height of Bethlehem makes for a cooler, more temperate environment—and partly the rich aquifer trapped in the limestone layers beneath Bethlehem, which keeps the fruit trees so lush and resplendent. The line between wilderness and hill farms has shifted backward and forward over the millennia. The climate changed and the desert grew after the Stone Age. But then, little by little, Bethlehem learned to use its water resources to claw some land back from the wilderness.

These are the hills where humans first decided to put down roots and stick in one spot. The first inhabitants were lazy nomads who found they didn't have to travel with the different seasons; they could just turn from desert to hills without stirring from the spot. In the spring, they could graze their flocks in the wilderness, which the rains briefly transformed into rolling, verdant grassland, while they could farm the flat, rich soil of the wadis between the hills. They learned to breed dogs, and then sheep, and began to plant trees. Almonds were probably the first trees to be domesticated, followed by olive trees. The wealth of Bethlehem's villages was built more than thirty-five hundred years ago when olive oil was carried on pack animals to the cities of the Nile, establishing a pack route that runs south along the present-day Hebron Road, through Beersheba to the Sinai and on to Egypt.

The majority of Bethlehem's orchards lie in a series of valleys that arc around the west of the town, moving counterclockwise from the wine-producing Cremisan Monastery in the north, through a valley of apricot trees named al-Makhrour, to the villages of Battir, Wadi Fuqin, and Nahalin. The valley terraces are artfully watered by natural springs that emerge from between the limestone layers. All the types of nuts and dried fruit inside my pudding are grown in these hills: almonds, apricots, figs, grapes—the different harvests coming almost month-by-month from spring to autumn. The picked fruit is laid on sheets to dry in the shade beneath the trees or, better, indoors so the sun does not make the skin turn tough. The English names of the fruit hint at their route to the pastry ovens. Almond is from the Greek *amygdala*, to which medieval Europeans added an *al-* prefix because they bought their nuts from Arabs; they assumed the word had Arab roots. The original English word for apricot, *abrecock*, is a direct transliteration of the Arabic *al-barquq*. Fig is from the Latin *ficus*, which derives from an older Canaanite name. *Sultana* is "queen" in Arabic; *raisin* comes from the Latin for grape, and *currant* from the Greek town of Corinth. The names read like a chronology of East-West relations through the ages.

THE SPICES IN A CHRISTMAS PUDDING may not grow in Bethlehem, yet in some ways they are the most distinctively local ingredients.

The words "cinnamon" and "*cassia*" (meaning "peel" and referring to the bark of the cinnamon tree) both come from Canaanite, the language spoken in Palestine and Phoenicia before the advent of the Persian Empire, two thousand five hundred years ago. The oldest varieties of cinnamon are grown in Ethiopia; ginger and cloves come from India; nutmeg is found on a group of mysterious islands whose whereabouts was once a closely guarded secret (spoiler alert: it is the Banda Islands, twelve hundred miles east of Java). Indian sugar molasses was traded as white gummy balls until crystal sugar was refined around the fifth century CE. This is how the crusaders first encountered sugar, which they referred to as sweet salt. The Crusades' chronicler, William of Tyre, recommended it for its health benefits.

The Nabataeans dominated the spice trade for a thousand years; they, along with the Idumaeans (or Edomites), were one of two proto-Arab groups that settled in Palestine before the Persian era. Both groups were semi-nomadic shepherds and livestock breeders. However, as early as 800 BCE, the Nabataeans began to roam much further than rival tribes thanks to a talent for finding, using, and storing water in inhospitable conditions. This laid the basis for an astonishing trading network: the Spice Route. The Nabataeans developed trade routes that stretched southwards to encompass India, Ethiopia, and Yemen and upward to their warehouses on the Bay of Naples in southern Italy.

The Spice Route, in turn, spawned cities founded by allies and rivals of the Nabataeans as way stations, customs houses, and markets. Everyone wanted to profit from the trade. In Palestine, this was not limited to spice, sugar, and incense. The fulcrum of the Nabataeans' commercial empire was the Dead Sea, a kind of natural chemical plant that produces bitumen, potash, fuller's earth, and other noxious elements. Bethlehem straddles an important trade route up from the Dead Sea known as Wadi Khreitoun that ultimately connects the Dead Sea to Jaffa and Gaza. At some point in the first millennium BCE, a new town named Tuqu' was created at the summit of Wadi Khreitoun, marking the point where the wilderness meets civilization. Tuqu' is a barren spot and so an aqueduct had to be scoured through the limestone, up the valley to the freshwater spring at Artas, a small village that might be the oldest in the Bethlehem district.

With the construction of the Tuqu'-Artas aqueduct, the Bethlehem area began to take the shape of an urban center. But it was only with the construction of a far more ambitious aqueduct, under Greek rule around 200 BCE, that the town of Bethlehem was born, making it one of the more recently established towns in the region.

EACH OF THE VILLAGES DOTTED across Bethlehem's hills is nurtured by springs erupting from the the aquifer in the limestone substrata, below. Only Bethlehem itself is dry, relying on water from the spring at Artas. The first of the three reservoirs that now stand above Artas was dug under Greek rule to feed Jerusalem. This Bethlehem-Jerusalem aqueduct follows the contours of a dozen hills from Artas to the great man-made chambers beneath Jerusalem's temple. Along the way, it tunnels under the hill on which the Church of the Nativity stands. The aqueduct brought water to this rocky outcrop for the first time, allowing us to date the town. The aqueduct enabled the creation of a town fountain, and Bethlehem grew around it.

Bethlehem is far younger than the traditional accounts allow. Indeed, the town was founded only around two hundred years before the birth of Christ. Like Tuqu', it began life as a buffer between the desert and farmland. Bethlehem sits on a small, round hill with fine vistas, making it a valuable military redoubt. But it was only the building of the aqueduct that allowed it to become a population center, unlike the older villages with their natural springs.

One of the ways we can date the Bethlehem aqueduct is by its mention in the "Letter of Aristeas," a short document that chronicles the creation of the Bible. Jewish scribes in Alexandria laid the ground work for a single book around the turn of the second century BCE, by shaping and polishing older stories. The letter connects the appearance of the Bible with the construction of the new aqueduct, as the Jewish faith was reshaped around the twin pillars of scripture and pilgrimage. The aqueduct allowed Jerusalem to accommodate the tens of thousands of pilgrims that visited the city each year from Alexandria and across the Middle East.

The Jewish faith has ancient roots in a military cult dedicated to a god named *Yehu.* The traditional Bible story is that these proto-Jewish warriors travelled to Canaan from Mesopotamia, now Iraq, in the distant past. Historians agree, however, that the new faith emerged in the Iron Age from the wider Canaanite-speaking region, an area that includes much of Syria as well as Israel and Palestine. Jerusalem was just one of many pocket kingdoms established by these proto-Jewish warriors. It was a temple-garrison to Yehu from where they ruled over the surrounding farmers and peasants, and paid tribute in their turn to yet more powerful kings and emperors. The Yehu faith spread as the warriors intermarried with locals, acted as governors and mercenaries for the era's great imperial powers, and gathered converts that cut across borders of language and ethnicity and tribe. When Alexander the Great conquered Palestine in the fourth century BCE, he allied with Yehu forces from Samaria but distrusted Jerusalem. As a result, the city was demilitarized. This had the unintended consequence of boosting the power of the city's priests, which led in turn to the emergence of Jerusalem's temple as a spectacular pilgrim destination, famous for animal sacrifices and the burning of a wealth of Nabataean incense.

Under the rule of its priests, Jerusalem became a boomtown, a place of both sanctity and entertainment. In time, the first Bethlehem-Jerusalem aqueduct proved insufficient for the multitudes of tourists, pilgrims, and newcomers. As Greek rule gave way to Roman, the Jewish King Herod the Great dug new reservoirs above Artas and built a second high-level aqueduct in the Roman style following a direct route north along Bethlehem's Hebron Road to Jerusalem. At the same time, Herod built a new summer palace above Tuqu', which he named Herodion, and renovated the original Tuqu' aqueduct to serve it. This is the Bethlehem that the Holy Family knew, a building site that tied the small town into Jerusalem's infrastructure, to support the grandiose visions of Herod.

Dating Bethlehem to the construction of the Jerusalem aqueduct introduces an ambiguity into the town's name. In the language of Canaan, Bethlehem means "House of Bread," while in Arabic it is "House of Meat." By the time Bethlehem was founded, Canaanite was a language of the distant past and "House of Bread"—*Beit Lechem*—is an ill-fitting name for the town. Bethlehem is set among water-rich hills at the edge of the desert. It is perfect farmland for orchards, not wheat. Of course, both wheat and barley have been grown in Bethlehem wherever the vertiginous landscape allows, but Palestine's breadbasket lies to the north in Jenin or on the plains of what is now Israel.

A history of Bethlehem should be able to answer the question: Was Christ born in this town? The most compelling evidence in favour is that pilgrims began visiting Bethlehem within a hundred years of his life, perhaps even within living memory of his crucifixion, and certainly close enough to establish a strong collective memory. The counterargument is that the gospel accounts are hard to square with each other and seem designed to establish a connection to the legendary David, the nomadic shepherd boy who rose to become a king. If it is impossible to come down on one side or the other, the Christian Gospels of Matthew and Luke nevertheless display a familiarity with the first-century city of Bethlehem that makes them invaluable historical accounts of the town.

Bethlehem's resources are its water and climate, and its proximity to the wilderness, El-Bariyeh, which bring the nomadic graziers to the town's market. The Gospel stories tell us that Bethlehem was a livestock market: the first people to greet the infant Christ are shepherds. The Bedouin sold their sheep for meat and the wool for processing into yarn. Thanks to Dead Sea chemicals, Bethlehem became a center for a range of icky processes, from cleaning to fulling and dyeing. It is likely that Bethlehem grew up around a sheep market, a fact reflected in the connection to David. The idea that David is a sheep grazier is not peripheral to his story; it is central. The design and construction of Bethlehem as a walled market town with a *caravanserai* (the biblical "inn") at its edge suggests it was conceived as a secure environment to do business with dangerous outsiders, and no one carried more of a threat to townsfolk than nomadic shepherds. At the time of Christ's birth, the shepherds who knelt before his cradle would have been Bedouin-like figures, either Arabs or proto-Arabs like the Idumeans who lived in the nearby city of Hebron. This connection to sheep and shepherds suggests that the name Bethlehem may be Arabic rather than Canaanite: *Beit Lahm*, the House of Meat.

Cities and even countries are often named by their visitors rather than by their inhabitants: America owes its name to Italians; Palestine to Greek and Egyptian neighbors who associated the land with the Philistine. It is the people who have to give directions to a place that need to give it a handle, not the people who live there. It is possible, however, that Bethlehem is a homonym of an older Aramaic word, such as *Beit Lamra*, which does means the House of Lamb. It is certainly the most appropriate of names for an ancient livestock market.

The ambiguity between the House of Bread and the House of Meat is reflected in my Christmas pudding, which contains both flour and grated suet, or rendered kidney fat. Suet has a high melting point and only begins to liquefy when the egg-and-flour batter has come together to bake. As the flecks of suet melt away, they leave air pockets that create a lighter texture, while the warm fat moistens the otherwise dry dough. In a Christmas pudding, at least, meat and flour become indistinguishable.

THE CITRUS PEEL IN MY PUDDING comes from both lemon and oranges. Lemons were developed by crossing bitter oranges with the fleshy "citron" mentioned by Pliny the Elder in his first-century CE *Natural History*. Though lemons may have reached Rome from India in the first century, the word is Arabic, and lemons only became widespread under Arabic cultivation in the seventh century. Sweet oranges arrived from China around the eleventh century and were introduced into Europe by the Islamic farmers who had colonized Spain and Sicily. The best varieties of oranges and lemons in Palestine grow in Jericho but, at Christmas, the tree in front of the Sansours' kitchen window held small, hard fruit, so unripe I could not tell if they were oranges or lemons when Leila used them as garnish in our Negronis.

The thousand years that separate the appearance of lemons and oranges saw the creation of many of the institutions, both cultural and physical, that define the Palestinian identity. The period divides neatly in two halves: the Roman era, and the Arab era. But even during the Roman age, Palestine already had a growing Arab flavor. Christianity had much to do with this. The first Christian emperor in 204 CE is Philip the Arab, an epithet he chose himself. Other Roman Arabs created Christian mini-kingdoms along what is now the Syrian-Turkish border—notably, at Edessa and Palmyra. In the latter half of the third century, Jerusalem got the first of several Palmyrene Arab bishops.

From the beginning of the Roman era, well into the Christian period, Bethlehem was home to soldiers and slaves. Rome's Tenth Legion was based in Bethlehem in order to guard Jerusalem's fragile water supply and ward off desert raiders. The silent multitudes who produced olive oil and wine were slaves. In a town of soldiers and slaves, the Christian heritage necessarily came from newer arrivals, and here there was a curious alliance between wealthy Roman women and Arab Christians. Both groups valued Bethlehem's proximity to the wilderness as much as its association with Mary and the birth of Christ. Roman heiresses were drawn to Christ's ascetic nature, reflected in the forty days he spent in the wilderness. Christ's triumph over the biological needs of his human form was inspirational to twenty-something divorcees and widows like Constantine's mother Helena and Jerome's sponsor Paula, who wanted to sidestep their biology to pursue the political power that their wealth and privilege could buy. Arabs were also drawn to the accounts of Christ's struggle in the wilderness, but in their case they saw a reflection of their own desert lives, already the focus of much of their poetry and songs. Christ's life in the desert was imitated by the early Arab Christian saints known as *boskoi*, wild-living hermits.

Roman and Arab influences conjoined in Bethlehem between the fourth and sixth centuries. St. Helena founded the Church of the Nativity, while St. Paula built the town's first monasteries. Arab benefactors and patrons who funded the many monasteries in Bethlehem's desert soon followed them.

The hierarchy of the Roman priesthood is designed to reflect the imperial Roman court with its ascending order of knights, dukes, and kings right up to the emperor. The sixth-century Emperor Justinian made the relation between Constantinople, the city of emperors, with Jerusalem, the city of God, explicit by recasting Palestine as the Holy Land, a term he seems to have invented. The Holy Land may have been a piece of heaven on earth, but it was organized on strict Roman lines with God conceived as the emperor of the skies. In contrast to this Romanized version of Christianity, the Arab desert monasteries represented a more alien and strange version of Christianity, deliberately set apart from this world. This was a fiercer Christianity that adored Christ because he rejected human frailty and found the spiritual strength to triumph over his mortal frame.

CHERRIES AND CITRUS PEEL are turned to candy through an expensive process that originated in Mesopotamia. Candied fruit is still wildly popular in gift shops in Amman, Dubai, and Jedda, and can be far more expensive than rival gifts like chocolate. The fruit is slowly simmered in sugar syrup until the cellulose turns to crystal and the flesh is jellified. These and other complex chemical processes like distillation reached Europe from the Islamic world via Arab merchants and conquerors. In the same period, European pilgrims were introduced to the new sciences as they visited the holy sites.

Roman-Arabs had long represented an important, even elite, class in the Roman *Oriens*, the Latin term for the Middle East. The term "Arab" only applied to Roman citizens at the time. The similar, tribal people who lived outside the empire were known as Saracens. A series of Saracens became allies, or *foederati,* of Rome who paid the tribes to guard the empire's desert borders from raiders and the Persian army. These foederati, the Tanukhids, the Salihids, and, finally, the highly trained and fearsome Ghassanids, were all devout Christian. Rather confusingly, the tribes they were paid to fight were often also either Christian or Jewish Arabs. Both faiths had spread through the margins between the Roman and Persian Empire and had deep roots in the Arabian Peninsula. The foederati were supposed to keep to the borders, not interfere with the life of Roman citizens inside the empire. However, when a revolt by the Samaritans in 529 CE led to the destruction of the church in Bethlehem, Justinian handed the Ghassanids responsibility for Palestine. The Samaritans are drawn from a community of Jews who never accepted the centrality of Jerusalem in Jewish life, and in consequence reject the stories of David and Solomon that underpin Jerusalem's preeminence. In the fifth and sixth centuries, the Samaritans were the largest community in Palestine, but they never recovered from this war against the Ghassanids, which saw their men slaughtered and their women and children sold into slavery.

The Ghassanids were defeated in their turn by the Islamic forces. The Battle of Yarmouk in the Ghassanids' stronghold of the Golan in 636 CE allowed the new Muslim forces to enter Palestine without obstruction. Over the next centuries, Palestine was cut off from the Roman Empire and from Roman-style Christianity. The Middle Eastern church evolved on its own course as the Arab Orthodox Church, part of the wider Eastern Orthodox communion, alongside a number of smaller independent Oriental churches, like Palestine's Arabic-speaking Melkite Church. Other Oriental churches developed in Syria and Lebanon, seeding traditions and cultures that strengthened the three countries' separate identities.

The one ingredient in the pudding with no local connection to Palestine is cognac, though the monks at Bethlehem's Cremisan Monastery distill a brandy they choose to call cognac (they also claim to make madeira, Marsala wine, sherry, and port, for that matter). There is a strong connection between the Cognac region and Palestine, however, hinted at in the fact that the science of distillation reached France via the Holy Land. The Cognac region borders Bordeaux and, first, tin merchants and, later, Christian pilgrims would sail from the British Isles to the inlet at Bordeaux, from where they would follow a pack horse route across country to the Rhône and then down river to Marseilles, the Provençal base for all voyages to the Holy Land.

Communications between Northern Europe and Palestine were carried by tin merchants, pilgrims, and also by slavers. Marseilles was a great slave market. However, it was the entrance of the Scandinavians into the slavery market that most decidedly changed the region. One of these Scandinavian tribes—the Normans—grew so familiar with the Middle East that they became the driving force behind the Crusades.

THE DISTINCTIVE SWEET-SPICED taste of a Christmas pudding is found in other Christmas dishes such as the German *stollen*, or the Provençal "thirteen desserts." The crusaders brought this very specific flavor combination back from Palestine. The flavor is perhaps best showcased in mince pies, which derive from a recipe dating to the time of the First Crusades: a meat confit is slow-cooked in fruit syrup so that the sugar will preserve the meat through winter.

The Crusades came at a time when the old Roman Oriens had split between three regional powers: the Roman Empire with its capital in Constantinople; the Abbasid Caliphate centered on Baghdad; and the Fatimid Caliphate based in Egypt. The buffer zones between these three powers became the door through which a new force arrived: the Seljuk, nomadic Turkish tribes from the remote Asian steppes. A few European mercenaries saw an opportunity for profit and adventure and began fighting in this region, at first on behalf of the Roman Byzantium, then alongside Armenian forces that had established an opportunistic mini-state in the hills behind Antioch. The mercenaries were the Normans who, almost simultaneously with their successful conquest of England, established kingdoms and principalities in Italy from where they staged forays into the Middle East.

The Normans' knowledge of the Syrian borderlands and their friendship with the Armenians gave them the leverage to become the de facto leaders of the Crusades. Better, the Normans also had a strong working idea of how to run Palestine once the fighting had ended. They already ran similar Arab kingdoms in Italy and knew how to govern the kind of ethnic and religious mix they faced in Palestine. In lands from Sicily to Puglia, the Normans retained the Arab civil servants as administrators, minted their own bilingual versions of Arabic currency, and even embraced the Arabs' lemon farming business. The Normans developed close ties and bitter rivalries with the Italian republics: the Venetians, Genoese, Pisans, and Amalfitans, all of whom were trading partners of the Fatimids in Cairo. Throughout the Crusades, the Italians traded with both crusader and Muslim states. After the Crusades were over, Venetian merchants leased land in the old crusader city of Tyre, where they began to manufacture sugar for a European market that had become addicted to the sweet stuff.

In Bethlehem, the Normans rebuilt the Church of the Nativity with a spectacular lack of sympathy for the original Roman building. Though Norman rule in Palestine did not last beyond the first generation of crusaders, they substantially altered the politics of the land because they deprived the local Christians of any say over the institutions they had run for a thousand years. Arab Orthodoxy survived in local parish churches, but not inside Jerusalem's cathedral or Bethlehem's monasteries. This situation persisted after the Ottomans reunified the old Roman Oriens in the sixteenth century. They did not restore power to Palestine's Christians but instead handed power to the Greek-speaking Orthodox Church. This was presented as a restitution of the old order, but in fact the Greek church had evolved far from its roots in the Roman Empire. In Bethlehem, the incoming Greek clergy was simply another alien occupying power.

THE HEAVY DOUGH CANNONBALL that forms the essential architecture of a Christmas pudding is based on savory porridges that medieval peasants would cook up by boiling meat and grain in a muslin bag suspended in a cauldron of boiling water. The fruit "figgy" pudding appeared before the seventeenth century after raisins became widely available in Britain thanks to the fast trading ships of the Levant Company. By the Victorian period, the Christmas pudding had become the centerpiece of the great national holiday, a celebration of family life.

In 1831, six years before Victoria ascended the throne, the army of Muhammad Ali, a renegade Ottoman general who had made himself supreme ruler of Egypt, invaded Bethlehem. Muhammad Ali, who was ethnically Albanian, claimed to be a herald of modernity, and to an extent he was: authoritarian, militaristic, and technocratic. Ali's invasion was met with some sympathy in Palestine because it threw off the Ottomans, but the enthusiasm soured and in 1834 Palestinians united in a revolution against Egyptian rule. This has been dubbed "The Peasant's Revolt" as the majority of the militias were drawn from the agrarian *fellahin* class. However, the rebels included fighters from all sections of Palestinian society, the Bedouin, townsfolk, and the fieldworkers. This was an age that prized national self-determination, and the revolt against Ali is a landmark in Palestinian nationalism.

The foundation of this broad national alliance had been laid by two nationwide political parties, a Palestinian "People's Party" known as the *Yamanis* and the rival conservative party, the *Qais*. Though these names derive from real tribes in the pre-Islamic past of Arabia and the Levant, they were drawn from folktales and represented fictive identities much like the nineteenth-century epithets Whigs and Tories, popularized by British and American political parties. Yamani forces from Bethlehem laid siege to Jerusalem, seizing the capital within a few days. When the city was recaptured in turn by the Egyptians, Bethlehem's sister town of Beit Jala suffered heavy reprisals. By midsummer 1834, the revolution was defeated, though the war left a legacy of popular Palestinian identity.

In the autumn of 1840, the British negotiated an alliance with the Ottoman government in Constantinople. The Royal Navy helped to drive the Egyptians out of Palestine. In November 1840, Admiral Napier fired on the Palestinian port of Acre. One of Napier's new exploding shells hit Acre's munition dump, destroying half the city. The Egyptians fled.

The British have always celebrated the unusual resemblance between their national pudding and a cannonball. A month after Napier's gunboat diplomacy, the young Queen Victoria celebrated her first Christmas with her husband, Albert. The couple had married the previous February and had their first child eight months later in November 1840. Their first Christmas saw the blending of German and British traditions, with the introduction of the German fir tree. In Palestine, this new Anglo-German friendship led to the creation of a joint Lutheran-Anglican bishopric in Jerusalem, and though the period of cooperation was brief, English and German Protestants substantially reshaped Palestine, supported by a keen audience back home ready to buy books and photographs and paintings, and fund the projects of evangelical missionaries, many of which verged on the lunatic.

The Victorians pioneered biblical archaeology as a theoretical sideline to the broader imperial project. The earliest and most famous book on the archaeology of Palestine was by a churchman: Arthur Stanley, the dean of Westminster. *Sinai and Palestine* told the story of his pilgrimage over Christmas and New Year, 1852–1853, and was such a huge success that it resulted in the British government establishing the Palestine Exploration Fund (PEF). The surveys carried out by the British army at the behest of the PEF were particularly helpful when Britain invaded Palestine in 1917.

The PEF portrayed itself as a modern, scientific project, but while Dean Stanley enjoyed hobnobbing with Darwinians, biblical archaeology was far closer in spirit to the Creationists than to Darwin-inspired scientists. The aim of the PEF was explicitly to reveal the original biblical "truth" of Palestine. The archaeologists it employed arrived in the country believing they knew what they would find, if they looked hard enough. Every field survey, every trench, every shard of pottery was merely a detour in pursuit of the stories they knew from Sunday school classes. However long the journey, they believed they would eventually get back to the world created by God and given to Abraham, Moses, and David.

The British captured Bethlehem's reservoirs on December 7, 1917. With the water supplies in British hands, Jerusalem fell four days later. Prime Minister Lloyd George described the capture of Palestine as "a Christmas present for the British people." The link between cannon and Christmas seemed entirely natural, even at the tail end of the imperial age.

The British saw the landscape of Palestine through the Bibles they carried in their knapsacks. The results of this original Christian-Zionism are visible around Bethlehem as the forty-two Israeli settlements that surround the city flow from the version of history manufactured by Dean Stanley and his followers. Though it is obvious that Bethlehem is nowhere near as old as the Bible claims, western archaeologists came armed with their own ideas of truth, and anything that contradicted their preconceived ideas was overlooked or erased.

WHEN I WAS PLANNING my Christmas gift for Anton and Raissa, I imagined a pudding with a traditional lucky coin baked inside. This is why I went shopping in Harrods: I hoped the fancier store would have what I wanted. I was really thinking back to the Christmases of my childhood, when my grandmother used to stir a silver sixpence into her pudding mix. The idea that Bethlehem needed luck was in the air in 1994, the year the Oslo Peace Accords were signed. Not to ruin the story for anyone who doesn't know how the Oslo Accords worked out, but I can tell you that Harrods does not sell a pudding with a lucky sixpence.

The story of Bethlehem is the story of orchards and shepherds, of farmers and nomads. These are not the kind of things that leave deep marks in the historical record. Inevitably, a history of Bethlehem is a history of the times that swirl around it and of the wider landscape that surrounds it. It's lucky, of course, that time *literally* hinges on Bethlehem, as we count forward and backward from Christ's birth. But there were moments in the research process when I worried that Bethlehem might disappear from view. I had all this material, some sweet, some stodgy, and I wondered if Bethlehem was in danger of disappearing from its own biography. My fears lessened as the work grew. Bethlehem was always there, like the lucky sixpence in my grandmother's pudding, glinting in the mix.

Focusing on Bethlehem brings a new perspective to a familiar story. Histories of the Holy Land revolve around Jerusalem, a city where history and myth are too easily confused. At the time the Bible stories were being collected into a single book, the importance of Jerusalem was by no means agreed, even among the Jews. Jewish warlords ruled over equally powerful cities such as Samaria and Amman. Understandably, these other rulers saw their own temples and priests as the equal of Jerusalem. The problem of telling a story that places Jerusalem at the center of both the land *and* its faith—as though this amounted to the same thing—is that one has already adopted a set of filters that blend myth and history together.

Placing Jerusalem at the center of the story forces the historian to circle continually back to the Bible. But by shifting the view to Bethlehem, the world begins to look very different. It's just a little hill town at the edge of the desert, yet the air is a great deal clearer. Shades of myth dissolve, and a historical perspective becomes possible. This is a history of the people who lived in Bethlehem from the year dot to the present day. It is a story with far more continuity than anyone might imagine. I have sifted the most current historical thinking, guided by my long love affair with the town and the surrounding countryside.

Bethlehem's orchards, like Anton Sansour's garden, are filled with apricots, almonds, figs, grapes, oranges, lemons, and olives. The Persian word for both garden and orchard is *pardes*, which gives us the biblical word "paradise." The story of Christ is shaped around two gardens, the garden "inn" at the edge of Bethlehem and the garden of Gethsemane in Jerusalem. The first Christians recognized the significance of Christ entering and leaving the world by way of two gardens. Just as these garden caravanserais were the entry points to cities, where locals and strangers could meet and talk, so gardens were also seen as the gateways to eternity. There is a short Jewish fable from around the fourth century that illustrates this. Four rabbis enter a garden paradise, a mystical space outside of earthly time. The first three rabbis are arrogant or destructive in one way or another. Only Rabbi Akiva treats the garden with respect: he enters in peace, and he leaves in peace. In reality, Rabbi Akiva's reputation as a man of peace may be undeserved: he was the military chaplain for the Bar Kokhba revolt and spent several years holed up in caves in the hills around the Bethlehem village of Battir. Nevertheless, the lesson holds; the best way to understand a problem is to approach it in peace.

The fable inspired a traditional Jewish reading technique, which also goes by the Persian word *Pardes*. As a formal reading strategy, Pardes refers to the four levels of meaning in a text. *Peshat* is the literal meaning (what the words actually say); *Remez*, the allegorical meaning (a way of appreciating and celebrating the poetry in the scriptures, as well as interpreting the "poetic" meaning); *Derash*, the comparative meaning (clarifying definitions by finding alternative uses of the word in parallel passages); and, finally, *Sod* or the mystical meaning (the spiritual interpretation, which will often be hidden and so require a higher level of wisdom or piety from the reader). These four levels, together, make up *PaRDeS*.

Since Victorian times, Christians have emphasized the literal meaning alone. The Victorians believed the Bible reflected a historical truth and viewed poetry and allegory as eccentric detours that had to be turned back around to the literal meaning. Metaphors were treated as annoyances to be squashed down and reduced to the literal: a kind of poetrycide. In my high school religious classes, my teacher had no problem recognizing that the story of the creation in six days was an allegory. Yet we were told the order nevertheless reflected God's work schedule. In a Pardes account, by contrast, the reader is supposed to keep the mystery alive, leaving the proper space between the levels of reading so that they do not simply blend into one. The reader is supposed to respect the layers, and also the margins that separate them.

I came across the idea of Pardes when researching the work of Jacques Derrida. Leila and I were philosophy postgrads when we met in England, and if I arrived in Bethlehem knowing nothing about her home or the Palestinian-Israeli conflict, it was because I had my head buried in Derrida. I was attracted to his work because he had garnered a reputation as an anarchic destroyer of meaning, and as a young PhD student I thought destruction was cool. As I immersed myself in Derrida's work, however, I discovered the opposite was true: his real interest was the way that communication and understanding persist in a world as violent and destructive as our own. In the early 1990s, Derrida wrote a memoir of his life growing up as a Jewish child in Algeria, which is where he revealed that the inspiration behind his philosophy was Talmudic exegesis, expressed in this notion of Pardes. At the time, I was not sure that I wanted a Derrida who was conservative and respectful of traditions, but this is what I found.

Pardes asks the reader to approach a text with sensitivity and intelligence, but also charity. If that applies to a book, it goes double for a city. Bethlehem is so suffused with history and myth that it feels like an unreal city even to the people who call it home. As I worried away at Bethlehem's stories, the biblical accounts inevitably began to unravel, but they never went away. They always had a kind of pull, tangled up with the true history of the town. The history of Bethlehem and the mythical version have to coexist. They have to live in peace. Like the saying goes, Bethlehem is not just for Christmas. We all have to live with Palestine and Israel, even if we don't actually live there.

You can get a lot out of a Christmas pudding. It works as a kind of soft archaeology of fruit, spice, and flour. But first and foremost, it is a symbol of goodwill and fellow-feeling. I know this because a gift card attached to the cellophane wrapper on my pudding reads: *Merry Christmas, with peace and goodwill to all.*

# CHAPTER 1

# NOMADS AND LOVERS

## *From the Stone Age to the Bronze Age*

*The Ain Sakhri lovers figurine.*

The Allenby Bridge is the border crossing for Palestinians leaving or returning to Bethlehem, and the other cities of the West Bank. The checkpoint is a large, shed-style construction, like a warehouse. Coaches arrive from the Jordan side of the river, where the passengers are funneled through a series of security checks by Israeli forces, to reconnect with their luggage before searching for a bus or taxi to Jerusalem. The cabs don't go as far as Bethlehem, and there was a time when I would arrange for Mustafa, a Bethlehem taxi driver, to meet me at a gas station in the desert near Jericho. He is a small, wiry man from the Ta'amareh Bedouin, with a Clark Gable moustache and a tough, angular head the shape of a paper water-bomb. Even after he started a successful car hire company, he continued to pick me up, so it was several years before I discovered he no longer drove a taxi.

The desert road to Bethlehem gives a Bedouin's-eye view of the town. In winter, around Christmastime, the ground is hard and bleak, and the sky above is an unremitting slate color. At Easter, the weather can be even worse. But within days everything changes. The wilderness is a miracle in spring. Grass appears from nowhere, covering the coarse surface like a green spray. The tightly packed hills have the happy look of a child's drawing: one hill swimming into another, with a third hill peeking between their shoulders. It feels as though no one could ever have seen the world look so fresh and new; it is the first day of creation.

At the outskirts of Ta'amareh, an area of the desert that takes its name from Mustafa's tribe, I would crane over Mustafa's shoulder to catch my first sight of Bethlehem. The low afternoon sun casts the city into shade. In outline, it looks like a cat stretching to get the last comfort from the embers in the fireplace. Imagine the bluntly rounded hill with the Church of the Nativity as the cat's head. Facing it is a long narrow ridge; the cat's back with its haunches in the air at the university, the highest point in Bethlehem. As the desert road climbs, the town blurs into a fuzzily gray silhouette. I know I am in Bethlehem when I see the outline of the church: the oldest-surviving working Roman temple and, as a direct consequence, the most mysterious building in the world.

The timeline of human history is ordered around Christ's birth. Every time I write a date BCE or CE, I am aware that the Church of the Nativity marks the fulcrum of human time, and all history revolves around it. In its first, BCE, life, the Bethlehem region was an unnamed aggregation of villages known for its fruit and olive oil, sitting within a world of empires and trade networks. In its second life, one of these villages became famous above all the others. Time seems to move so much more slowly inside the church, like a black hole at the center of a frantically spinning universe. Maybe this is why, in the hidden depths at the heart of the church, in the cave where Christ is said to have been born, the site of the nativity is marked by a fallen star.

The Emperor Constantine commissioned the Church of the Nativity in 327 CE. When it was completed in 339 CE, it sat at the edge of a bustling hilltop city. As new monasteries and guesthouses were added, the actual town ended up being shuffled onto the ridge opposite. Now, town and church face each other across a short saddle that has been built up to make the open plaza of Manger Square. The walk from the summit of the ridge at the university to the church square takes about fifteen minutes, depending on the crowds, the day of the week, and the length of your shopping list. The road slopes, tilting more steeply as it descends. The street ends at the souk with a flight of marble steps, flanked by a ramp that is scoured with raised ridges to give the wheels of the stallholders' carts some traction as they haul their goods up to market. A wide smooth gutter runs down the center of the ramp that the local children use as a luge run. They come hurtling downward on sheets of cardboard, to collide at the bottom in laughing, mangled piles.

This is Bethlehem: an old town facing the site of an even older town, sitting at the edge of the desert, just six miles south of Jerusalem. Throughout all its cat's lives, Bethlehem has been defined by this position. The desert is the home to the Bedouin and the pathway to an ancient world of nomads and caravans, shepherds and Magi, and the great, lost civilizations of the Middle East. Jerusalem is the gate to the west, an open door that too easily gives way to occupiers and invaders. Today, it is the road into Israel, described in the language of the 1949 Geneva Convention as the "hostile occupying power." Bethlehem is caught between its past and present; its face turned to the desert as though stretching out for warmth or perhaps hoping for a new day.

IN 1935, A LOCAL DOCTOR bought a house at the top of town, opposite the Catholic seminary that later became the university. The doctor hired workmen to dig a cistern in his garden, and as they dug, they turned up some mysterious bones, including what looked like the tusks of an elephant. The discovery brought the pioneering archaeozoologist Dorothea Bate and her colleague Elinor Gardner to Bethlehem. Bate was the daughter of a Welsh policeman who picked up her knowledge of zoology while cataloguing fossils at the Natural History Museum in London. She started as a teenager and was paid piecework rates for every fossil she filed away. By the time she arrived in Palestine in the late 1920s, she was almost fifty and widely respected—though also feared for her habit of carrying sticks of dynamite, which she used with enthusiasm. The relics in the doctor's cistern were the remains of an extinct species of elephant, and Bate and Gardner soon discovered other surprises, including an early horse and a prehistoric giant tortoise, as well as evidence that at least some of these animals had been hunted by Bethlehem's first inhabitants. The tortoise bones showed signs of being drilled for bone marrow to suck.

Dorothea Bate came to Palestine at the invitation of Dorothy Garrod, a younger woman who later became Cambridge University's first female professor (of anything). In the late 1920s and '30s, during British rule in Palestine, the military governor put Garrod in charge of a dig at Haifa. She recognized that Palestine had been settled earlier than almost anywhere else, and for the reasons that later attracted the Bedouin. The area offers a variety of landscapes and climates bundled into a single compact area. There was no longer any reason to pick up sticks with each season, when it was possible to stay in a single location. Garrod gave the laidback Stone Age nomads their name: the Natufian, after Wadi an-Natuf, the site of her dig. The most important relic of Natufian civilization was found in Bethlehem, however, and a shepherd from the Ta'amareh discovered it.

The Ain Sakhri lovers figurine is carved from a rounded calcite cobblestone, the size of a fist, discovered in 1930 in the cave networks of Wadi Khreitoun. A lively market in archaeological treasures grew up in Bethlehem after the 1840s, when the Ottoman government's liberal reforms encouraged foreign tourists. The Ta'amareh saw a business opportunity and began exploring the local caves while their sheep were grazing. They are responsible for the most celebrated finds in Bethlehem, including some of the earliest examples of Jewish religious writing, the Dead Sea Scrolls. The Ain Sakhri lovers figurine was discovered twenty years earlier and is just as important a find.

Calcite is a crystalline stone found in limestone. I imagine the shepherd seeing a glint in the cave's shadow, brushing the dry desert dust from the cobblestone, then realizing with a jolt what he had. The figurine depicts a couple, facing each other, one sitting on the other's cock. I can see the shepherd passing it to his friends to test their reaction, maybe trying to play it cool as he masks his own response. The Ta'amareh like to mess around. They tell jokes. Though they are clannish—they actually are a clan, after all—they also have the self-confidence to trust their instincts. Maybe he would ask the other, straightfaced: *What do you think of that?* but breaking into a grin a fraction too early. The carved faces of the lovers merge together, the thighs of one wrapped tight around the other's waist as they embrace. The sexual theme continues. Turn the figures around and the faces meld to resemble the head of a penis; their embracing arms form the twisted ridge of a drawn-back foreskin. Turn the cobble over, end to end, and it could be a vulva. Turn it again and you might decide, now, it looks like two breasts. It seems impossible that any sculptor could have intended so much, but once you hold the actual figurine it is all there in one tightly packed lump of sexual significance.

In fact, I am not allowed to hold the actual stone; there is a strict no-touching rule at the British Museum where I see it, nestled in tissue paper inside a Tupperware lunchbox in a study room. The curator, Jill Cook, allows me to handle a cast-resin copy. This is what I take and hold, turning it around and around as I wish that I had someone to show it to. If they have the sense of humor of a thirteen-year-old schoolboy, so much the better.

The sculpture arrived at the museum via a crooked path. The Ta'amareh boys sold the sculpture to a small, private museum run by the Fathers of the Sacred Heart of Betharram, a Basque Catholic order with a monastery in Bethlehem. In 1933, a newly appointed French diplomat named René Neuville took an interest. Neuville was an amateur archaeologist who, aside from wartime service in North Africa, passed his entire diplomatic career in Jerusalem. (In 1946, on his return to Jerusalem, Neuville was a key witness of the attack on the King David Hotel that killed ninety-one people. The hotel was then the headquarters of the British military in Palestine and was targeted by a Jewish terror group led by Israel's future prime minister, Menachem Begin. The French consulate sat next door to the British headquarters.)

Neuville spent all his free time on digs, especially at a Paleolithic burial site close to Nazareth. The visit to the museum at the Betharram mission came because he was hosting Father Henri Breuil, a celebrated fifty-seven-year-old professor of prehistoric ethnology at the College de France. Breuil would become infamous during his time working in apartheid South Africa when he claimed a sixty-thousand-year-old cave painting was too sophisticated to be the work of black Africans, and must be proof of a

Neolithic European presence. However, in the 1930s, Abbé Breuil's reputation was still high. He was regarded as the leading expert on prehistoric humans and was a personal mentor to Dorothy Garrod, who had served a two-year apprenticeship under him. He was in Palestine to inspect Garrod's dig in Haifa, and his visit to Bethlehem was something of a day excursion to visit the Holy Sites. It was Breuil who saw the significance of the stone, and called Neuville over to admire it.

Inside the British Museum's study room, curator Jill Cook explains that dating the stone is difficult because it is one of a kind; nothing quite like it has ever been found. Breuil believed it was around 11,000 years old. This puts it at the beginning of the period when humans first began to pick wild wheat, build settled communities, and domesticate animals other than just dogs. (Humans started sharing their lives with dogs twenty thousand years ago, Jill tells me. We really love our dogs.) Wheat is a kind of grass, and most grass seeds blow away in the wind; identifying the few species where the seeds cling to the stalk is a crucial step in human evolution: it allowed humans to harvest the stalks, take the seeds home, and eat them plump and ripe, or store them until they were dry and could be ground to make flour. So Jill tells me. As she speaks, I am thinking about one my favorite Palestinian dishes: a kind of ripe wheat called *frikeh*, which can be eaten like rice, or cold in salads like bulgur wheat. The idea that recipes could be passed down over eleven millennia is almost vertigo-inducing, as though the floor of history has just given way and I am staring into a precipice.

The sculpture of the Ain Sakhri lovers also feels like proof that Stone Age life is not so distant from our own. Here was an artist with enough free time to carve a sculpture, and who chose to make a piece about sex and human love. The subject says a lot about leisure and creativity, as well as about friendship and family life. Yet it is difficult to spin too much out of a single object. Jill is a small, blond woman with bright eyes and a definite no-nonsense style. She has heard extravagant theories about the Ain Sakhri lovers that hope to prove the root of all religions lie in fertility cults and the mysteries of human love and sex. They do not impress her. The problem, she says, is that we have nothing to compare to the Ain Sakhri lovers; there is no way to understand what it might have meant to its sculptor. The only other carved objects comparable in size and skill are stone pestles and carvings of dogs. (You can see carved pestles and sculptures of dogs in the Palestine Archaeology Museum in East Jerusalem, now renamed the Rockefeller Museum.) Perhaps, though, the stone did celebrate fertility, and the Natufians had just realized there was a connection between having sex and producing babies. Jill has some sympathy with this view. The Natufians had learned to domesticate sheep and so, she says, "If you have a flock of docile sheep, you quickly learn to keep away the wild rams, or else you have to start domesticating all over again." The figurine is both eloquent and sexy, yet it remains somehow impenetrable.

Jill's fascination with the Ain Sakhri lovers led her to turn detective. She uncovered a series of letters between Neuville and Breuil and learned that Neuville was never entirely sure that the stone had been found in the Ain Sakhri caves. He wrote to Breuil to relate how he tracked down the shepherd and asked to be taken to the spot where he found the stone. Wadi Khreitoun is the original desert road to the Dead Sea. The valley sides are peppered with caves, and Neuville claims that he scoured the area but found nothing else of significance.

Despite the problems establishing the proper site and context for the stone, Jill stands by Breuil's evaluation. It is Neolithic, and so far as we know it is the earliest depiction of human lovers. The unanswered question is: how did the stone come into Neuville's possession? The stone was in his private collection when he died in Jerusalem in 1952. His children sold the piece at auction in 1958, which is when it was bought by the British Museum.

Staring at the Ain Sakhri lovers in its paper-lined box, I am conscious that the Elgin marbles hang in a wing on the other side of the museum. It occurs to me that this stone might be Palestine's equivalent of the marbles and, one day, a Palestinian minister of antiquities will demand its return. So I decided to play detective myself. On my next visit to Bethlehem, I go to the monastery and make my enquiries. The monastery stands in the grounds of the Carmelite convent of Saint Mariam Bawardy, a Melkite nun canonized by Pope Francis in 2015. Bawardy's convent overlooks the edge of Wadi Ma'ali and the eastern side of Bethlehem's ridge. The large square Betharram monastery lies a little further back, surrounded by neat flower beds. When I pull at the bell, a young African priest appears to tell me we have caught them at lunch. At once, I am in a canteen with all the monks, eating maftoul, often called Palestinian couscous, which they eat with chicken stew. I am disappointed no one wears robes. The monks are a mix of Africans and Europeans, and all are dressed more causally than me. The abbot is away, but I am invited to return and a few days later we meet inside a small study. Father Pietro Fellet is a quiet man with a neat, gray beard, wearing slippers. There hasn't been a museum in the monastery in his time, though he once saw a typewritten catalogue of the collection. This was some fifty years ago, he says, when he was a teacher at the local Catholic seminary. He had seen the catalogue while browsing the Betharram library. Today, even the library is gone. Father Pietro tells me that the artifacts in the museum were sent away during the 1948 war for safekeeping, and ended up in Italy and France. It is also possible, he thinks, that parts of the collection were sent abroad during the 1936 Arab Uprising.

I suggest that René Neuville might have offered to help the monks transfer the collection to Europe. He was the consul, after all. Father Pietro is adamant this could not have happened. The Betharram movement is a Pays Basque order and on poor terms with the French state. After almost seventy years, it is impossible to say how Neuville acquired the Ain Sakhri lovers. It may have happened as the collection was broken up and shipped abroad. It is possible that Neuville was given the piece, and just as likely that it simply found its way into his pocket in the chaos of war.

THE AIN SAKHRI LOVERS FIGURINE makes a poignant starting point for a human history of Bethlehem. This is where it all began, eleven thousand years ago. They had already managed to domesticate the dog and prepare wheat to make frikeh, perhaps eaten with a salad of tortoise bone marrow (I am guessing), so it was a short step to becoming either farmers or animal breeders—but which?

Many of our ideas about human prehistory are predicated on the idea that humans divide between the safe-but-dull life of farmers and the wild and unpredictable existence of a nomadic grazier, driving their flocks ahead as they move between grasslands. The biblical historian Karen Armstrong proposes a universal model of prehistory based on the movement of nomadic warriors. Armstrong examines a number of civilizations across

India and the Middle East and sees a repeating pattern as farmers succumb to raids from nomadic shepherds. As the nomads stick around to build feudal mini-states, the farmers are reduced to slaves. Eventually, the nomads transform themselves into an aristocratic caste. What they had taken by force, they learn to hold and maintain by bureaucracy and custom, all the while camouflaging their aggression behind a facade of sophistication and spirituality. At its base, however, these kingdoms rest upon slavery, as an incoming warrior caste rules over the indigenous peasants.

Armstrong applies this abstract model to periods when there is little or no written documentation, and it proves a powerful and seductive explanation of the way that cultures, languages, religions, and goods are transmitted across seemingly disconnected expanses. The earliest states are simply garrisons, pinpricks in the wider landscape. There is no sense of territory in the modern sense, and certainly no idea of cartography and mapping. Each kingdom extends only as far as its strength and supply lines allow, at which point it fades into a hinterland. Beyond this point, the warrior king can no longer safely post his soldiers, nor tax the peasants, nor levy tolls from the passing merchants. Over the horizon, there will be another armed garrison, in which another king declares himself the ruler of all he surveys.

By their nature, these early garrison states always already operate in a multinational and multiethnic environment. Each kingdom is born in competition with others, lying just over the horizon, while inside the kingdom the rulers and subjects have separate and private cultures, foreign to each other. Armstrong notes the farmers will often retain their own gods, which serve as a constant reminder that the master and their slaves are literally different people.

These dots, strung across a landscape, join together to form trade routes or political alliances. The children of one ruling dynasty may head off to found their own garrison states. Kings may marry into another dynasty and assume power as a dowry or claim an inheritance by bloodlines. One king may become the vassal of a more powerful neighboring warlord. So the earliest empires begin to take shape as networks. There are still no maps, but if there were, we would not see the solid blocks of color we associate with empires. Rather, we would see lines squirming in every direction. These baby empires would spread like veins beneath pale skin, forming bundles of bloodlines that grow to form organs and muscles.

Armstrong's hypothesis is powerful because it explains not only the peculiar mismatch of cultures found between peasants and their masters, but also how globalized trade networks emerged at an early point in human history. In his powerful account of the way trading networks shaped our world, the historian Peter Frankopan notes that trading routes are also the military supply lines of nomadic armies. But before we focus on Bethlehem and its place in this networked world, we should note two paradoxes that flow from this model.

The first is that a theory of movement makes it difficult to speak of an origin for any particular dynasty. These are nomads, setting up kingdoms in series, and who is to say where the series began? When an established dynasty sets out to write their story, there is a strong incentive to construct an origin story to make a mythical connection to the land they have seized, such as the tale of brothers Romulus and Remus. Roman mythology states that wolves on the Tiber suckled their founders, when the truth seems to be that an alliance of disparate outlaw tribes made their home on Rome's Palatine Hill. Imagining the shape of a state's prehistory is difficult, because only when we have written documents do we have something approaching a real history, and these records are a product of a state-sponsored bureaucracy. In the case of Rome, it is all but impossible to give an account of the city before the creation of the Republic in 509 BCE. Prior to the Republic, everything is propaganda and myth; after it, events come into focus as there are corroborating documents, produced by an effective government with a state bureaucracy and a working legal code.

We might even say that states do not have prehistories. Armstrong gives us a story of how nations form, but her model says more about the international environment than the organization of any particular state. It is all about flows of armies, the emergence of trade routes, the sharing of technologies, and the spread of languages. It is an abstract model and provides no insight into what these garrison states might have been like, or even if they deserved to be described as "states" at all. History begins with documents: legal documents, tax records, sales receipts, births, deaths, and marriages, property registers, and, perhaps most importantly, correspondence and treaties with other, similar states. It is difficult to get back to the day before the emergence of writing. As Jacques Derrida observed, at some level all history turns out to be the history of writing. If we want to argue that a proto-state existed prior to the emergence of a historical, record-keeping city, we risk becoming lost in the myths that the warlords told about themselves. This is particularly hazardous in Palestine, where the Bible so often tempts writers to turn myth into history.

Armstrong's nomadic model explains the emergence of garrison states. Yet it is so abstract that once we turn to a specific culture and try to account for its duration, we are at a loss. Perversely, perhaps, this may actually be one of the model's strengths. The French philosopher Gilles Deleuze was also attracted to the idea that nomadic warriors are the engines of history. But he favored the theory precisely because it is an abstract model. If the first paradox of the model is that it is impossible to talk of a nation's origins, the second paradox is that it is not a history of states at all but rather, as Frankopan also shows, a history of the world. In his books, Deleuze speaks of nomad graziers as "Nomadic War Machines" and argues that the movement of these shepherd warriors creates the framework that allows us to imagine both historical space *and* historical time. The routes created by these nomads as they traverse the world lays the groundwork for a networked *space* of trade and cultural exchange, while their attacks on settled communities create the *timeline* by which we mark the changes of regimes and dynasties. If history is the story of the rise and fall of kingdoms, it is because nomads put the notches on this timeline by deposing one regime and either replacing them or laying the city to waste. It is in this sense that nomads are the abstract motor of history: they create the graph paper on which we chart human history.

Nomads create a sense of history as movement: their world begins with sheep and ends with empires. A theory embraced by figures as diverse as Karen Armstrong, Peter Frankopan, and Gilles Deleuze is a powerful tool for imagining the prehistory of states, even if it only allows us to talk about towns like Bethlehem obliquely. It is easier to say who passed through Bethlehem and boasted of ruling over it rather than describe the lives of the people who actually lived here. By focusing upon nomads, we gain a tumultuous theory of the rise and fall of civilizations.

This abstract story of ceaseless change and movement necessarily contrasts with the archaeology of Bethlehem, which paints an entirely different picture: one of continuity and stability. The archaeology suggests that the lives of peasants, farmers, and slaves bumbled on across the millennia, even as their masters changed. The people of Bethlehem, or many of them, are likely to be the descendants of its first inhabitants.

CITIES BEGAN TO APPEAR between nine and ten thousand years ago. These walled communities held thousands of people yet were still part of the Stone Age. My route to Bethlehem takes me through Amman, in Jordan, before crossing the Jordan River at Jericho, passing by the two oldest surviving cities on earth. Amman and Jericho emerged from *Tell* sites, cities of the plain that played an important role in the evolution of the trade networks that supported smaller hill communities like those around Bethlehem.

I learn more about these Tell sites from James Fraser, the curator of the Levant collection at the British Museum. James is a tall Australian with bright blue eyes and black hair. He talks rapidly, speeding up when he gets on to a subject he likes: and Tell sites top the list of things that he likes. James gives a vivid account of a dig in Amman's Ain Ghazal archaeological site. Tell sites were built from sunbaked clay bricks that crumble easily. However, the walls around the Tell sites could contain the debris as one generation of buildings crumbled and a new generation was built, so these cities grew upward rather than sprawled out across the plains. As each new neighborhood was built on the dust of the old, the Tell would rise over the decades and centuries to form a giant, artificial hill. James describes the excitement of standing at the foot of a trench sunk straight through the city mound and staring upward to see the weight of history given physical shape, towering above in clearly stratified layers. Ain Ghazal once held three thousand people: a Stone Age metropolis.

The timeline of the Neolithic Age is divided between pre- and post-pottery eras, and the British Museum has two plaster sculptures from Ain Ghazal, in the period before high-temperature ceramic kilns were invented. The sculptures are half-sized mannequins of children, spooky-eyed twins made by slathering diluted clay over a reed skeleton and leaving the sculpture to dry in the sun. They are nine thousand years old and stare out of a glass case into a world that they could not have known, though they appear to see straight through it.

James tells me that the division of human time into Stone, pre-pottery, post-pottery, Bronze and Iron Ages is imprecise because older technologies always coexist with newer ones. Canaanite farmers found it was easier and cheaper to make a DIY flint scythe or a knife than buy a metal version, especially when access to metals was jealously controlled by kings and warlords.

I know elements of Stone Age technology survived into the modern era because I have seen Palestinian threshing boards studded with sharp flints that date to the nineteenth century. The freshly harvested wheat and barley was scattered over a circular outdoor threshing floor, and the flint-studded threshing board was dragged over the drying crop, pulled by a donkey that walked in circles around the edge of the circle. There is an example in the ethnographic museum run by the Bethlehem chapter of the Arab Women's Union (AWU), a social club founded to promote welfare and education, much like America's equivalent Women's Clubs. The museum lies in the old town's souk, split between two buildings, and shows traditional home life in the nineteenth century. I am given a tour of the preserved kitchen by Helen Loussie, a small woman in her sixties with sharp eyes and a formal manner that in no way dims her natural warmth. She is an expert on all the kitchen implements, drawing my attention to a taller cylinder made of plaster, about the size of a kitchen trashcan. It is a hopper used to store dried apricots, another example of the way ancient technologies can persist into the modern age. The hopper is constructed over a reed frame, in exactly the same way as the Ain Ghazal twin mannequins. Helen tells me that the hoppers were never manufactured commercially; a woman would simply make one for her home. They would also make small clay braziers to keep pots warm. A couple of these charcoal-burning braziers stand by the kitchen door, like scaled-up versions of the incense oil burners that use a tea light to warm the oil. Both the braziers and the hopper were sun-dried rather than kiln-fired. The hopper is fascinating because, though simple, it combines great character with a unique and sophisticated design. Helen explains it was lined with a muslin bag and filled with dried apricots. There is a flap at the foot of the hopper, and when the cook needed dried fruit, she would reach a hand through the flap and take a handful.

THE TELL CITIES OF JERICHO and Amman survived when many other cities of the plains were abandoned to the sun and the winds. The next generation of cities were based on river networks. Five thousand years ago, life along the Tigris, the Euphrates, and the Nile went into "turbo-drive," so James Fraser tells me; new and emerging civilizations sent tentacles up- and downstream to create the earliest of the "networked" empires. Though Amman and Jericho are far away from these big rivers, they were uniquely placed to survive in the new era, thanks to a metal-trading road that came to be known as the King's Highway.

The route of the King's Highway is marked by a modern motorway that begins at Aqaba on the Red Sea and leads north to Syria, where teeming refugee camps have sprung up because of the current Syrian war. In ancient times, the King's Highway spanned the known world from the Nile in Egypt to the eastern cities of Assyria and Mesopotamia. It became a diplomatic route that connected the great imperial centers, but first and foremost, it connected the copper mines of the Negev with the tin mines of Anatolia in modern-day Turkey. Together, copper and tin make bronze, a metal so wonderful that it gave its name to an entire age. Bethlehem lies on a parallel road to the King's Highway that runs north from the Negev through Hebron, Bethlehem and Jerusalem before forking right to Damascus via the Golan Heights or left to Tyre and the Lebanese coast. This is still the main road through the Bethlehem district, known as Hebron Road. In the great world of empires, it may be a "B" road, rather than an "A" road. Yet it is significant, and by joining up with the King's Highway, it can get you to Babylon or to Cairo.

A clue to the earliest life of Bethlehem emerged only recently with the discovery of a Bronze Age necropolis between Tuqu' and Artas, deep inside a hill known as Khalet al-Jam'a. A team of Palestinian and Italian archaeologists excavated the subterranean chambers within the hill in 2014, and besides the desiccated corpses of five-thousand-year-old farmers they found a number of distinctive chocolate-colored jars. The dark-brown surface was burnished with white patterns, created by rubbing powdered lime into scoured marks before applying the darker slip. The style is known as Tell el-Yahudiyeh ware, or "City of the Jews," after the Egyptian city where they were first discovered. (The name is purely coincidental. Tell el-Yahudiyeh is a relatively modern name for a city that was known as *Ney-ta-hut* in the Bronze Age.) Despite being first discovered in Egypt, they are known to be a Canaanite design; indeed, the English word "jar" derives from the Canaanite name for these jars. They were used to transport Canaan's olive oil. Pottery and metalworking technologies emerged in tandem because the high-temperature kilns necessary to smelt Negev copper could also fire ceramics, which in turn allowed olive oil to become a tradable commodity five thousand years ago.

I catch up with Lorenzo Nigro, leader of the team that excavated Khalet al-Jam'a, in London. He tells me that the Bethlehem necropolis would have faced the farmer's homes, which suggests that the oldest inhabited parts of Bethlehem were centered on Artas and may have extended as far as a heavily built-up area known as Wadi Ma'ali, just below Bethlehem town. The houses run along the wadi in parallel lines, one above the other, giving a clue to the shape of the orchard terraces that predated them. The water from the spring at Artas could have been channeled through the terraces, as is it in the nearby village of Battir. For what it's worth, Saint Mariam Bawardy chose to build her Carmelite convent at the end of Wadi Ma'ali when a voice came to her in a vision and told her the site overlooked the home of Jesse, the father of David. Thanks to her vision, Bawardy may have inadvertently identified the oldest part of Bethlehem.

The Egyptians named this land Canaan, while Greek-speakers used the name Phoenicia. Both words mean "purple," though the reason why is open to speculation. It may be named after the *Murex* sea snails from the coast between Gaza and Lebanon whose shells produce a purple dye if crushed and left to decompose. Whether or not the people saw their home as "the purple," or even as any kind of homeland at all, we cannot know. The olive oil producing villages of Canaan's hills were tied together by the Hebron Road, and by the brown and white jars carried along this pack route on donkeys, strapped to the sides of wooden frames. As the money flowed in, the people from around Bethlehem and other olive regions followed the road all the way to the Nile, where they established warehouses and trading posts to sell directly to their customers.

As though to prove that trade routes are also military supply lines, a group of Canaanite raiders known as the Hyskos followed the olive oil trail and conquered the entire Lower Nile. The Hyskos were highly mobile charioteers. The Egyptian kingdom they created thirty-eight hundred years ago lasted for around a hundred and fifty years until it was overthrown by a powerful new Egyptian dynasty imaginatively called the New

Kingdom. The new regime was not content with merely defeating the Hyskos. They chased the Canaanite interlopers all the way across Canaan/ Phoenicia to expand Egyptian territory well into what is now Syria.

Today, Bethlehem olive oil is rarely sold outside the city limits. The yield isn't high in such an urban area. The olive groves that once surrounded the villages have disappeared, as much of Bethlehem's countryside has been confiscated to build Jewish settlements, and the rest has been declared closed military zones. Nevertheless, Bethlehem oil is valued in other Palestinian cities, where it has a reputation as a delicacy. I ask a cousin, Vivien Sansour, why Bethlehem oil is so unusual, so different, so rare. She tells me: it is because it is rancid. This sounds like a bad thing, though Vivien assures me it is not. She is an agriculturalist and has studied French olive oil production. She explains that olives are supposed to be picked quickly to get the crop to the press in the shortest time possible. The technique in Bethlehem, however, involves exposing the olives on groundsheets for a few days, which mildly toasts the olives before they are crushed. I have always thought that Bethlehem oil is excellent. It is not as peppery as some, but has a definite bite and a taste that I might have described as nutty, complex, maybe even dense.

Definitely not musty.

Being classified as rancid means the oil cannot be sold in Europe, but this does not seem such a hardship when there is now barely enough for the people of Bethlehem.

THE NEW KINGDOM CONQUERED Canaan c. 1550 BCE lending it a greater landmass than any subsequent Egyptian empire. However, the new pharaohs ruled their acquisitions with a light touch via a series of vassal kings—the term they used is rather closer to "mayor" or "governor." We might think of these governors as franchise-holders. They lived in garrison palaces and enjoyed a kingly lifestyle provided they kicked a slice of their profits back to the head office in Egypt. There are written records in the form of letters from many of these franchise-holders, including one named Abdi-Heba who ruled from the rocky outcrop where Jerusalem would be built. His name translates as "the servant of the goddess Heba," which suggests that he may have originally come from what is now Anatolia, and may perhaps be a forefather of the Armenian people. There is no older historical account of this city, so the Armenians might claim to be the founders of the fortress that became Jerusalem.

The Egyptians not only recruited foreign rulers, but also co-opted an alien writing system to communicate with their franchisees. This script, known as Akkadian cuneiform, is a product of one of the world's longest-lived institutions, the civil service of the Akkadian-Sumerian Empire. Though the empire had disappeared six or seven hundred years earlier, its bureaucracy lived on. The cuneiform script is "written" with a sharpened stylus used to impress wedge-shaped indentations into a soft clay tablet. The various combinations of indentations make up symbols, and these symbols comprise the written text. Once the text is completed, the tablets are baked or dried. The system requires the coordination of highly trained scribes across innumerable cities, along with the technicians who will prepare the tablets, the couriers who operate the postal way stations, and all the ostlers, stable-hands, and saddle-makers who keep the postal service moving.

The cuneiform script welded the Egyptian New Kingdom together. This is all the more striking because it was developed to transmit a language that neither the pharaohs nor their governors, such as Abdi-Heba, spoke. Cuneiform had become an abstract symbolic system that existed to facilitate empire-building, entirely divorced from actual spoken languages. James Fraser arranges to show me a selection of cuneiform tablets in the British Museum. I repay this courtesy by reaching the room late and breathless, because I entered from the wrong end of the building. The entrance is almost hidden by stepladders and paint cans, but once through the door I find a high-ceilinged Victorian room that looks as though it ought to be described as dusty, except, of course, it is spotless. The shelves reach to the rafters, each one filled with boxes and all containing Akkadian tablets. I have only seen examples of the tablets in photographs, and had imagined they were Moses-sized tombstones. The tablets are closer to the size of jam jars, easy to stack together, wrap in cloth, and pack in a horse's saddlebag. Half a dozen translators are working at a long desk beneath the vaulted ceiling, holding magnifying glasses over the dry-brittle clay forms. James tells me that the majority of the tablets are yet to be translated.

In 1915, a German philologist named Otto Schroeder translated letters written by Abdi-Heba to Egypt. Schroeder was hoping to find corroboration of biblical texts and was quite ingenious in constructing a mention of Bethlehem that did not exist. He focused on a letter in which Abdi-Heba complained that a city named *Beit Ninurta* had switched allegiances. Be-it-Ninurta, or the "House of Ninurta," references an Akkadian god of war. Schroeder knew it was unlikely that a long-out-of-date god would be worshipped in Canaan's hills, and this led him to make an improbable speculative leap: he suggested that Abdi-Heba was referring to Bethlehem.

Schroeder seems to have been working on a hunch that the logogram used to symbolize Ninurta, a god of war, had been borrowed by Canaanite-speakers to represent the everyday word "fight": *lakham*. On this basis, he suggested that Beit Ninurta might actually be read *Beit Lakhem*, a homophone for Beit Lekhem. There are an outrageous number of steps in Schroeder's translation: from the symbol of a god of war, to the word for fight, which then functions as a pun on *lekhem* (the Canaanite word for "bread"). Yet, though far-fetched and oblique, there is a visible thread running through Schroeder's translation. Even this slim thread of plausibility was lost when the American archaeologist William F. Albright, the most influential biblical archaeologist of his day, embraced his translation in 1921.

Albright was quick to pick up on Schroeder's claim to have found the first mention of Bethlehem. But he offered a different and far simpler translation. He argued that the cuneiform symbol Beit-Ninurta could be read *Beit-Lahmu* because "Lahmu" was an alternative for Ninurta among the Sumerians. No one else has ever suggested this, and as Lahmu is only ever mentioned in conjunction with his twin sister, Lahamu, the connection is highly dubious. In truth, Albright seems simply to have misunderstood Schroeder's reading, which had only been published in German. Albright recanted in 1968, when he identified Beit-Ninurta with Beit Horon, yet his fanciful interpretation of the Abdi-Heba letter is still cited in guidebooks and archaeological studies to date Bethlehem.

The events of the Bible are set in a time of myth that places them outside of historical time. William F. Albright's great innovation was to link myth and history by creating a biblical timeline that maps onto the timeline of human history. This invention proved his lasting legacy: that, and the fact that he hired and trained the first generation of Israeli archaeologists. Albright locates the story of the patriarchs, the Egyptian exile and the rise of King David, within the context of the rise and fall of the historical empires like the Egyptian New Kingdom. As his interpretation of the Abdi-Heba letter shows, his methods are no more reliable than Bawardy's visions, based on wishful thinking rather than any facts. Perhaps the temptation to see only what you want to see is inevitable when interpreting a writing system as hermetic and ancient as Akkadian cuneiform, with its near-random mix of symbolic and phonetic elements.

The good news for historians is that Akkadian cuneiform was on its way out. At the start of the first millennium BCE, it began to be replaced by a more transparent phonetic system, the ancestor of our own present-day alphabet. An early example of this new writing—possibly the very first—was found in Bethlehem.

## CHAPTER 2

# SCENT, SPICE,
# AND CHEMICALS

## *The Iron Age*

*Tell el-Yehudiyeh
Ware.*

Asquare stone church dedicated to St. George sits at the edge of
the vineyards in the village of al-Khader. The church used to be a
monastery, but in the nineteenth century it became a mosque,
which is when the village got its current name, al-Khader, or "The Green."
Al-Khader is a Muslim saint who has blended so well with the figure of St.
George that the two are indistinguishable. The mosque was reconverted to
a church in the late nineenth century thanks to a donation from Russia.
On the back wall of the courtyard there are old chains hanging from a
rusting bolt. The story is that St. George was chained to the wall as a

prisoner, and if a lunatic is chained to the wall overnight, then St. George will bless him and exorcise his demons. I try the chains on for size, but not for long enough to feel the benefits, unfortunately.

There are more modern kinds of madness in al-Khader. The soccer stadium rising above the church is home to the al-Khader Boys, one of the twelve teams in the West Bank Premier League. The stadium is also used for an annual grape festival. It was built with a grant from Portugal in 2007, and is squeezed into a space between the church and the eight-meter-high concrete wall that Israel began building around Bethlehem in 2004. A bypass road for Jewish settlers lies on the other side of the wall. The wall is there to mark territory rather than prevent people from crossing; there is an underpass beneath the wall that leads to al-Khader's orchards, as well as the stop for the number 23 bus to Jerusalem. The wall traces the limits of Bethlehem's built-up urban area, and where the farmland begins—the beautiful hills and valleys that are home to Bethlehem's villages and forty-two Jewish settlements. In July 2004, as the route of the wall was published, the International Court of Justice (ICJ) gave an advisory opinion. The fifteen judges voted fourteen to one that the wall is illegal; the route is not determined by security concerns, they said, but is intended to "create a 'fait accompli' on the ground that could well become permanent . . . tantamount to de facto annexation." At the moment, Palestinians can move freely from one side of the wall. There is always the fear that one day the underpass will be sealed.

IN 1953, TWENTY-SIX BRONZE spearheads were discovered in al-Khader. The jagged, leaf-shaped pieces were dated to the late twelfth or early eleventh century BCE. The fact that they came bundled together suggests they belonged to an armory. Al-Khader lies at the crossroads where the Dead Sea trail through Wadi Khreitoun bisects the Hebron Road. The find of spearheads suggests al-Khader was a military garrison and toll station over three thousand years ago. The spearheads tell us that the Dead Sea trade was so lucrative that it warranted taxing or defending at this early date. The find is all the more significant because five of the spearheads are inscribed in an alphabetic phonetic script, perhaps the earliest examples of this script ever found. The spearheads stand at the start of a revolution that freed human potential like no other invention before or since. Once literacy is common, we become equals, at least in the sense that we are all able to weigh evidence and make judgments. The spearheads stand at the beginning of a process that leads to the idea of human rights and universal justice, as well as to a fourteen-to-one advisory opinion at the ICJ.

The word "alphabet" comes from the Canaanite letters Alf 𐤄 and Beit 𐤍, which are also the words for "cow" and "house." A large quantity of documents have now been found using this alphabetic script, including blessings and invocations, legal documents, and shopping-style lists as well as exercises designed to teach children to read and write. After a short education, anyone could write the new script, unlike the Akkadian system it replaced. Moreover, the script could be written on anything. Instead of clay tablets people began to scribble on papyrus, parchment, and slate tiles, scratching figures into ceramic glazes, carving legends into ivory, stone, or jewelry, and even engraving blessings onto weapons. Lorenzo Nigro from the team exploring the nearby burial site tells me that although iron was beginning to come into use for weapons, bronze remained prized as a more precious metal. The spearheads are beautiful objects, elongated leaf-like shapes that would have been fixed to a javelin by inserting the "stem" into a drilled socket. Given their relatively small size, they were likely to have been used on short spears for close combat; high-status, elegant, and perhaps slightly out-of-date weapons, like the cavalry officers' swords of a later age. The inscriptions honor Anat, a goddess worshipped in what is now Syria. The Egyptians and Hittites had fought a great battle in Syria in 1274 BCE. Six thousand chariots took to the field beside the Orontes River in the largest chariot battle ever known. The fight exhausted both armies. Soon afterwards, the Egyptians pulled back to the Nile while the Hittites fragmented into smaller operations, rather like a giant industrial behemoth hit by federal antitrust laws. The result was a power vacuum in Canaan.

Some archaeologists see this period as a time of crisis, favoring the term Late Bronze Collapse and looking for evidence of droughts or floods to explain the retreat away from a long period of earth-encircling empires. However, there are many signs pointing in the opposite direction, to a time of innovation. In Canaan, this proved to be an exciting time as the land was released from an imperial system that no longer served progress. Perhaps what we read as a collapse is actually a sign that existing empires were too slow to cope with changing technology in weapons, trade, and, of course, writing—which gave smaller rivals a competitive advantage. The dominant trade in Bethlehem had been olive oil destined for Egyptian markets, but al-Khader stands on a route up from the Dead Sea, which implies different products: wool, of course, from the desert graziers but also chemicals like bitumen, alum, and fuller's earth. The destination for these chemicals was new, too. The trail from al-Khader continues west toward the port cities of the Mediterranean: for the first time, goods were being trafficked to the sea.

A new warrior alliance had arrived on the Mediterranean coast and built southern Canaan's first ports. More than this, they supplied the territory with a name. From now on, the neighboring powers would call this land after them: Palestine, Falestin, Pelest, Philistia.

WHEN I FIRST VISITED ISRAEL in the mid-1990s, three-quarters of the population lived between Jaffa and Haifa, on a narrow band at the sea's edge, as though an entire country had been laid out on a beach. In the years since, aggressive government funding has attempted to tilt Israel's center of balance away from these mixed, multi-faith cities toward the Jews-only settlements in occupied Palestine. Yet even now the most desirable real estate lies on the Mediterranean in cities like Jaffa, Tel Aviv, Haifa, and Acre. We all love the beach life, but it is a relatively new fashion, made possible by engineering projects so familiar that we no longer appreciate their scale or ambition. The sea brings strong and unpredictable weather. The coastline is *wiggly* in all directions, both up and down and in and out. Rivers are at their widest and swampiest where they flow into the sea, which means they cannot be easily bridged or forded. Anyone who chose to live on the coast was quite literally off the beaten track. This isolation bred a different kind of people: fishermen, smugglers, pirates, people torn between sea and land. A coastal highway through Palestine did eventually develop, called naturally the Way of the Philistine, but the main road connecting Egypt to Syria remained the longer route along the King's Highway. The relative inaccessibility of the Lebanese coast, which sits behind a mountain range, provided a protective enclave where Canaanite/ Phoenician seamen would one day make their own leap into empire: the

North African Punic Empire of Hannibal. But before them came the Philistine, the Mediterranean's first sea people.

The British Museum has a collection of sarcophagi used by the Philistine to bury their dead, modeled and painted with friendly, big-featured faces. It is disconcerting to find that the Philistine may have resembled the Flooglies from the film *Spy Kids*. The sides of the sarcophagi are decorated with Egyptian hieroglyphics, but the words are meaningless. The Philistines are brash newcomers who do not understand hieroglyphs; they just like the effect, like basketball players who misspell the words tattooed on their bodies. The Philistines are a mystery, in part, because they seem to have so few particular ethnic traits, only the absence of identifiers: they borrow their culture, they cannot read or write, and they do not speak Canaanite. They are sailors, when hitherto all nations have been land-based. At different times, they have been confidently identified as Sardinian or Sicilian or some other kind of Italian, as well as Doric and Hittite. There was a group called the *Palastin* among the Syro-Hittites in Anatolia who ought to represent a good match, though the evidence is rather weaker than one would expect. Perhaps, like their exact contemporaries, the Trojans, the Philistine had their roots among the downsizing Hittites. Wherever they came from, they made their way by sea, island hopping across the Mediterranean and picking up comrades as they went. Like the later Romans, they are probably best seen as a multiethnic alliance of men who had been cast out of their own societies. They are outlaws, maybe even the sea version of the Hells Angels. They appeared over the horizon, on boats with single sails and wide stable hulls that were chiefly propelled by oarsmen.

The Egyptians first encountered the Philistines as raiders on the Nile delta. They had no cavalry, as they could not carry horses, but used their ships as landing craft and attacked as infantry. They may have been the first people to use swords. In Canaan, they built their cities on riverheads, which made them inaccessible to chariot attacks. According to the biblical tradition, the Philistines were restricted to the five cities they built: Ashkelon, Gaza, Jaffa, Gath, and Ekron. In fact, the Philistine settled throughout Palestine, as discoveries of sarcophagi and ceramic pots from what is now northern Israel show. However, the famous five cities appear to be the first Philistine strongholds. Their number may hint at their earlier life as a coalition. If they had internal divisions, this may have been their strength: an alliance based around a string of coastal cities is far stronger than one large city. The five cities are each a day's march from each other, ensuring that reinforcements were never far away.

If the Philistine arrived abruptly, they disappeared just as quickly, around a hundred and fifty years later. However, as the cities they built continued to thrive, they probably became invisible through assimilation. They adopted the local culture, and then they disappeared into it. Yet despite their mystery, the Philistine did create a strong impression on all the neighbors. From this moment on, southern Canaan was seen as their land. In Egypt, it becomes known as Pelest, in Greek it is Philistia, Falastin in both Canaanite and later Arabic, and Palestine in Latin. The Greeks began to reserve the name Phoenicia purely for the coastal cities of what is now Lebanon. The Bible stories especially reflect the Philistine's elevation into a powerful myth, treating them not as a historical people but as an eternal and ever-present dark force. They are there back in the mythical days of Abraham. They are embodied as Goliath, whose Achilles-like invulnerability had the tiniest weak spot that only a nomadic shepherd could exploit. At other points in David's story the Philistine are said to be the rulers of Bethlehem, and are still credited as the enemy when the Bible narrative turns to an actual historical character, Hezekiah, who governed Jerusalem long after the Philistine had faded into the landscape.

The goofy-face sarcophagus with the nonsense hieroglyphics could make anyone warm to the Philistines. Their great achievement was to pull off the classic trick of the poacher who turns gamekeeper. They went from being pirates to becoming the Palestinian Port Authority.

AN IRISH CLERGYMAN NAMED Dr. Joseph Barclay began his visit to the Holy Land in 1861 with a shopping expedition and came away with a seventh-century BCE bathroom ornament carved from a giant clamshell, *Tridacna squamosa*. Once again, I go to see it in a study room in the British Museum. It is solid, though delicate, colored in a pearly cream: the kind of shell that carries Venus to the shore in Botticelli's imagination. It once held face cream or powder: the cosmetics business is one of Palestine's earliest indigenous industries. The cream would have been scented with perfume oils, probably from Yemen or the Arabian Peninsula, though the bulk of the product would be olive oil or even mutton tallow, combined with alum from the Dead Sea. Alum is a natural astringent and has anti-fungicidal properties, important in the days before the invention of lathering soap.

Barclay served two stints in Palestine with the London Society for the Promotion of Christianity Among the Jews, and later became the third joint Anglican-Lutheran Bishop of Jerusalem. He donated this shell and the other objects he had purchased to the British Museum in 1865, where they are displayed beside the Philistine sarcophagi. The pieces, which also include amulets and perfume flasks, are all in good condition, suggesting that they were found in a burial chamber. Barclay said the local dealer had told him that the objects were discovered close to Rachel's Tomb, a Roman Christian pilgrimage site that had become a Muslim cemetery by 1861. It is unlikely that the pieces were found at Rachel's Tomb. We cannot know if they actually came from Bethlehem or even represent a single cache. But they all date from around the same time, the ninth or eighth century BCE, and they all have a certain beauty department flavor. No trace of perfume remains in the flasks, so there is no way yet of saying if they once contained frankincense from Arabia, myrrh from Ethiopia, or balm from Jericho. Nevertheless, the perfume flasks are evidence that the long-range trade along the Spice Route was already in full swing by this date. And it is not the only evidence.

The shell, *Tridacna squamosa,* is native to the Indian Ocean and would have reached Palestine along the Nabataean Spice Route with the perfume oils and incense. Hundreds of examples of carved Giant Clam shells have been found across Palestine, and exported as far as Italy, Sicily, and Sardinia. The shell represents the height of fashion in Iron Age home furnishing; this is *Elle Decor,* spring 800 BCE. The shells have never quite gone out of fashion: my mother used one as a soap dish in the 1970s. I have to wear medical gloves to handle the shell, actually a half shell, as a clam is a creature of two halves. My strongest feeling on picking up the shell is that I have seen contemporary examples in Bethlehem. Bethlehem craftsmen have been carving Christian devotional scenes on shells since at least the sixteenth century. The technique uses the layers within the shell, accumulated year by year as the shell grows, to produce iridescent three-dimensional scenes in the mother of pearl, usually of religious scenes and Christ's Nativity. They are typically carved from oyster shells, though I have also seen carved nautiluses and conches. There are valuable examples of Bethlehem mother of pearl in church museums, including the Vatican, and the Topkapi Palace of Istanbul, but I have seen nineteenth- and twentieth-century examples in a display in the Bethlehem Museum and in glass cases of the older souvenir shops, many of which are run by families who have been in the trade since the sixteenth century: Lama, Giacomen, Dabdoub, Rock, Zougbi, and others. Holding Barclay's cosmetic dish, it seems possible that this trade does not just date back six hundred years; it could go back almost three thousand years.

Once again, James Fraser talks me through the carving. It depicts a goddess known variously as Astarte, Ishtar, Ashareh, or Ashtoreth. He points out the goddess's features in the small, raised nodule that forms the shell's hinge. At last, I see a nose following the central line of the shell's hinge, and then oval eyes placed on either side. The goddess has a hawklike aspect, narrow and querying. All at once, she becomes as clear as day. I turn the shell around, and the shell's deep corrugations reveal themselves as the folds of her cloak, traced with feathery patterns like a peacock's tail.

The skills required to carve a clamshell are transferrable to ivory, and carved ivory was a major industry in Palestine by the eighth century BCE. Finds of ornate ivory buckles and amulets show the sophistication of Palestinian craftsmen. There is a particularly glorious carving of palm trees, once the decoration on a piece of furniture, now in University College London's Petrie Collection. The piece suggests that the fashion in interior design favored remote and exotic scenes. Palm trees are not particularly Palestinian: they belong to the warmer climates of Jordan and Arabia. This kind of ivory-embellished furniture was a specialty of Palestine, and held in such high regard that ivory pieces are specifically itemized in a long list of valuables demanded as tribute by the Nineveh-based emperor of the new Neo-Assyrian dynasty. The report specifically singles out ivory beds and chairs.

The entry of Nineveh into Palestine ended the long period of No Overall Control, and the emperor's demand for ivory furniture came at the end of a short-lived rebellion by Jerusalem. The ivory furniture was a penalty payment for bad behavior, and tells us the kinds of items for which Palestine was famous. The list also includes ebony, which came from India and its islands, and gold, which, like ivory, came from East Africa. Then there are also chemicals, both fabric dyes and kohl. These items are also part of the Nabataean trade: they carried a far wider variety of goods than spice and incense.

The Nabataeans used Jerusalem as a free port—or perhaps as an Amazon-style warehouse. The city was a distribution center for goods that had been imported from much further afield. The trade made the city rich and, as the emperor's demands show, Nineveh kept a greedy eye on the inventory. It is impossible to overstate the wealth of goods travelling through Palestine in the eighth and seventh centuries. When Nineveh was succeeded by a Babylon-based regime, a new city named Tayma was built in the desert purely to block the Nabataeans' trade route. Taxing the Nabataeans was not a perk or a marginal benefit: entire empires were funded by Nabataean wealth.

In the late eighth century BCE, the governor of Jerusalem, Hezekiah, rebelled, backed by Nabataean fighters. The neo-Assyrians record an Arab force inside the Jerusalem garrison alongside Hezekiah's "mercenaries." The term Arab then referred exclusively to the Nabataeans.

THERE IS NO CLEAR ETYMOLOGY for the term Arab, and trying to trace one is complicated. In the classical age, Greek and Latin writers would invent etymologies to add color to their accounts of people or places, or else to foreshadow their destiny, mixing myth and history together. Thus, the word Arab has been associated with the desert, with terms meaning "outsiders" or "the west," and also with the name of the biblical Patriarch Abraham, which also gives us the Greek word "Hebrew." But to the neo-Assyrians and neo-Babylonians, "Arab" simply meant Nabataean.

The Nabataean kingdom with its capital in Petra began to take shape in the sixth century BCE. However, their network of trade routes is considerably older, dating back before the eighth century BCE. The Nabataeans were not only traders; they also had an unparalleled reputation as engineers: the archaeologist Avraham Negev suggests the word "Nabataean" means "water-finder." Nabataean aqueducts and cisterns have been found in the Arabian Peninsula, the Negev, Jordan, and Palestine. The signature element is a lime-based hydraulic plaster, a combination of quicklime and silica. When it comes into contact with water, the mix undergoes a chemical change and creates a waterproof barrier. The Nabataeans used their plaster to coat the insides of the cisterns they dug in the remote dry desert, and then began to coat the watercourses and aqueducts they constructed to fill their cisterns. Nabataean chemists found a way to produce quicklime at relatively low temperatures, but the great leap forward came with the discovery of a fine, naturally occurring silica, found in remote desert locations. The need to produce a very fine silica is a key reason why so few civilizations mastered hydraulic cement. The Greeks would grind up ceramic pots, which made their plaster as lumpy as *taramasalata*. The Romans used silica-rich ash from Mount Etna, ground to a powder. Only the Nabataeans had a ready source that was already fine enough to make cement plaster.

The Nabataeans kept their techniques secret, so the discovery of an ancient cistern is a marker of their influence. The cisterns begin to appear in Palestinian cities during the Assyrian period. In Beit Shemesh, for instance, we see the construction of an entire system of elaborately joined cisterns by the eighth century BCE. Around the same time, Hezekiah's fortress was linked to a spring in Silwan via a subterranean channel. The presence of a Nabataean force in Jerusalem suggests they acted as contractors, not only selling the latest municipal water systems but also sticking around as consultants to implement the technology. To use cisterns effectively, it is not sufficient to dig chambers into the ground and paint them with waterproof plaster. It requires a new attitude toward urban space, ensuring that run-off water is directed to the cisterns to be conserved. Every drop of rainwater hitting the roofs of the city, skittering across the pavements and splashing into the gutters, has to flow into the cisterns, and this requires fundamentally rethinking a city. This is why it makes sense to see the Nabataeans as contractors as well as salesmen or warriors. Whenever a Palestinian city begins organizing its urban fabric around cisterns and the conservation of water, we see the hand of the Nabataeans.

The influence persists: all homes in Bethlehem have underground cisterns, and the roofs and balconies are arranged to keep the cistern filled with rainwater. Digging a cistern is such a familiar part of Bethlehem's way of life that no one makes anything of it, until they turn up a prehistoric elephant. It is simply a part of the urban infrastructure, an unrecognized influence from three thousand years ago that blew in from the desert, to shape Palestine's distinctive culture.

THE SUFFIX TO THE NAME Hezekiah, or *Hizkiyyahu*, denotes a worshipper of Yehu, the god that gives us the root of the word "Jew." Hezekiah is presented in the Bible's Book of Kings as one among a long line of Jerusalem-based rulers that stretch back into a time of myth. These passages, written centuries later, show the influence of Greek and Roman writing, when it had become a part of the rhetoric of kingship to link real kings to mythical forebears: Romulus and Remus, for instance, or Ilos and Tros. In tracing their rulers back to gods and heroes, classical writers were not doing genealogy in the modern sense. They were not scholars or genealogists, they were myth-makers. The Bible traces Hezekiah's family to a mythical founder, *Yehudah* (Judah). On the face of it, this story downgrades the god Yehu to the level of a mortal, Yehudah. By the second and first centuries BCE when the Bible is written, God is regarded as a hidden figure about whom nothing can be said. The myth of Yehudah, a founding mortal father, serves to edit the old god from the story, while giving Hezekiah's family a touch more vintage. From the historical standpoint of the real Hezekiah, however, all this takes place five or six hundred years in the future. His god is Yehu and his allegiance to this figure is independent of any attachment to any particular land or even any people.

Hezekiah's rebellion against Nineveh makes him the earliest proto-Jewish figure to appear in a datable historical source. It is notable that the Nineveh report into the siege of Jerusalem makes no mention of civilians or even local forces. It speaks only about Hezekiah, his mercenaries, and the Nabataean Arabs. If Hezekiah was a proto-Jewish ruler, whom did he rule over? Was he a king without subjects? Or were the Assyrians ignoring the civilian non-combatants, the slaves and farmers who fed his garrison?

Writing about the relation between Iron Age warlords and their subjects, historian Ephraim Stern states: "While each nation's chief (male) god had a distinctive name, the chief female deity had the same name in all these cultures: Asherah or its variants Ashtoreth or Astarte." The distinction between the male "nation" and the female "culture" is dubious. There are no nations at this time: the actual distinction is between incoming warlords and the existing peasants. However, Stern's basic point is sound: warlords arrived with their own gods, and though they would not tolerate other male gods, if the peasants worshipped a female deity, warlords were happy to co-opt her. As Stern notes, the goddess across Palestine was always Astarte, the figure carved on the Giant Clam soap dish and on a thousand other objects. Trying to keep track of the numerous male gods can be tricky. They have names like Baal, Marduk, El, and Yehu, each favored in a handful of cities, and each with his own origins myths. Keeping these gods straight is rather like memorizing a collector's pack of Iron Age superheroes. Only Astarte is always the same. The peasants were allowed their own identity as long as it was feminized and passive, and so could be symbolically bound in submission to a god king. Across Palestine, Astarte was married off to these male gods in hastily arranged shotgun weddings.

The marriage of Yehu and Astarte produced many shrines and temples. The couple was worshipped in Jerusalem, Bethel, Beit Semesh, Samaria, the Sinai, and elsewhere. In Bethlehem, there is no evidence as yet of any shrines to this male/female union, though traces of the Astarte cult can be detected. The traditional henna night at weddings in Bethlehem sees the hands and feet of the bride traced with henna paint—an echo of Canaanite-era ceremonies that honored the union of Baal and Anat, continuing into later marriages like those of Yehu and Astarte. A Jewish tradition sees Astarte represented by a wooden "Asherah pole" that is intended to signify a tree. The Bible contains several appeals to destroy these poles, and not to set them up near altars, yet at Jewish weddings and at the harvest festival of Sukkot, the poles are used to raise canopies, a ruse to smuggle the goddess of fertility back so that she can perform a surreptitious blessing. In Bethlehem, both Christians and Muslims celebrate weddings and the harvest with an initial open air feast beneath trees. At local Muslim weddings, as in Jewish weddings around the world, brides and grooms are lifted on chairs in a wild and celebratory wedding dance. The use of chairs might seem to have more obvious roots in sedan chairs and the thrones of kings and queens, yet the way that each of the four chair legs are lifted up high by individual guests suggests to me the raising and carrying of Asherah poles. I remember a wedding between two of Anton Sansour's students, when he was Vice Chancellor of Bethlehem University, and seeing the bride and groom tossed about so violently that the groom's head went straight through the polystyrene ceiling tiles.

Astarte is often portrayed holding her breasts, combining fertility and love in the figure of a nursing mother. Behind the Church of the Nativity, on the aptly named Milk Grotto Street, there is a chapel dedicated to the moment Mary breast-fed Christ. The story is that a couple of drops of milk fell to the ground, turning the ground white. The chapel is carved from a series of small caves, their intimacy enhanced by the warm light that plays off the limestone. A vein of soft white stone runs against the deeper amber rock. It is believed that if a little was scraped away and mixed with water, the milky drink can cure infertility or help with nursing problems. A grain of an older folk religion, once repressed, bubbles back to the surface to offer comfort.

THE REVEREND BARCLAY'S little cache of objects has been dated to the seventh century BCE, around the time of Hezekiah's rule. It includes a small figurine of Astarte, known as a pillar statue, which makes it sound grander than it is. She is only a few inches tall, made in two pieces. Her body is a molded clay pipe, while her head and breasts are modeled separately and attached to the stem. She resembles a Pez dispenser with boobs, and like a Pez dispenser she is a mass-produced object. More than four hundred of the eight hundred pillar statues recovered have been found inside Jerusalem, indicating that the center of production was inside the city. The worship of Astarte evidently had official sponsors. The authorities were not simply co-opting the local religion, they were making an effort to reach out—perhaps even to woo the locals. Warlords were discovering that political control was no longer a simple master-slave dynamic. Brute force was not enough; regimes had to learn to act politically.

The period between the eighth and the sixth centuries BCE sees rulers beginning to pay attention to the beliefs and traditions of the populace. Kings and even emperors find that respecting the traditions and culture of their subjects confers legitimacy on their claim to kingship. The Neo-Assyrian emperor Ashurbanipal builds the first national library in his capital, Nineveh. In Babylon, the emperor Nabonidus sets about conserving the city's ruins, in the process earning a reputation as the first archaeologist.

When Babylon falls to the Persian Cyrus the Great in 539 BCE, even Cyrus declares that his first aim is to protect and preserve the city's old traditions. Nothing resembling the Jewish nation of the Bible yet exists, though we have firsthand accounts of the proto-Jewish Yehu forces, thanks to a cache of letters written from a Yehu garrison stationed on the Nile, as part of the Persian occupation force. It is striking that the letters show no particular interest in Jerusalem. The Yehu faith crosses borders of ethnicity and language, but as yet has no geographic center. In his book *The Invention of the Jewish People*, Shlomo Sand argues that Jewish history has multiple origins, emerging not only in Palestine, but also from communities in Babylon, Iran, Arabia, and elsewhere. The one Palestinian ruler that the letter writers do respect is the king of Samaria, known as Sanballat. The letters target him for a charity appeal—they ask for funds to rebuild their temple by the Nile.

The Sanballat dynasty recurs in an account of Alexander the Great's conquest of Palestine, written by the Roman-era Jewish historian Josephus. Alexander conquered Palestine in 332 BCE, while Josephus wrote his history some four hundred years later. The Sanballats of Samaria joined forces with Alexander, but Jerusalem resisted, remaining loyal to Persia. Josephus tells us that Alexander was so angry that he marched on Jerusalem, intent on destroying the city. Only at the last minute, in a kind of miraculous conversion, he changed his mind. He used Jerusalem as the site of a speech addressed to the Persian Jews of Babylon and Medea, assuring them that they will find a friend in him. It is impossible to say what is fact and what is fanciful in Josephus's account. Whatever his sources, they no longer exist. It is certain that Jerusalem was not a significant city in Alexander's day. Yet it shortly became one. As the Yehu faith spread under Greek rule, these diverse communities came to see Jerusalem as the key Palestinian city, and the area around the yet-to-be-built Bethlehem as its ancient heartland. The fact that Jerusalem grew into a priestly city and a focus of pilgrimage is due to a confluence of reasons, not least of which is that it stood on the Nabataeans' incense route.

But the one great reason for Jerusalem's rise is Bethlehem. All of the water for the rapidly expanding Jerusalem lay below its hills. All it needed was someone to take notice and build an aqueduct.

# CHAPTER 3

# BETHLEHEM AND CHRIST

## *The Classical Age*

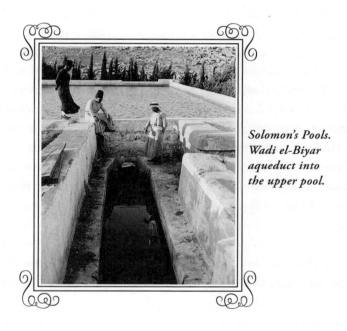

*Solomon's Pools.
Wadi el-Biyar
aqueduct into
the upper pool.*

On a bright day in early November 2016, I stood on a rocky terrace at Mar Saba Monastery in Bethlehem's wilderness staring down to the bubbling stream in the Kidron Valley below. When I first visited Bethlehem, more than twenty years earlier, the writer William Dalrymple was also in town, staying in Mar Saba as he wrote his debut book, *From the Holy Mountain.* He reports that the Greek abbot warned him that on the Day of Judgment the river would turn to blood as devils chased the Pope, the Freemasons, and other sinners through the valley to hell. This terrace was the perfect place to watch the fun at the End of Days, he learned.

I was too early to catch the devils and the Freemasons, but I thought the fast-flowing Kidron Stream was miracle enough. It was a raging hot day, Bethlehem had seen no rain for eight months, we were in the middle of a desert, and yet water was tumbling and frothing as it ran through the ravine eighty feet below the monastery. How was it possible? I was told that the stream was not carrying water; it was pure sewage, and if I stood any closer the stench would be overpowering. Palestinians in occupied East Jerusalem are not hooked up to the Israeli sewage system, and more than eight million gallons of untreated sewage are pumped into the Bethlehem wilderness each day, before emptying into the Dead Sea.

The Kidron Stream has long been an open sewer, which is perhaps why the valley was seen as a conduit that would one day sweep away the worst of the world. At the turn of the second century BCE, Alexandrian pilgrims were visiting Jerusalem in their tens of thousands. The city's infrastructure was crumbling and the single spring at Silwan was inadequate. Worse, the channel from the Silwan pools had been cut directly beneath the temple mount, allowing raw sewage, offal, and blood from the temple sacrifices to pollute the water supply. An aqueduct intended to bring water to the temple had become a sewer, poisoning the the inhabitants of Silwan—as it does again under Israeli military occupation.

PILGRIMAGE TO JERUSALEM began under the rule of the Ptolemies, a dynasty founded in 305 BCE by Alexander's general, Ptolemy I Soter. The new Egyptian capital was the port city of Alexandria, built with the help of Sanballatian forces who became the city's founding community. Throughout classical antiquity, Alexandria was the city with the world's largest Jewish population, larger than any individual city in Palestine. Alexandria's original community came to regard themselves as Jewish rather than as Samaritan: the doctrinal split between Jews and Samaritans did not happen until much later, driven by the rise of Jerusalem. At the end of the third century BCE, however, Jerusalem's chances of becoming a powerful city even within Palestine, let alone on the international stage, would have seemed slight. The city had no military forces. It was ruled from Amman, whose Yehu-worshipping Tobiads collected its taxes, and it was overshadowed by the Sanballat cities of Northern Palestine. Yet Jerusalem's weakness became its strength as the city's aristocracy focused on religion rather than warfare. It became a city of priests.

A document known as the Letter of Aristeas connects all the elements of Jerusalem's rise together: the Alexandrian pilgrims, the new religious doctrines, and the aqueduct from Bethlehem. The real Aristeas was a Jewish advisor to the Ptolemaic court in Alexandria, though the author of the letter is an imposter. The document is usually dated to the turn of the second century BCE, and certainly existed by 160 BCE, because fragments from this date are preserved in the writing of the Christian scholar Eusebius. The link to Ptolemaic Alexandria via the name "Aristeas" strongly argues the document was written before the Damascus-based Seleucids seized Jerusalem in 200 BCE.

The Letter of Aristeas recounts the story of the writing of the Jewish Bible, a book known as the Septuagint—or "the Seventy"—because it is credited to seventy-two translators. The story goes that each was asked to turn the original Jewish scriptures into Greek, and all miraculously produced an identical text. This myth disguises the fact that the Septuagint is not really a translation: it is better regarded as an original work. In many cases, there are no other older versions of the Bible. Even when extracts have been found in the local languages—whether Canaanite or Aramaic—these fragments are not necessarily more authoritative than the Greek. The Dead Sea Scrolls are the chief source of non-Greek fragments of Jewish scripture, and few if any predate the third century BCE, making the oldest among them roughly contemporaneous with the Septuagint. The Septuagint is the first edited and collated Bible, and it continued to be updated and revised well into the first century CE.

The Greek-language Septuagint was the sacred text read in synagogues until the Islamic period, when an Arabic translation became standard for Jews in the Arabic-speaking world. It is conventional to use the term "Hebrew" to refer to Jewish scripture written in ancient Canaanite, though the first full-length Hebrew translation of the Jewish Bible—known as the Masoretic Text—was only created in the Middle Ages. The edition regarded as the most authoritative is even more recent. It is a Renaissance document published in Venice after the invention of the printing press.

The Letter of Aristeas speaks about the pilgrim trade, the water resources and the bible in the same breath, linking together the three factors that underpin Jerusalem's new preeminence. The letter reassures travellers that there is sufficient water to wash away the blood of the "many thousands of beasts" sacrificed in the temple, and that the water drawn from distant sources constantly replenishes the cisterns below the temple. The aqueduct from Artas to Jerusalem is fourteen miles long, tracing the contours of every hill to make its path almost double the direct route along Hebron road.

Two reservoirs were dug by the spring at Artas to feed the Bethlehem-Jerusalem aqueduct. Today, there are three reservoirs, known as Solomon's Pools, an epithet they gained later, possibly under crusader rule. The higher pools were built in the Roman era, around the turn of the first millennium CE. The lower pool was constructed by combining the two original Greek reservoirs in the reign of the Mamluk sultan Khushqadam in the 1460s. It is by far the largest of the three, with a capacity of 113,000 square meters. The original Ptolemaic reservoirs may have been smaller, yet the water pressure had to be sufficient to raise the water through an inverted siphon to the mouth of the aqueduct, which followed the hill track between Artas and Bethlehem along the valley wall of Wadi Ma-ali.

The interiors of the pools descend in a series of stone terraces, like steps designed to allow a giant to waddle down to the water's edge and bathe his feet. The Artas spring is buried inside the lower reservoir, so there is always a little water in the pool. This spring also supplied water to Tuqu', the customs post at the head of the Khreitoun Valley. The upper reservoirs are fed by more distant springs. I remember a picnic in the forest around the pools when I first noticed the aqueducts running down the rocky hillside between the pines. I had joined a scavenger hunt for 'aqqub, a thorny cactus-like plant that is carefully de-spiked before it is cooked in stews. It looks a little like rhubarb and tastes like sour celery. Scrambling up a slope through the pine needles, I saw a trench-like water channel—deep, dry scars that snaked through the trees around the reservoirs. This was the al-Arrub aqueduct, which takes its name from Ain al-Arrub, a spring on the outskirts of Hebron. It takes a slow twenty-five mile route to go just twelve and a half miles. The Wadi al-Biyar aqueduct is fed by its headspring at Ain Faghour, which also lies south of Bethlehem, on Hebron Road. Both aqueducts have side branches that collect water from the other springs along their routes. It was one of those balmy days when the air is thick with resin from the pines, and the sunlight plays between the shadows of the surrounding trees on the surface of the water. The forest seems ancient but was planted by the British in the early twentieth century.

The three reservoirs descend toward Artas in steps, one after the other. From around 2012, the pools have been fenced off behind chicken wire, and you have to buy a ticket from the conference center across the road if you want to picnic at the water's edge. The conference center was commissioned in the optimism of the Oslo Peace Accords, but was unfinished when Israel invaded in 2002. It sat semi-built and semi-derelict for a decade. It is now open for business, and there is also a nice little ethnographical museum in the sixteenth-century fortress that overlooks the highest reservoir—which is all good, except that you can no longer wander freely across the pools. In spring, after the winter rains, the water in the lower pool hovers ominously above the village. Most of the year, though, the levels are low. I once happened on three boys with fishing rods standing at the water's edge at the bottom of an almost-dry pool, where some sheep were grazing on bushes that grew out of the stonework. To my amazement, the boys caught a small fish and stood waving it proudly. It might have come all the way from the spring in Hebron.

The original Greek siphon is long gone. The British replaced it with a pumping station, which served Jerusalem until 1967 when Israel conquered the West Bank. The Israelis chose to bypass the reservoirs entirely by drawing water directly from the aquifer at an army base and settlement they called Kfar Etzion, built at Ain Faghour. The reservoirs are not much higher than Jerusalem, only thirty meters above the temple. In Greek times, the water flowed by gravity alone. The aqueduct dropped by about eight inches for every hundred and twenty yards it traversed on its fourteen-mile journey to the temple. In its understated way, the lower aqueduct is an impressive piece of engineering. It is certainly the most important man-made structure in all of Palestine, judged by its impact on the course of history. It became a pipeline rather than a stone watercourse during Ottoman times but, in total, it remained in use for something like twenty-three hundred years.

In late October 2016, I tried to walk the route of the aqueduct. The road skirts above Artas, a densely packed little town that grows cabbages on the bed of wadi inside a series of polytunnels. As the road bends toward Bethlehem, I scoured the hillside for traces of the aqueduct on the hill-face. At the summit of the hill is the Palestinian president's helicopter pad, used only with Israeli permission and almost exclusively by foreign leaders visiting the church: the Italian president was expected in the morning. As the road entered Wadi Ma'ali, I followed the route on the best map I possessed, photographed from a 1907 edition of the Baedeker guide to Syria and Palestine and stored on my phone. (When I opened the copy in the British Library, a first-class train ticket bought in Cleopatra Station in Alexandria, Egypt, fell out. I would have liked to take that journey.)

The aqueduct runs northwest into Wadi Ma'ali then makes a sharp turn below the Carmelite convent to follow the southern flank of Bethlehem's long ridge. At the end of the street, where the road forks left up a short, steep hill to Manger Square, there is a fountain named *Al Ain* (The Spring). It is fed by the aqueduct, and covered by an Ottoman-era stone pavilion that contains a row of troughs for washing clothes. The fountain is derelict and padlocked behind steel bars. In the 1940s, archaeologists began to research the aqueduct. A photograph from the dig shows a well-dressed man crouching inside a tunnel that had been discovered by removing part of the fountain's façade. When I first saw the photograph, I had a feeling I knew who he was, a hunch I confirmed by asking a retired archaeologist named Kay Prag. When we met, she recognized Robert Hamilton, a British archaeologists who worked in Palestine from 1929 to the late 1960s. Hamilton excavated the Bethlehem aqueduct with the leading Palestinian archaeologist of the day, Dimitri Baramki, famous for his excavation of the fabulous Hisham's Palace near Jericho (the site of the world's largest mosaic). Baramki and Hamilton fell out after Hamilton wrote a monograph on Hisham's Palace that failed to mention Baramki at all.

Kay is a small, warm Australian woman who also has a forty-year relationship with Palestine. She worked with the doyenne of Middle Eastern archaeologists, Kathleen Kenyon, as well as with Hamilton, and is still saddened by the rift between Baramki and Hamilton, because the men had once been close. Kay got her first job on a dig in Jerusalem in 1963, travelling from London by train with one of Hamilton's son. Two years later, she was hired by Kenyon to supervise a dig, and this time she drove alone from London to Jerusalem in a second-hand Land Rover she bought for the journey. In those days, Bethlehem and Jerusalem were under Jordanian control; Kay remembers the only route between Jerusalem and Bethlehem was the desert road, because Jewish soldiers on the Israeli side of the border would take potshots at passing vehicles on the direct Hebron Road. This desert road is named Wadi an-Nar, the Valley of Fire. Kay had to take her driving test in the wadi to get a Jordanian license. The test comprised a hill start and nothing else. The police colonel told her that it was enough; if she could do a hill start, she would be all right.

Kay and I arrange to see each other in Manchester, her home since the late 1960s. We meet in the Whitworth Art Gallery and talk like old Mancunians, agreeing that the view through the drizzle of Victoria Park is stunning, and that the tea in the cafe is first class. The photograph of Hamilton on my phone shows a tall man in a pale suit: a little dressy for a man inside an underground tunnel. The sides of the tunnel are rough and uneven. Bethlehem limestone is called the "royal stone" or *Meleke*. It is so soft that it can be cut from the quarry with a knife, but then miraculously hardens on contact with air, changing color with the years to mature from yellow cream to pearly amber.

When I first visited Bethlehem in 1993, Manger Square was a wide, dirty parking lot, paved with crumbling asphalt that would collect the oil drips from the visiting tourist coaches. I had no idea that there was a tunnel below my feet, though I had heard local legends that there was buried treasure beneath the square. In the run-up to the 2000 millennium celebrations, Bethlehemites had a chance to see if the legends were true, as the square was dug up to be re-laid with local marble. A team of archaeologists was on hand to take a look. Kay Prag surveyed the work. She discovered that the saddle between the town and the church was far deeper than she expected. The saddle was on a slant, so it was higher at the point where the aqueduct entered the hill. In Greek times, the tunnel would have emerged closer to the center of what is now the square.

There is an obvious conclusion, and both Kay and I recognize it. The Bible places Bethlehem's water source at the city gates. The original shape of the land suggests an aqueduct emerged in front of the town, and so perhaps there was once a fountain outside the city gates, supplying drinking water for the traders visiting the market and a trough for the animals they were selling. A seventh-century account by the Bishop Arculf describes the water flowing out of a stone in front of the church, into a trough, by the low wall surrounding the town. Bethlehem was a dry, rocky summit and only the water from the aqueduct allowed the town to develop into a market town. Religious scholars have followed William F. Albright in fixing the stories of Bethlehem's town well to the late Bronze Age. Dating the water source more accurately to the Greek-era aqueduct not only changes assumptions about Bethlehem's age, but means that the descriptions of the town in the scriptures should be read as a picture of a Greek or Roman-era life.

From Manger Square, the aqueduct turned toward Jerusalem, following the path of a road everyone calls New Road, though it is labeled Manger Street on tourist maps. New Road is a bypass on the eastern side of Bethlehem's long ridge, replacing the shorter but narrow and hilly Star Street. A section of the original Greek aqueduct was discovered on New Road at the back of a gift shop with the misleading name Roman Canal Stores. It is a small shop by Bethlehem standards. The largest are built to accommodate several coach parties at once. Yet all available space on the floor-to-ceiling shelves is filled with olive wood statuettes and the pretty blue-and-white plates made in Hebron. At the rear of the shop, a small section of the aqueduct is visible through a glass viewing-window. I find I need a stool to peer inside, and the view is so dark that I can make out a layer of cut stone but not much else. I resist telling the owner that the aqueduct is not Roman: no one likes a smart alec. There is a coffee shop next door, part of a Palestinian chain called Stars and Bucks, which has no connection to Starbucks. As I drink a coffee I try to decipher the flash photograph that I took through the viewing-window. The flare from the glass pane obscures most of the image, but I can see the cut ridge of the water channel.

The route of the aqueduct continues along New Road past the main road to Beit Sahour, known as Karkafa Street, and then bears right toward the Caritas Baby Hospital. I could continue following it, but just beyond the last houses in Bethlehem the route is blocked by two rows of electrified fences separated by a strip of dirt road. This is the border of a new settlement named Har Homa, built in 1997 by razing a popular forest park in Bethlehem. The original aqueduct burrowed beneath this hill on its way to Jerusalem, but the fence is as far as I can follow it.

BETHLEHEM SPRANG INTO LIFE around two hundred years before the birth of Christ. The stories about the town in the Jewish Bible may not reflect the Bronze Age, but they do have enormous historical value for what they tell us about Bethlehem in the period from the second century BCE to the first century CE.

The town gates feature in two of the three stories about Bethlehem in the Old Testament. In the Book of Ruth, the landowner Boaz sits down by the gates to negotiate the ownership of Ruth after he has fallen in love with this young farm girl. In the other, three of David's best warriors creep into Bethlehem at night and steal a jug of water. The city they depict is a defensive stronghold, and the city gates and its delicious water are the most important parts of town: the only things worth mentioning. The town gates represent an airlock between the inside and the outside. They are a neutral place of formal negotiation, which is why Boaz waits at the gates rather than visiting the men at their homes.

The story of the theft of water includes a preamble in which David and his men are hiding in the hills as outlaws. David reminisces about the sweetness of the water in Bethlehem. David is always depicted as a shepherd, and a shepherd would only taste the fountain's water on his sporadic visits to trade wool, mutton, and tallow. Just as the city gates provide an airlock between the inside and outside of the city, so Bethlehem is itself an airlock between the farming towns of Palestine's hills and the encircling wilderness of the Bedouin. Bethlehem is a safety valve between these two different cultures—the place where they can meet and do business.

The fact that Bethlehem is mentioned less than a handful of times in the Jewish Bible is striking because it reflects a city with almost no history, and absolutely no pedigree. What is more, all of the stories are addendums and asides to the larger narratives. The story of the water fountain pops up out of sequence, tacked to the end of the section about King David. It is less a story than a preamble to a list of notables and recalls nothing so much as the thank-yous found at the very end of the credits of a film. The names are presumably those of the Greek- or Roman-era aristocratic families, and their inclusion in the Bible is to flatter them with a connection to David.

The Book of Ruth is a folktale with an obvious allegorical theme. A family flees its home because of poverty and famine, signaled in the names of Ruth's late husband and his brother: Sickness and Famine (Mahlon and Chilion). The story also includes a claim that Ruth is the great-grandmother of David, a connection that has no bearing on the tale, though it means it earns its place in the Bible. In the Christian Old Testament, the story is inserted after Judges in what would be its approximate chronological place; in the Jewish Bible it is relegated to the Writings section, below the status of a genuinely sacred text.

The only other story is the tale of the Levite and his concubine. The Levite has gone to Bethlehem to buy a sex slave, and her murder on the way home sparks a civil war between the Israelite tribes. The war story turns into a close reworking of the Roman legend of the Rape of the Sabine Women, an indication of the influence that Roman culture was exerting over Alexandria at the time that the Bible was being constructed.

Taken with the story of Ruth, the picture that emerges of Bethlehem is a little town famous chiefly for its women. All the stories depict Bethlehem as a largely foreign, non-Jewish city, either because the majority of its population are slaves (as in Ruth), or because a foreign power governs it (as in the David story), or both—as in the tale of the Levite and his concubine.

THE THREE STORIES ABOUT Bethlehem may echo older folktales, but as scripture, they would only have entered circulation a century or two before the birth of Christ. Bethlehem in Greek is Βηθλεεμ, which leaves us no wiser as to whether the name as the locals knew it has Canaanite, Aramaic, or Arabic roots. Bethlehem enters the literary record as a place where locals are available for purchase as workers, wives, and concubines. This reflects a Hellenic world: the emergence of large, multiethnic imperial cities has led to the rise of a class of urban free men and their opposite, the slave class. The Greek conquest condemned agricultural peasants to slavery, where they became the property of landowners. This was a subtle difference to the pre-Hellenic world where warlords ruled over peasants who might also be tied to the land but were not necessarily available to be bought and sold. Commercial slavery underpinned the Greek political economy.

In Bethlehem, there was another reason to enslave people: security. Thanks to its aqueduct, Bethlehem was heavily militarized throughout antiquity. The Bethlehem aqueduct is a kind of metaphysical proposition: it created the conditions for the possibility of Jerusalem as a Holy City and pilgrimage site. Yet the aqueduct is also a weakness, even a quiet act of sabotage. Jerusalem began life as a military fortress, but after its elevation it became impossible to defend. All it takes to conquer Jerusalem is to seize its water supply, as history has proved, again and again. This is what every future invader did, from the Seleucids to the crusaders, the Mamluks and Ottomans to the British Army, ending with the 1967 conquest of Jerusalem by Israeli forces.

The security of Jerusalem requires that the whole of the Bethlehem district be militarized, not simply the area around the reservoirs or the route of the aqueduct but also the hilltop springs of al-Arrub, Ain Faghour, Battir, Artas, and others. The territory is 700 square kilometers, and incredibly hilly, making it difficult to mobilize forces or search the terraces and valleys, or the desert wadis. Worse, from the standpoint of a policing army, the land is riddled with caves. On walks around Bethlehem, the caves are one of the great attractions for an explorer, because so many show signs of long-gone habitation, including dug-out sections and man-made lintels and hearths. Throughout history, outlaws have hidden in Bethlehem's hills and the surrounding wilderness, from the Jewish wars against the Romans in antiquity to the Palestinian wars against the Egyptians at the birth of the modern era, to the Israeli invasion of 2002 when wanted Palestinians disappeared into the hills, reappearing only when ordered to by the Palestinian leadership in the deal that ended the war.

The Egyptian-based Ptolemies had placed power in the hands of the Tobiads of Amman. In 200 BCE, the Damascus-based Seleucids conquered Palestine and allowed Jerusalem's aristocrats to build their own forces. Two of the Bethlehem stories, Ruth and the Levite and his concubine, tell the story of a power transfer from Amman to Palestine: in Ruth, the Ammanite Ruth humbles herself as an available slave to the Palestinian

Boaz; in the story of the Levite and his Bethlehem concubine, the civil war ignited by the murder of a girl purchased in Bethlehem ends with the rape of the women of Amman in order to repopulate the war-torn Palestinian cities.

The Seleucids must soon have regretted the policy of arming local notables: an early consequence was an uprising remembered as the Maccabean Revolt, spearheaded by a family from Modi'in, an agricultural area to the north of Jerusalem. The Seleucids regained Jerusalem, however, and continued to trust local notables. The longest-serving Seleucid governor was the high priest and warrior John Hyrcanus, a close ally of the Seleucids who earned his unusual Greek name while fighting as part of a Seleucid-led alliance. Hyrcanus is credited with consolidating power in Jerusalem, first by destroying a rival temple of Samaria and second by converting the Idumeans of Hebron. It is possible that the proto-Arab Idumean were already Jewish, but the need to make them submit to Jerusalem reflects the issue of water security. Al-Arrub spring is in Idumean territory, and many of Bethlehem's springs lie closer to Hebron than Jerusalem.

Histories of this period conventionally describe the era of Seleucid rule over Palestine as the Hasmonean period, referring to the dynasty of Jewish priest and warlord John Hyrcanus. His reign lasted thirty years, and Hyrcanus certainly ruled with a great deal of autonomy. But taken as a whole, the Hasmonean period is marked by intra-communal strife. Hyrcanus's legacy is less a dynasty than a nasty feud. (The Hasmoneans are conventionally associated with the Modi'in Maccabees, though this connection might be figurative or, indeed, might be a later invention.) After John Hyrcanus died, power shifted back to Amman. For this reason and others, speaking of a Hasmonean era lends the dynasty a solidity that it notably lacks. It is difficult to credit a sense of unity of purpose or agency to its various rulers.

It is notable that the Seleucid shift in policy that sees Jerusalem become independent of Amman receives the approval of Rome. The Romans were the rising power in a region they termed the Oriens throughout the Seleucid/ Hasmonean period. In the beginning, Rome is in de facto political control of Alexandria, but is content to work behind the scenes in a back-seat role. Roman foreign policy at this time extends no further than ensuring a balance between the Ptolemies and Seleucids. The period ends, however, with Rome developing its world-encircling ambition. It takes direct control, seizing both Egypt and Palestine.

The forts constructed under the Seleucids contain cisterns and aqueducts lined with Nabataean-style cement. Evidently, the Nabataeans remained Palestine's plumbers. The Nabataeans had been allies of the Ptolemies. The rise of the Seleucids in Palestine saw a short war over mineral rights in the Dead Sea. It was an improbable naval battle: the Nabataeans attacked Seleucid forces from across the salt lake using specially constructed coracles. After the dispute was settled, however, the Nabataeans forged new agreements with the Seleucids. When the Romans replaced the Seleucids, the Nabataeans experienced another rocky period under the unsympathetic Pompey the Great. Yet they bounced back as control of Palestine passed to the Herodian dynasty, a new political alliance between the Nabataeans and Idumeans. Herod the Great was not simply the King of Jerusalem, Hebron, and Amman, but the ruler of an entire Roman province. Thanks to the Roman convention of honoring mythical founding fathers, and perhaps a confusion over the root of the word *Yehudim* after its translation into Latin, the name the Romans gave to this province was Judea: or the Land of Judah.

JERUSALEM'S RISE CAME because it was a focal point for a religion that already crossed regional borders and tribal identities. Herod the Great reflected this multiethnic Jewish identity. His family was Jewish Idumean on his father's side and Nabataean on his mother's. As king, he deftly reflected other strands of the Jewish identity by marrying into the Hasmonean dynasty based in Amman and Jerusalem, as well as into the Sanballat dynasty of Samaria. In the past, aristocratic Jewish families had run individual cities as warlords or as governors. Herod was the first king of a Jewish "nation," albeit a province of the Roman Empire.

The journey from Nazareth to Bethlehem credited to Mary and Joseph in Herod's reign would cut through this new nation from top to bottom, and in the process reveal all the different ways that one could be Jewish in Judea. We imagine Mary and Joseph making the hundred-mile journey from Nazareth to Bethlehem by donkey. A few other options were available, notably sedan chair or horse, but portraits of Mary and Joseph agree they come from families of modest means, and that they lived or settled in the Nazareth-Galilee area. In fact, the modesty is about all that is agreed upon. Joseph varies in age from youthful to geriatric, either a widower with adult children or a first-timer with no children. He is either a carpenter or something closer to an odd-job man, and guesstimates about his income vary accordingly. Most accounts agree that Mary is young, perhaps very young: in the apocryphal writings known as the "Infancy Gospels" she is a twelve-year-old newlywed. The key point, however low their income, is that Mary and Joseph actually do have an income. They can travel and pay for things they might need along the way.

Almost all of Christ's disciples are depicted as modest tradesmen, like his parents. They could hardly be otherwise; in a world where most people were slaves, the only people with the freedom to suspend their everyday lives and follow Christ would have been tradesmen and aristocrats, and Christ's message is certainly not aimed at aristocrats. To borrow Marxist terminology, the Galilee had become home to a bourgeois revolution: a class of independent tradesmen had risen above the peasant class and enjoyed a measure of independence from the ruling aristocrats. This freedom allowed them the space to think about their faith, and the leisure to listen to the debates of itinerant preachers. It is notable that every significant historical Jewish figure in Palestine from the century before Christ's birth and for six hundred years afterwards is from the Galilee.

The Holy Family would see how Herod's other subjects lived as they travelled to Jerusalem. Inside the city, Herod's new temple dominated the landscape. It straddled the saddle between two high ridges, a polished Roman citadel built of the same yellow stone as the outcrop below it, yet so highly worked that it formed a startling contrast with the raw bedrock. The architects conceived of Herod's temple as a series of broad horizontal lines, divided into piazzas, shallow pitched roofs, flights of stairs, and wide terraces. On their way through the city, Mary and Joseph would spend the night in a garden hostel. The obvious choice is Gethsemane, the same campsite Christ and his disciples favored on the night of the Last Supper. It lies below the temple at the point where the rocky hill is at its steepest and most forbidding, at the cheap end of town, close to Silwan, the poorest and most polluted part of the city.

Gardens like this functioned like the gates to Bethlehem in the story of Boaz and Ruth: the neutral entry points into cities (inspiring the later use of the word for garden, pardes, in literary exegesis as the entry point into a text). Visitors would camp under the trees, while vendors would sell street food from barrows or wood-fired ovens. There would be water for the animals, stable boys to sell animal feed, and ostlers to treat lame donkeys or sell fresh ones. There would even be entertainment: songs and poetry, perhaps shadow shows and, of course, religious debate. The Jewish faith was spread from caravanserai to caravanserai across Arabia, Persia, and the Mahgreb.

The temple above the garden was a city within a city, and an economy within an economy. Visiting pilgrims had to change their money into a specific temple currency, essentially exchanging cash for tokens that only could be spent within the temple precincts. The money was used to buy birds and lambs for sacrifice, to pay the priests for their services, and to buy the incense that was burnt in great, colored clouds. The temple took cuts from both ends, from changing money into tokens, as well as a slice of the sale of temple goods. When the adult Christ revisits Jerusalem and overturns the tables in the temple, he is attacking this kind of profiteering. Inside the temple and its environs, most professions would be tied to the pilgrim trade, whether as guards, functionaries, money-changers, vendors, hostel workers, civil servants, or, of course, priests. This contributed toward a conservative mind-set, as the hereditary priesthood controlled the livelihoods of everyone through favors, nepotism, and perhaps bribery. It is a different story in the Galilee, which is geographically and temperamentally closer to Samaria than Jerusalem. Indeed, the road from Nazareth leads through Samaria, passing directly beneath the rival Samaritan temple on Mount Gerizim. The apostles, like all Galileans in general, share something of the Samaritans' cynicism about Jerusalem. Galileans enjoy the freedom to question the priest's dominant role in Jewish life, while Jerusalemites recognize which side their bread is buttered on.

The heart of the temple is the inner sanctum, the Holy of the Holies, the focus of temple life. The sanctum contained a square stone altar and nothing else. Jerusalem was a city caught between Greek and Arab worlds, and it embraced the most extreme iconoclasm of both cultures. The priesthood condemned all representations of God, in any form, whether written or visual. In the Greek world, this puritanical approach had its roots in the philosophy of Plato and its deep distrust for artists and sculptors. As the myth of Pygmalion shows, Greek sculptors were making work that was ever-more lifelike, and this was a source of both pride and anxiety. The philosophers worried that these gifted artists looked no deeper than seductive appearances; they were content with a facsimile of the truth. Plato argued that painting and sculpture dazzle us, leading us away from virtue into a world of falsehood. The Pygmalion story showed the evil that came with taking pride in mimicking nature, a mimicry that revels in luxury without understanding.

Meanwhile, just as the Greeks turned against representation, the Nabataeans worshipped a god so abstract that he could not be represented at all. On their epic journeys through the desert, the Nabataeans would nominate a suitable stone, cut it into a cube, and make it the focus for their prayers. At first, this sounds impossibly primitive: a stone is eternal, but it is not our kind of eternal; it has no memory and no past or present. Yet the Nabataeans offered a subtle and profound solution to the question that so bothered the Greeks: how do we worship a god that passes human understanding? The Nabataeans' abstract approach was enthusiastically embraced by the Jerusalem priesthood, who used stones in funeral rituals to reflect the mystery of death, and made a cut, square stone the focus of the inner sanctum in the temple, the heart of the mystery of their faith.

The chief purpose of the temple at an everyday level, however, was the processing and killing of animals. There was a sacrificial animal to suit every income bracket, from birds and sheep, to expensive heifers. The animals would first be butchered and skinned, before portions of the flesh were burned. The temple would be awash with blood, but it was efficiently sluiced through the temple's killing floor with clean Bethlehem water. From there, the blood washed into the old *qanats* or cisterns below the temple and flushed as sewage into the Silwan water supply. The animal skins, too, would end up in Silwan, where they were processed into vellum parchment. The production of parchment was part of a vertically integrated publishing industry and as the quantity of scrolls found in Bethlehem's caves bordering the Dead Sea show, the Greek and Roman periods were a boom-time for publishers. Turning animal skins into vellum was a dirty process that required skins to be soaked and treated in chemicals such as urine and alum, then split into near-transparent sheets and dried on wooden frames. Silwan is thought to be the location of a Seleucid-built suburb named Antiochia, and it may once have been a desirable city quarter; but by Herod's time it had deteriorated to become an industrial slum. Just as the Victorian publishing industry gave birth to the modern novel, thanks to twin improvements in printing technology and education, so the spread of the Jewish faith gave birth to the idea of scripture, helped along by an endless supply of cheap animal skins from the temple sacrifices and a booming market in literary souvenirs for the pilgrims. The Silwan neighborhood was ground zero for Palestine's publishing industry, but a neighborhood that lives off tanning and vellum is not somewhere any one would choose to set up home.

The Holy Family's route to Bethlehem would take them from Gethsemane, past Silwan to the Hebron Road recently rebuilt by the *Legio X Fretensis*: Rome's Tenth Legion. The road began just below a new suburb of luxury homes that enjoyed a safe water supply, separate from the polluted water of Silwan. The water came from Bethlehem, stored in new reservoirs at Artas and brought to Jerusalem via a new aqueduct that followed Hebron Road in the no-nonsense direct style of Rome's military engineers. The Hebron Road dips sharply as it enters Jerusalem. The meandering Lower Aqueduct turned rightwards to cross the valley and tunnelled beneath the old city to reach the cisterns below the temple. The Upper Aqueduct simply sailed on, carried by a series of high arches toward Herod's new suburb.

For the next five miles, as their donkey plodded along the well-paved Hebron Road, the Holy Family would follow the Upper Aqueduct. Water was carried inside a sealed pipeline of prefabricated stone blocks. The identical blocks fitted one next to the other, like square beads on a necklace, and the water ran through the hollow center. There are examples of these blocks all around Bethlehem, both in the Bethlehem Museum, and at the museum in Murad's Fort next to the Solomon's Pools center. The construction of the aqueduct fell on the legionnaires, but the job of making the many thousands of blocks depended upon local labor. Herod was a contemporary of the great city-building emperor Augustus, and he shared the emperor's building bug. Herod not only rebuilt Jerusalem and Jericho, but also created Tiberias, the capital of the Galilee, and Caesarea, the

Mediterranean port city of Roman Palestine. The Holy Family's journey from the Galilee took them through a landscape that Roman influence had changed beyond imagination. The Bethlehem district was, once more, the secret heart of these changes, because it was home to the best quarries. The marble-like stone is the equal of anything in Italy. The quarries lay in southern Bethlehem, as they still do, dotted among the same hills whose springs fill Bethlehem's reservoirs. The Roman Tenth Legion was based in Bethlehem for centuries and built hundreds of miles of roads across all of Palestine, the best paved with Bethlehem stone. The men working these quarries, however, were slaves.

The Holy Family's route forked left off the Hebron Road, beside a fountain whose waters sprang from the new aqueduct. The couple might drink at the fountain and water their animals, before turning onto a simpler track skirting the eastern flank of the Bethlehem ridge. After a half mile, the road climbs suddenly. This is Star Street, so called because it is said to be road that the Magi followed to greet the infant Christ. The view over the desert from here can be bewitching. When the sun is at its brightest, every contour is outlined by the play of sharp sunlight and the tight shadows of the folds of the hills. Way off to the south where the sightlines begin to dissolve into the desert haze, the visitors would see Herod's summer palace on its conical, man-made hill above Tuqu'.

Herod funded his grand projects by taxing the Spice Route. This is why the Gospel of Matthew depicts the Magi arriving with gold, frankincense, and myrrh. The luxury items that underpin Jerusalem's wealth are being offered in tribute to a different kind of king. The gold comes from Ethiopia, frankincense from Arabia and Somalia, and myrrh from the Yemen. If the Magi are not intended to be actually Nabataean merchants, then they are at least allies who are travelling on the Nabataean's highway. Matthew is declaring that even Herod's family and friends do not think he has what it takes to be King of the Jews. The Gospel of Matthew was written at least a hundred years after the events it purports to describe, at a time when Jews across the empire were in open revolt against Rome. Rather than see Herod's reign as a time of peace and coexistence, the writer blames Herod for leading Jews astray with his ambition and his excesses. He was a king who sought worldly glory by creating palaces. The Magi pointedly refuse to give Herod his due, instead handing the tribute intended for a king to a poor child. Vanity of vanity, as the preacher of Ecclesiastes says. The treatment of Herod also reflects the long-simmering difference between the Galilee and Jerusalem. Galileans believed Jerusalem was shoehorning the faith into too small a space: Jerusalem and its temple. Under Herod, the Jewish faith was a squalid compromise between earthly authority and the priesthood, a trade-off that valued grandeur, centralization, and a notion of orthodoxy that placed religious authority solely in the hands of Jerusalem's priesthood. The Magi honor a version of Jewish leadership that is un-showy, poverty-stricken, and innocent—as child-like as Herod is worldly. But by including the Magi among the faithful, the gospel is also saying that the Jewish faith is broad and universal, it cannot be corralled into the narrow and selfish politics of a single city.

Walking along the track toward Bethlehem on market day, the Holy Family would hear the sound of mewling sheep long before they reached the end of the track. The market sprawled across the dip before the tightly packed town of Greek-style multistory houses with tiled roofs. Bethlehem is always described as having a gate, so must have been a walled town. But a newish and small town would not have a wall of quarried stone blocks. Arculf describes a low wall, more like an animal pen, and though he visited seven hundred years later, his account feels like a true picture of the town in Herod's day. Bethlehem would have a low dry stone wall of the same jagged, reddish surface rocks that support agricultural terraces. This was all that was needed to corral livestock, and was perfectly adequate as a defensive measure. A low wall makes a good barricade when under attack, and if the raiders break through, the defenders can switch to the other side and attack again as the raiders try to escape.

On market day, Bethlehem would look as though it was sailing on the back of a giant flock as the saddle between the ridge and the town filled with sheep and goats drinking from the famous fountain. The sight of so many Bedouin shepherds might be alarming to a visitor. These are men with bony heads and burning eyes, which they exaggerate by lining their eyes with kohl. The women decorate their faces with tattoos. These desert graziers have little in common with the lyre-strumming shepherds of Greek myths, though they spend their free time reciting poetry. A lot of the traditional Jewish laws are devised to separate the nomads and the city dwellers: for instance, the prohibition on tattoos, or mixing dairy and meat. (The great Bedouin banquet dish is *mansaf*: goat or mutton cheese sauce on lamb. It took me a while to love this dish, as the sauce is so strong-tasting. It was a specialty of Raissa Sansour, a modern Russian woman capably undertaking a Bedouin dish that was many thousand years old.) The gospels place the shepherds at Christ's nativity to remind contemporary Jewish readers that these uncouth tribesmen more closely resemble King David than any of the High Priests of Herod's Jerusalem. David was also a shepherd, standing apart from civilization, living in the wilderness as a nomad and warrior.

The Holy Family would have to skirt the market, taking the lower path to the garden beside the town. Bethlehem's counterpart to the hostel in Gethsemane was a very different proposition to the biblical inn of the English imagination, yet an innkeeper of sorts would run it. When the family entered, a couple of slaves would run out to set out tables and cushions. If it was a hot day at noon, they might hoist a sheet into the trees to make a sunscreen, billowing like a sail tethered to a mast. Bethlehem is high enough that there is often a breeze, even when the sun is scorching. The garden stood lower than the town, which meant that it was framed by a bank studded with caves that had been enlarged to make stables and storerooms, as well as the inn kitchen. Large ceramic jugs sunk into a stone countertop would be filled with olives and pickles. Down a few steps, a wood-burning oven would tunnel straight in to the hillside. Casserole pots and shoulders of lamb rubbed with herbs would be pushed into the oven on long wooden paddles. When the oven was full, its entrance would be sealed with bricks and wet clay.

There are a few sparse references to Bethlehem's garden caravanserai from long after the events described in the gospels, at a time when Christianity was the rising religion. In Hadrian's reign, the garden is described as a shrine to Tammuz, the god of the harvest. A statue to Tammuz might have stood inside an arbor: not a large figure, perhaps as little as eighteen inches high. Tammuz is usually presented as a prince with a tall crown, standing erect and holding his thresher like a royal scepter, similar to figurines of the greatest of Canaanite gods, Baal. Tammuz is a little like the English pagan god John Barleycorn, a deity who suffered the indignity of being kidnapped, beaten, and ground to dust at harvest time, only to re-emerge in the New Year. In a fruit-growing town like Bethlehem, a shrine to Tammuz may have taken the form of an ornamental orchard containing symbolic examples of figs, almonds, apricots, and lemons. Some modern historians have suggested that it was because the garden was already a shrine to Tammuz that early Christian pilgrims chose to identify the garden with Christ's Nativity, overlaying one god on top of another.

The first reference to Christ being born in a cave dates to around the year 145 CE, in a letter written by the Nablus-born Christian, Justin Martyr. Devout early Christians were happy to identify a cave in a garden shrine with the Messiah's birthplace because of the obvious parallel with the story of his death, beginning with a meal in the garden of Gethsemane. This is how important the garden as the symbolic air-lock to a city had become. The one place that mutually suspicious communities, insiders and outsiders, could sit down and do business had been adopted by Christians as a symbol of the "way" between all of life's contradictions.

The attempt to keep a distance between city-dwellers and the Bedouin is apparent in the Jewish laws that prohibit tattoos or mixing meat and dairy. During the 2002 invasion of Bethlehem, I worked on Bethlehem's ambulances, and one day helped take an elderly Bedouin woman for kidney dialysis. The family lived in Zatara, one of the new villages in the desert where the Ta'amareh Bedouin put down roots in the mid-twentieth century. The woman was elderly, perhaps ninety, quite tall and so swollen that lying on the gurney she resembled a beached dugong. She had facial tattoos on her forehead and chin, the only time I have seen the tattoos outside of books. She may well have been the last tattooed woman in Bethlehem. Though Jewish religious laws are designed to re-enforce the boundary between desert and townsfolk, the two communities were nevertheless locked in a relation of mutual dependency. The meat in the inn's oven came from the nomads' flocks, the cloth used in the sunscreen from their goats. They needed each other, and the place they met was the garden at the city gates. Early Christians would have seen the poetry in identifying Christ's birthplace to this inter-zone at the edge of the desert. Where else might one find the Son of God—a figure who exists between two worlds?

The Gospel of Luke tells us that the Holy Family were visitors in Bethlehem and that the first people to pay their respect were shepherds (the Gospel of Matthew assumes that the family lived in Bethlehem and only later emigrated to the Galilee). Again, Luke was written a hundred years after the events it describes. The passage with the shepherds is intended to carry a visceral shock: the reader is confronted by an image of a young Jewish mother and child sharing the animals' quarters, cheek-by-jowl with wild, kohl-eyed strangers. The Gospel of Luke is also the gospel that contains the story of the Samaritan: a key theme of the book is that a stranger may often know our hearts better than the people demanding our loyalty and respect. Like the Gospel of Matthew, Luke chooses to highlight people who would remind the reader of King Herod. Where Matthew uses the Magi to underscore Herod's Nabataean heritage, the shepherds in Luke reflect the king's Idumean father, Antipas. The Idumeans were no longer Bedouin-style nomads, though they remained notable livestock breeders. In effect the gospels tell us that even the Nabataeans and Idumeans believe that Christ is a better King of the Jews than their kinsman, the Roman-appointed king of the newly coined province, Roman Judea.

Passing the night in the garden in Bethlehem, Mary and Joseph would see tough-looking traders strike deals, count profit, write contracts, and exchange their sheep and wool for fruit or olive oil. As visitors from the Galilee, this might make Bethlehem a wild and strange kind of town. Nevertheless, it was clear that Bethlehem was far less free than the Galilee. There were soldiers everywhere. The Tenth Legion was charged not only with protecting many miles of aqueducts, but also with policing the desert, the empire's international border, as well as the profitable trade in livestock and Dead Sea chemicals. In addition, Bethlehem's quarries and Herod's summer palace were all very obvious military installations. Bethlehem was supposed to be part of the Jewish ancestral homeland. Yet, as the scriptures tell us, it was not a place where one was likely to find many Jews. By the time the Christian gospels are being written, there would be even fewer. The Tenth Legion paid its soldiers' pensions in farmland, which meant that Bethlehem's farms and orchards fell into the hands of retired legionnaires, who relied on slaves to do the work. Romans did not much care what religion their slaves followed. Jewish and Samaritan landowners, by contrast, always converted their slaves in order to ensure their food was prepared according to religious law. Indeed, the Jews may have been the first faith to insist on the conversion of slaves, though the practice was adopted by Christians and Muslims and lasted into modern times.

The Jewish Festival of the Booths, Sukkot, reflects the one clear instance when a Jewish slave-owning class interacted with the customs of their workers. Sukkot's open air feast has its roots in the harvest time customs. Anton Sansour's mother would spend most of the summer living in the family's orchards of al-Makhrour where she and other smallholders would sleep in stone bothies or simply under the stars with a sheet hung from the branches of an apricot tree to make a screen for the morning sun. During the various harvests, which fall every month through Bethlehem's summer, she would be joined by her children and grandchildren as whole families would decamp to the hills to help pick fruit—almonds, apricots, figs, olives—and eat barbecues beneath the balmy night skies.

The gospels were written after the first Jewish War of 66-73 CE. This was a civil war fought across the empire, but the focus ultimately narrowed to a sacrificial defense of Jerusalem. Fighters arrived from every corner of Rome, thought the most fearsome of the fighters are thought to have been local Idumean zealots who wielded knives that earned them the name Sicarii. The war went on for seven years and was characterized by reckless attacks and mass suicides such as the one in the Galilee described by Josephus, its only survivor. Volunteers knew what they were walking into in Jerusalem: they had come to die. The battle ended in unimaginable horror. The long siege saw the defenders eat the bodies of the dead, before the end came with a general massacre. The city, starved of Bethlehem's water, was a charnel house of putrefying corpses and swarms of flies. But this was not even the end of the war: there was another bloody battle at the southern fortress of Masada, where the Dead Sea meets the Negev, which also ended in a mass suicide.

The global character of the First Jewish War is confirmed by the second, in 115-117 CE, which was fought across the southern Mediterranean, with notable rebellions in Alexandria, Cyprus, and North Africa. The Second Jewish War is known as the Kitos Rebellion after the Berber general who suppressed it. General Kitos had previously been stationed in Bethlehem as the commander of the Tenth Legion, a reminder of just how diverse the Roman army could be. The connection between the Syrian St. George and al-Khader village probably emerged because Syrian soldiers had settled in the area.

The third and final Jewish War, by contrast, was completely parochial, fought entirely in Bethlehem, though the rebels came from the Galilee.

This is the Bar Kokhba revolt, 132–135 CE. The rebels hid out in the hills around Battir, where the caves that peep between the olive terraces are perfect for guerrilla warfare. When Bar Kokhba faced defeat, he did not melt away into the caves but followed the example of earlier martyrs in Galilee, Jerusalem, and Masada, ending his war in a sacrificial death. Bar Kokhba is commemorated as the "Father of Lies" in the Talmud. The reputation of another figure from the revolt, Rabbi Akiva, fared better; he is remembered as the wisest of the early rabbis.

The scriptures gave Bethlehem a narrative and a historical weight that matched its geo-physical importance as Jerusalem's reservoir. In the coming centuries, however, Bethlehem would achieve real religious prominence as Bethlehem's wilderness filled with the desert monasteries that gave shape to the new Christian faith.

# CHAPTER 4

# HELENA'S CHURCH

## *Christian Rome*

*Dürer, Albrecht.*
*St Jerome.*
*Woodcut. 1492.*

I n 327 CE, a woman in her late seventies stepped down from her sedan chair, dirtying her feet on the pavement of the livestock market. This was the *Augusta Imperatrix*, the Empress Helena. As she walked across the marketplace, she was followed by a procession of bishops and princes, and watched by the crowds that had joined her long pilgrimage on its way toward Bethlehem. The mother of the Emperor Constantine approached the site of Christ's birth as humbly as any other pilgrim. When she reached the cave, she kneeled in prayer. Helena had announced the building of many churches on her journey, but the one she built in Bethlehem was so unique it must have a personal significance. The chapel was a hexagonal rotunda positioned above the cave, allowing the faithful to look down from a gallery into the heart of the mystery below. There was nothing like it anywhere in the world.

Helena was a twenty-year-old barmaid c. 270 CE when she met her future husband, Constantius, in what is now Izmit, Turkey. He was a young Roman officer who whisked her to his hometown, now Nis in Serbia, where she gave birth to their only child. Constantius was too ambitious to remain married to a commoner and he soon divorced Helena to make a more political alliance. She was sent to live in the household of the jealous Emperor Diocletian, where she was allowed to oversee the upbringing of her son, Constantine. Helena might have traded on her status within the emperor's household; instead she made a virtue of being a single mother. She embraced Christianity, a faith which gave value to a celibate, even virginal, woman.

When her son finally maneuvered his way to Roman emperor, Helena enjoyed the rewards. Her title of Empress allowed her to maintain her own court at the Sessorium, a campus of palaces on the outskirts of Rome. It also allowed her to issue her own coins. There is quite a variety of Hellenic loose change showing a woman with a stern but kindly face and a long nose that lies almost flush with her forehead, as though she is leaning into a plate glass window. Helena looks bruised, perhaps, but solid and serene. The coins show how she shaped her public image. You would have to say that Helena was a politician in that she recognized her real power was persuasion. She played the role of a second Mary, the mother of a child born to be a king.

The coins had another significance. For a hundred years, inflation had destroyed faith in Rome's monetary supply, and the empire had retreated to a barter economy. At the start of the fourth century CE, Diocletian had issued the first new gold coin in centuries. But this positive measure was accompanied by more misguided reforms such as devaluations and price-fixings that encouraged people to stick with barter and hoard the new coins. The economy only began to recover when Constantine minted a new gold coin, the *solidus*, in such large numbers that it was actually used. Whether by design or by accident, Constantine had hit upon a modern solution to kick-start the economy. Step one was minting a trusted currency. Step two was finding a way to ensure that the new coins were pumped through his empire. The program of major works spearheaded by his mother was a masterstroke.

Bethlehem was affected by the long economic stagnation in distinctive ways. Jerusalem was no longer a pilgrimage spot after the Jewish wars, so there was no knock-on effect as wealth spread to surrounding communities. The spice trade avoided Jerusalem by going through the Negev, where Roman roads sped the goods to the port at Gaza. Raiders in the desert lands would soon force Rome to relocate the Roman Legio X Fretensis to Aqaba, and so Bethlehem's farmers lost a valuable market for their food. The Talmud shows that family farms were disappearing in the Galilee, where the land was bought and consolidated into larger estates. This was also the story in Bethlehem. Retired Roman soldiers were invariably poor farmers, and once the army was gone they lost the friendly military market upon which they depended.

As economic chaos undermined the empire's reputation for stability and security, Constantine looked to Christianity to instill a new common purpose. He knew the broad expanse of his empire more intimately than anyone alive. He had governed and fought from the North of England to the Persian plains; if he believed Christianity could supply the thread to tie all these lands together, no one else could claim to know better. Helena was central to the project, because Constantine was not trusted. Twenty-five years earlier, his protector Diocletian and his father Constantius had purged the Roman army of Christians. Arab military saints like St. Sergius, St. Bacchus, St. Damian, and St. Cosmas were witnesses to these purges—all martyred by the emperor that they had served. Eusebius's predecessor as bishop of Caesarea had been taken to Antioch in chains, where his tongue was ripped out with pincers. Both the army and the growing community of Christians would doubt Constantine's faith and sincerity, but they would never question his devout mother.

Helena's mission was cast as a pilgrimage, the most ambitious and expensive the world had ever seen. She presided over a travelling city, accompanied not just by her soldiers, household servants, and the civil administration that ran her affairs, but also by squads of clergy, provincial governors, and local princes and bishops that joined her retinue as she travelled. Her journey led her through the Balkans and the enormous building site at Byzantium, soon to become the new capital of the empire: Constantinople. Her arrival in Nicaea is usually dated to 326 CE, the year after the Council of Nicaea, though it seems odd that she was not in attendance. Constantine had called the council. Helena may have chosen to avoid it because she knew she would not like its conclusion. Like many Roman women, Helena placed Christ rather closer to his earthly mother than his divine father. The Council of Nicaea decreed that Christ was consubstantial with the father: that is, composed of the same substance and essence. Constantine's sister Flavia had spoken in favor of a flesh-and-blood Christ at the council, to no effect. Perhaps Helena was wise to sidestep a defeat, but it did not do her any good in Antioch where the city's bishop, Eustathius, was openly hostile towards her. He was a fierce defender of the new Nicene Creed, who felt threatened because Antioch was flanked by two semi-independent Arab Christian kingdoms, Edessa and Palmyra, which were also hostile to the new Nicene Creed.

After leaving Antioch and its obnoxious bishop, Helena continued to Palestine where she found the bishop of Caesarea a far more pleasant companion. Bishop Eusebius became the official chronicler of Helena's journey. His city was the administrative capital of Palestine, as it had been for three hundred years. It was the most diverse of Palestine's cities, with Christians, pagans, Samaritans, and Jews all living within a beautiful Mediterranean port capital. The salaries of civil servants in Caesarea were said to be higher even than in Antioch, and the city attracted the brightest graduates from the pagan rhetoric schools in Gaza and Ashkelon, which were the equivalent of the elite universities of the day. Caesarea was a world center for Christian scholarship, thanks to a library founded by the brilliant Egyptian scholar Origen. This reputation of learning also attracted Jews, and the next century would see the composition of the Jewish Talmud by scholars hoping to revolutionize the Jewish faith.

Helena is likely to have taken the best Christian and Jewish scholars with her, to help her interpret the land. She was shown the shrine to Christ's Nativity, where a carved niche in the shrine held a terracotta and plaster "manger," a description that makes it sound rather more like a water trough. Helena's architects turned this shrine into a temple by opening up the cave. Worshippers gathered on a gallery that ran around the internal wall where they could look down into the subterranean hole below.

This innovative design became the model for a number of Palestinian churches. The Roman heiress Poimenia built the Church of the Ascension on the Mount of Olives at the end of the fourth century. On the outskirts of Bethlehem, a widow named Ikelia built the Seat of Mary, or *Kathisma*, in the fifth century to mark the place where a heavily pregnant Mary rested on her way to Bethlehem. None of these churches now exist, though the outline of Ikelia's octagonal church lies a few yards off Hebron Road. You can see it from the bus as you leave Bethlehem, just after the Mar Elias monastery. There is no ticket kiosk and no sign, just a piece of stone floor among a few olive trees. The area is undergoing an enormous amount of construction work, including the construction of a new settlement named Givat Hamatos, so I am not sure in what form the site will survive.

What links the three churches is that they were built by women, and each has a rotunda above an opening to a cave or, at Kathisma, a view to the bedrock impression of Mary's seat—literally, the heart shape of a pair of buttocks. It feels a little explicit to commemorate shadowy glimpses into the mysteries of a woman's body and childbirth, but perhaps a taboo was being deliberately breached. The most spectacular version of this design, however, is the mosque of the Dome of the Rock, which is built over the rock altar said to have been used by Abraham when he came close to sacrificing Isaac. Fathers and sons, this time, not mothers and babies.

The rotunda at the Church of the Nativity stood at the end of an open-air colonnade that retained the garden aspect of the original shrine. Helena's mosaic pavement survives, discovered beneath the floor of the later basilica by the British after the First World War. The design interweaves organic and geometric shapes, as though attempting to synthesize the great theological dispute of the time: Christ's biological inheritance plaited seamlessly with his ideal divinity. The mosaic's rainbow colors have dimmed over the eighteen hundred years since they were set in place, but at the right time of day, when sunbeams pierce the narrow lights in the basilica roof, you can see that the tiles are arranged as a spectrum. When they were lit by the full glare of daylight, they must have glowed as though reflecting the divine light.

WHEN HELENA VISITED BETHLEHEM, she was the most famous woman in the empire. Forty years after her visit, the world's most famous woman was a nomadic raider, Queen *Māwiyya*, the leader of a Christian-Arab confederation known as the Tanukhids. It was Māwiyya's raids on the spice and incense routes that forced Rome to relocate its forces from Bethlehem to Aqaba. In 378 CE, she launched a rebellion that ended with the Tanukhids and Romans agreeing to enter a formal alliance. The church in Constantinople recognized the Tanukhids' bishop, Moses, as the bishop of all the Arabs. Though the deal with the Tanukhid was short-lived, it set a new pattern for Rome after which Arab tribes served as an official border force in Palestine. The forces were known as the *foederati* and distinguished from Roman-Arabs by the name Saracen or, among Christian writers, as *Ishmaelites*.

In January 383 CE, shortly after Māwiyya concluded her treaty with Rome, a Roman-Spanish woman named Egeria visited Bethlehem to celebrate Epiphany. This is the eight-day feast that marks the announcement to the Jews of Christ's birth. The announcement by the Magi was more of a slip-of-the-tongue than a formal announcement: King Herod responds with the Massacre of the Innocents. Epiphany is a passive-aggressive kind of festival, because the whole point is that the Jews did not welcome the announcement. Egeria's account of the Epiphany celebration suggests that Bethlehem had only a small Christian population, the rest being pagan and slaves. A law dating back to the First Jewish War banned Jews from Palestine's three central military districts: that is, Herodian (Bethlehem), Gophne (Ramallah), and Oreine (Jerusalem). However, the ban did not cover short visits: Helena had used Jews as guides, Jerome later employed Jewish translators while he served as abbot of Bethlehem, and of course there was no longer a huge military presence to enforce the ban. Egeria describes the Bishop of Jerusalem leading the psalms by the priests in the underground shrine, watched from the rotunda above by the congregation. At dusk, the majority of the celebrants left for Jerusalem with the bishop, "who must always be in Jerusalem on these days." The local priests and the visiting hermits kept vigil in the cave, singing and chanting until the dawn broke above them.

Egeria was writing some time before the church devised formal rules to govern monastic life. The Arab bishop Moses had been a kind of solitary hermit known as *boskoi*. In Egypt, where the Nile delta touches the desert, a monk named Pachomius had set about organizing these hermits into a community. The idea of a formal monastic order was still some way off. The hermits that Egeria describes chanting in the cave in Bethlehem would not have taken holy orders. Even in the fifth century, the greatest of Bethlehem's monks, Saint Sabbas, was only ordained late in his long career when it became necessary for political reasons. The term hermit comes from the Greek word for desert: *eremos.* They were mendicants who lived by foraging. The boskoi seem to have been proud of being mistaken for wild animals, either chased or shot. Pachomius and the monks of Egypt were following the example of Saint Anthony, a hermit who had sold his parents' farm and abandoned society to live alone in the desert. In Egeria's time, a biography of Anthony had become a bestseller in Rome, inadvertently creating a tourist industry to the Egyptian delta.

The growing interest in monks was the reason why Christians like Egeria visited Palestine, and why wealthier women like Paula, Poimenia, and Ikelia built churches and guesthouses. They were less interested in the country's traditions and history than its wilderness. Palestine lay at the edge of the world, where the empire faded into the surrounding desert. Roman pilgrims would typically sail to Alexandria, where they would travel through the delta to visit the monks of Nitria, or *Wadi el-Natrun.* This is the route followed by Poimenia, who sailed into Alexandria with a mini-fleet of ships and an entourage that included a number of bishops as well as her household and its slaves. In Alexandria, she chartered an armada of riverboats to sail into the desert delta in search of a hermit named John of Egypt, who she hoped could help with unspecified health issues.

From Nitria, these women would take the road through the Sinai, where they could experience the hardships of desert life at the inaccessible spot that Helena had identified as Mount Sinai. Once in Palestine, hospitality was provided at a guesthouse on the Mount of Olives established by Melania, another Spanish-born Roman noblewoman and a central figure in the history of monasticism. Melania connects the spiritual asceticism of Roman women with the physical asceticism of the hermits. Like Poimenia, she had also visited Nitria, but not as a tourist: she actively embraced the lifestyle. She lived in a number of Egyptian desert communities before she moved to Jerusalem where she ran a guesthouse or proto-monastery with her private confessor, Rufinus, a close friend of Jerome. When Rufinus and Jerome later fell out, Jerome suggested that Rufinus was a kind of intellectual beard for Melania, the real brains behind their partnership. Melania's establishment might fairly be called the first formal monastery.

The rise of Christianity is so entwined with the centuries-long Roman economic crisis that the two should be seen in parallel. The early monks showed how a spiritual seeker could embrace poverty. This ought to have made them unsuitable partners for super-wealthy Roman women. It proved a fruitful symbiosis, however, shaping the developing Christian faith.

These Roman dowagers invented monasticism in its most formal sense, though the credit is often given to the confessors they sponsored like Rufinus and Jerome. The irony is that these men were not natural hermits. Jerome and Rufinus had nothing in common with illiterate hermits in the Arab or Egyptian desert. They became monks because the women who supported them dragged them to the desert. Rufinus and Jerome were graduates of an educational system that looked to Greek-style philosophical schools. The Greek-style academies did not admit women, which provided further impetus for wealthy, intelligent women to create intellectual establishments that embraced men and women on almost equal terms.

The role once occupied by Roman heiresses is now filled by western Christian charities. Caritas, the Catholic development fund, opened a baby hospital, now run as a local Bethlehem charity. The Knights of Malta, the heirs to the medieval Hospitallers order of military monks, took over the maternity hospital at Bab al-Zqaq when it was forced to close in 1985. The Lutheran Christmas Church opened by Kaiser Wilhelm II in 1898, created a theatre and arts complex known as Dar al-Nadwa in the late 1990s. The Russian President Vladimir Putin built a complex of arts, sports, and social centers in Bethlehem in 2013, after a road was renamed after him by the Palestinian Authority (PA). At a more personal scale, individuals have begun exporting heritage products from Palestine, like olives or *za'atar*, the mix of spices and herbs that Palestinians eat for breakfast with oil-soaked bread. Others import local wine from the Cremisan Monastery, as Communion wine for European churches, for instance. Civil rights groups in the States and Europe work with groups that offer language schools, educational tours, and even opportunities to join protests and marches. For some, this work is pro-Palestinian advocacy, or about supporting the Christians of Palestine, while others focus on abstractions and absences like international law and human rights. Bethlehem is the most famous little town in the world, which provides a spotlight and a megaphone that other Palestinian cities lack; Qalqilya, Jenin, even Nablus, subsist in forgotten isolation. But when there has been so little good news coming out of the Middle East, the city shows that multi-faith communities can be resilient, continuing to function under hardship and occupation. In the summer the clubs and nightspots are full of young volunteers, interns, students, pilgrims, dancing and mingling with local families, as well as the many visiting Bethlehemites who work or study abroad but spend their holidays in the town. The warren of streets that make up Beit Sahour's old town echo with Arab techno music, the clink of bottles of the local Taybeh beer, and thick clouds of metallic-tasting smoke from shisha pipes.

THE ROMAN WIDOW PAULA entirely rebuilt Bethlehem, bankrupting herself in the process. She travelled to Palestine in 385 CE with her daughter Eustochium and her confessor, Jerome. In her previous life in Rome she had been part of a circle associated with the intellectually gifted widow Marcella, who was close to Pope Damasus I. It was Damasus who sponsored Jerome, an ambitious and mercurial rhetorician from what is now Bosnia who had a talent for invective and highly personal attacks. When Paula and Jerome met in 382 CE, both were in their mid-thirties. Eustochium was not yet a teenager. Two years later, in 384 CE, Damasus died. Jerome was suddenly without a sponsor and found himself arraigned before an ecclesiastical court and expelled from Rome. The charges against Jerome were secret, and though he downplayed their seriousness in a letter to Rufinus, he admitted that the judgment was banishment. Marcella's circle remained loyal, however, and Jerome continued to write to Marcella until her death at the age of eighty-five in 410 CE.

Jerome left Rome for Syria. Paula and Eustochium followed with their extensive all-female household. The new life of exile began with a year-long tour. They visited Egypt, where Paula made the desert communities of Nitria their first stop. Rufinus had visited the delta a few years earlier, and in his report he estimates that there were three thousand monks living among the scattered lauras. Eighty years after Paula and Jerome's visit, a monk named Palladius put the figure closer to five thousand, spread among fifty separate communities. This figure is likely to be accurate:

Palladius spent a year in Nitria. So Jerome's claim that he counted fifty thousand monks is a wild exaggeration; he cannot help adding that not one among them would keep their vows of celibacy if they saw any encouragement from Paula or her party. All of Jerome's multiple character flaws are revealed in a couple of sentences: he is entirely unreliable; he is consumed by jealousy, and he is always looking for his own angle. We might add that he does not much like monks.

Jerome was a pompous, thin-skinned man, far from being as clever as he wished to appear. He had all the faults of an ambitious writer, including the inability to hide them. It is fitting that he is the writer's patron saint. Inevitably, Paula's reputation has suffered as a result of her loyalty to Jerome. She is a woman who appears to have thrown away everything—money, health, her daughters' futures—for her attachment to a charismatic and petulant man. Yet Paula and Jerome were a forceful double-act. We should make some effort to understand the ways in which Paula was often the leading partner, as well as the things that she achieved alone.

Their life in Palestine began at Melania's monastery in Jerusalem. Paula soon decided to create a similar institution in Bethlehem. She planned two urban monasteries and a guesthouse that she named Mary's Inn. She may also have built a villa as her personal home. For the first two years, however, her household had to tough it out in the existing guesthouse. This was a rough establishment that catered for visiting pilgrims and hermits like those Egeria had met during the feast of Epiphany. John Cassian stayed in this guesthouse as a young man, years before he founded the famous pilgrims' monastery in Marseilles.

Paula built at the edges of the town, even on its slopes, suggesting that she was utilizing land at the edges of an existing urban core. Her new, larger guesthouse stood on the western side of the town, now Milk Grotto Street. She constructed her monastery complex on the far side of the town, beside Helena's church where the Catholic church of St. Catherine's now stands. The hill is so steep that it is almost a sheer drop (the flight of steps beside St. Catherine's gives an idea of the gradient). Paula divided the women's monastery into three houses, and her women were allocated rooms depending on their social class: upper, middle, or lower. Each house had its own mother, with Paula acting as the abbess or Mother Superior. Despite these hierarchies, the women lived largely as equals, dressing alike and attending services together. It is not clear where the men's monastery sat, or if it was part of the same complex.

The flow of pilgrims into Bethlehem underpinned a growing tourism industry, replete with souvenirs. Jerome recorded the short stays of their grand Roman guests, but there were also pilgrims from the East: India, Ethiopia, and Persia, beyond Rome's borders. The majority came in steady and regular tour groups, from Armenian Anatolia, Egypt, Syria, and Asia Minor. They would take away small, locally-made flasks known as *eulogiae*, or blessings, which contained samples of the earth on which Christ had walked or olive oil to remember that he was the "anointed one," the meaning of *messiah*. The flasks were metal or ceramic and were flattish, with pictures embossed on the surfaces, either biblical scenes or famous saints and pilgrims. Manufacturing flasks and catering for pilgrims created the conditions for a new class of urban Bethlehemites.

Life in the monasteries revolved around prayers and Jerome's literary production. The business of publishing Jerome's essays, biographies, and translations required editors, secretaries, and copyists. Women often carried out this work, as they had at Origen's school in Alexandria. Copying texts by hand was the only way to publish books. Once completed, the books would be sent to libraries and subscribers across the empire. Jerome's work was well known even in his lifetime, so the monastery must have kept up high production levels. When not transcribing his books, the women would do needlework, while male monks may have done some modest gardening. Unlike the Egyptian monasteries, however, Paula's monastery never aimed to be self-sufficient, and Jerome was scathing about agricultural work.

It is likely that Paula was a landlord and slave-owner; she was responsible for a great many nuns and monks, and they required feeding. A letter she wrote to Marcella, her elderly mentor in Rome, contains some of the few personal scraps Paula gives of her life in Bethlehem. She describes her joy at hearing the slaves in the fields: "All is silent, except for the psalms . . . for wherever you turn, you hear the ploughman turning in his furrow and singing, 'Hallelulah!' . . . or the man in the vineyard singing the songs of David. These are the ballads of this country, these are the love songs as they are called." Paula was not a woman given to idle strolling: when she heard the peasants' songs, she was probably overseeing work on her own farm. Victorian pilgrims such as Arthur Stanley, Dean of Westminster, took this passage at face value and assumed that Paula was hearing the psalms of the scriptures, sung in Biblical Hebrew. In her letter, Paula is looking for financial investment, so she is anxious to sell an idyllic Bethlehem experience. The phrase "songs of David" is carefully chosen and more vague than it sounds: it is a poetic way to describe a joyful song to God. Moreover, by way of clarification, she adds that the singers believe they are singing story-ballads and love songs. In the two hundred years since Hadrian's ban on Jews living in Bethlehem, the local slaves had been cut off from any kind of organized Jewish faith. They may have retained a folk memory of songs from holidays like the harvest festival, but Paula is saying only that the singing reminds her of the psalms. Hearing the songs, she believes that she is glimpsing the life of the exiled Israelites at work in the fields of Babylon. Of course, if she imagines her slaves are like captive Israelites, she really should picture herself as a new Nebuchadnezzar.

Paula's descriptions of life in rural Bethlehem were intended to persuade the older woman to visit. As Paula's money ran out, both she and Jerome worked hard to find new sponsors for their monastery. They almost snagged a wealthy Roman heiress by the name of Fabiola, who lived with Paula through the first half of 395 CE. However, that summer, news came that the Huns had swept into Syria, destroying every city they passed through. With the Roman legions far away in Aqaba, Palestine was unprotected. Both Paula in Bethlehem and Melania in Jerusalem packed up their monasteries and fled to Caesarea. Boats were chartered for a full-scale evacuation to Rome. When the danger passed, Fabiola had second thoughts about a life in the desert fringes of the empire. She returned to Rome, where she continued Paula's work by establishing a pilgrims' guesthouse at the river docks.

Paula was a stern abbess. She supervised the women, punishing any sign of quarrelsome behavior, immodesty, or undue cleanliness. Almost all her punishments involved extra fasting. She was shaken by a romance between one her young charges and an older deacon who had left Rome in a hurry after an affair with the wife of a foreign diplomat. The deacon had arrived with letters of introduction, so Jerome must have known the man's crime. Perhaps he believed that the man had turned over a new leaf, or he hoped to curry favor with his sponsors. The deacon's attempt to seduce the novice was discovered when a love letter was found wedged between two stones in the cave of the Nativity, actually inside the shrine to Christ's birth. The deacon wrote that he had bought a stepladder, which he needed to reach the girl's window.

Jerome was mortified, yet would have kept the deacon at the monastery. It was the man who chose to leave. What was more galling was that he only went as far as Jerusalem. Jerome gives a final account of the deacon as an aging Lothario strutting about the city with his thin hair plastered across his pink scalp. It is a well-drawn caricature, though Jerome cannot hide his rage at being made to look a fool.

Paula's favorite parts of the scriptures are the lyrical poems, the romantic and sensual elements of the Psalms and the Song of Solomon. She hears echoes of their poetry as she passes through her lands, and she reads and discusses the texts with Jerome at night. Jerome never underplayed or disavowed the powerful, erotic content of the Song of Songs. Like the hermits of the desert, he saw asceticism as a struggle and actively recommended these love songs to Paula and her daughter Eustochium. He always sought to acknowledge the hardships of the sexless path they had chosen, which in turn reflected and reaffirmed Paula's choices.

The long and intimate relationship between Paula and Jerome suggests a romantic connection. They are the inspiration behind Chaucer's story of the Wife of Bath, for instance. It is notable that Melania and Rufinus never attracted gossip or speculation, though on the surface they appear to have an identical relationship to Jerome and Paula. Somehow, they seem more levelheaded and independent of each other. Paula and Jerome are different. They are both intense and passionate, and they clearly needed and relied on each other. At a personal level, Jerome was a catastrophe, but in her own way, Paula was just as difficult. She was given to sudden excitements and low depressions, and dedicated so much to a higher life of prayer and theological speculation that she would only wash if her health depended upon it. Once she decided to be a benefactress and monastery-builder, she went at it with such enthusiasm that within ten years she was bankrupt. Rebuilding Bethlehem cost her entire personal fortune.

Early in their relationship, Paula's older daughter Blaesilla had died after embracing her mother's ascetic lifestyle. Jerome was blamed as a bad influence on the family. Paula never wavered in her support, however.

When Jerome wrote in favor of asceticism. he provided an intellectual justification for a path that Paula had already chosen. Far from brainwashing her, he was either supporting or enabling her: take your pick. Jerome's most tender description of Paula and Eustochium depicts them moving through their monastery in threadbare dresses, sweeping the day's dust away, setting tables and going to the kitchen to boil cabbage heads. This is on top of their intellectual and literary work, which he never omits to mention or praise. Jerome is unstinting in his praise of Eustochium, whose intelligence and language skills he relied upon as she became the editor of his work, playing a key role in his greatest achievement, the new Latin edition of the Bible, an immediate sensation that would become the basis of all later western Bibles.

In Paula and Jerome's day, as much as our own, Bethlehem was caught between the great conflicts and contradictions of the time. In 410 CE, Jerome records that Ishmaelite raiders had occupied Bethlehem. In a letter to Marcella, he quotes the Bible to say that they swept through the region "like a torrent that carried everything before them." The Visigoths sacked Rome in this same year, and it takes a special kind of character to tell an elderly widow that something worse has happened to you. No other writer mentions a large-scale invasion at this time, though it is unlikely that Jerome is actually lying. There was an interruption in Rome's border defenses between the end of the Tanukhids' role as Rome's foederati and the rise of their successors, the Salihids. This encouraged wide-ranging raids by the Lakhmids, a Christian Arab tribe that worked for Rome's enemy: the Persian Sassanids. If the Lakhmids occupied Bethlehem briefly sometime before 410 CE, it is a reminder that the desert was not simply a symbol of a hard and testing environment—it still was a place of danger.

By the end of the fourth century, relations between Paula and Jerome and the Christian elites of Jerusalem had fractured beyond repair. The problems were political, though as ever they were manifested through doctrinal arguments. As young men, Rufinus and Jerome had bonded over their mutual regard for Origen, not only for his brilliant work as an interpreter and translator, but also for his philosophy. Origen is responsible for a novel form of Platonism that argues God's love is a material force that drives the human thirst for truth and beauty. This force can be felt in physical forces such as sunlight; though, it will only be experienced in its purest and most intense form in the presence of God, because God is all love. Origen agreed that Christ is the same substance as God, yet he places Christ slightly lower down the energy scale, like a light bulb glowing at a milder intensity.

Origen's interpretation seemed to diminish Christ and so had become heresy by the end of the fourth century. Both Rufinus and Jerome repudiated the philosophy, though Rufinus continued to defend the less contentious parts of Origen's oeuvre: his translations and interpretations. Jerome did not. He would acknowledge some value in Origen, but his qualifications were drowned out by his forceful condemnations of the key heresy. At the same time, however, he was more than happy to pass off Origen's insights as his own. Origen's big idea was to read the Old Testament as a lengthy allegory on the coming of Christ. Jerome took this up, and recycled many of Origen's observations as his own insights. In a letter to Rome, for instance, he notes that of the three books credited to Solomon, Proverbs is for children, Ecclesiastes for adults, and Song of Songs for old folks, while a letter to the Roman dowager Principia unpacks Psalm 45 to show that an address to a man on his wedding day is an allegory pointing to the love between Christ and the church. This was extremely galling for Rufinus, who knew full well there was nothing original in Jerome's thought, and nothing interesting that did not come from Origen.

Jerome's tireless ambition was all directed toward Rome. The few of his correspondents who were not actually living in the old imperial city were Latin-speaking figures, like Augustine of Hippo. Similarly, Paula's standing and influence flowed from her membership in a family of powerful Roman senators, and when she looked for donors, it was to her own aristocratic circle. Jerome and Paula gave Bethlehem a Latin tinge that it has never lost, continuing with the work of Amalfitan merchants who organized pilgrimages to Jerusalem and Bethlehem before the Crusades, and later with the Franciscan fathers and Venetian traders who partnered Bethlehem's souvenir traders in Ottoman times. Bethlehem has a strong Latin tradition; the Sansour family is Catholic, for instance. This Latin strand runs against the main theme of Palestinian Christianity, which is eastern and Arab. Jerome represented the western church and this ultimately brought him into conflict with the local church embodied in the figure of John II, the Bishop of Jerusalem. Their violent disagreements were an early warning of the schism that would split Christendom into eastern and western churches.

While Paula was alive, the arguments with Bishop John were contained, or at least they simmered at a manageable level. On her death, Christians from across Palestine came to her funeral, including Bishop John and all of Palestine's other bishops. She was laid to rest in the caves below her monastery. Eustochium was laid beside her. Though the buildings above the cave have been rebuilt many times, the chapel mausoleum must be largely as it was when all the notables of Roman Palestine gathered here to pray over her body. The subterranean chapel is accessed from the Latin church of St. Catherine, above. A staircase leads down from a nineteenth-century chapel of marble and gilt, to a chalky limestone cave. In the milky gloom, there is a niche in the wall that marks Paula's likely resting place, opposite her daughter. At its quietest, before the coach parties arrive, it is one of the most peaceful of the chapels in Bethlehem, and aside from the grotto of the Nativity, it is probably the most ancient. Jerome was also buried here, though his remains were taken to Rome and now lie within the Vatican. The burial chapels are under Franciscan control, and connect directly to the grotto of the Nativity, though the connecting door is always locked. If you press your eye to the keyhole, you can spy on the Greek priests and the pilgrims kneeling at the spot dedicated to Christ's birth.

A passageway from Paula's chapel leads to a larger square underground chapel that is supposed to be Jerome's study, the room where he created the Latin Bible. It is possible to sit in this room and imagine Jerome as he appears in Dürer's print, bent over his desk with the weight of the monastery above him. Indeed, I have often done it. It was something of a disappointment to learn that his actual study was a bright, upper-story room with a view over the desert. Of course it bloody was.

After Paula's death, John banned Jerome from attending the services in the Church of the Nativity for a while. Jerome describes looking down on Helena's chapel and commenting that he consoled himself in his misery with the view across to Herodion and Tuqu'. Jerome ultimately became the abbot of Bethlehem, which formalized his role as the town's leading cleric. When the crusaders arrived in Bethlehem six centuries later, they were surprised to discover that Bethlehem had neither its own bishop nor answered directly to the Bishop of Jerusalem. Instead, it had a semiautonomous status within the diocese of the more distant city of Ashkelon. It is likely this was the compromise solution to the destructive relationship between John and Jerome.

The conflict with John reached its peak with the arrival in 415 CE of Pelagius, a Celtic monk from the British Isles who had developed a strong theory of free will. Augustine had condemned Pelagius in Carthage, but the sanction only applied in North Africa. Pelagius fled to Palestine, where he enjoyed the support of Bishop John. Jerome took Augustine's side and went on the attack in his inimitable style; he called the ascetic Pelagius fat, "stuffed with Irish porridge." In the course of the disagreement, an armed gang from Jerusalem descended on Bethlehem. Eustochium had become the abbess after her mother's death, with an estimated fifty nuns under her care. The number of monks led by Jerome is not known; a visitor put the figure at an unhelpful "multitudes." However, as Jerome oversaw five priests, his monastery might also have had fifty monks. The gang from Jerusalem set Paula's monastery on fire and killed a deacon. Jerome and Eustochium had to shepherd their entire party to the safety of a local fortress, probably Herodion. They stayed there for months, as the monasteries were rebuilt. Eustochium was traumatized by these events, and her subsequent decline ended in her death.

THE STATUS OF PALESTINE'S JEWS was becoming ever more precarious as the empire embraced Christianity. The Jewish patriarch in Palestine was recognized by the imperial authorities as a hereditary prince, with a court and a palace in the Galilee. This made him the senior figure in Palestine in Jerome's day, with the power to dismiss senior Roman administrators. Yet his position was under threat as new discriminatory laws were passed, notably one forbidding Jews from converting their slaves. The great Christian patriarchs of the day, Cyril of Alexandria and John Chrysostom in Antioch, saw Jews as sinners who were deaf to Christ's message; at times, both men encouraged the burning of local synagogues. The greatest threat to the patriarch, however, came from within the Jewish community; not only from the independent Samaritans, but also from Karaites and Talmudic Jews, who both in their way rejected the patriarch's authority in favor of a return to Jewish texts.

Jerome was part of this literary revolution. Christian and Jewish scholars felt justified in questioning the authority of kings and princes on the basis of their own texual analyses. Jerome outraged local Christians with his decrees, and like contemporary Talmudic scholars, he believed his scholarship gave him a greater authority than any patriarch. Jerome claimed his version of the Bible represented a return to the older Jewish wisdom, which had been obscured by poor Greek translations. His slogan was "Back to the Hebrew." However, he overlooked—or perhaps simply did not know—that the Greek-language Septuagint was an authentic Jewish work. The Christian gospels, moreover, were originally written in Greek; there were no more authentic older versions.

Jerome's claim to take the church back to the Hebrew is fanciful, but even if it were possible, Jerome would not be the man to do it. He was not a talented linguist. Early in his career, he could not even distinguish between Aramaic and Hebrew. His literary fame took off when he claimed to have discovered a lost Christian gospel in a monastery library in Chalcis, Syria. It was, he said, an original version of the Gospel According to Matthew. Origen had mentioned such a work, and it would have been the find of the century if it existed; but Jerome was lying and not very convincingly. He claimed that the text was written in Hebrew, but in his day the Greek words *Hebraois* and *Hebraisti* were used to refer to all Jewish texts, whether written in Greek, Aramaic, or Canaanite. Jerome's inability to specify the actual language suggests that he never saw the text. Today, we know the Gospel of Matthew is a compilation from various sources and no "original" exists. Jerome invented the book to make his name. He was a young man in a hurry.

Jerome's knowledge of Ancient Canaanite/Hebrew has been debunked many times. This is not to diminish his talent as a writer. By the thirteenth century, Jerome's version of the Bible was *the* Catholic Bible, the *versio vulgata*, or common version. It is a beautiful work, but his sources are not hidden or obscure. It is composed entirely from a work known as the *Hexapla*, Origen's astonishing assemblage of all the known versions of every biblical text. Jerome had access to Origen's copy of the Hexapla in the library at Caesarea: reason enough for Jerome to move to Palestine. Jerome's synthesis of Origen's work into a single Latin version gave the western church its founding text, and ultimately the King James translation, too. But the idea that this version is more authentic than any other is simply fanciful, a product of Jerome's shifting relation with the truth.

Jerome also wrote biographies of early desert fathers. Among these works is one that purports to be a biography of a monk named Malchus. In fact, it is a love story, a work of fiction that describes the lives of a devout man and woman who respect each other as companions but choose celibacy and isolation over marriage. It is impossible to read it as anything but an oblique love story to Paula, the woman who supported and loved him.

Once upon a time, all I knew about Jerome was that he was the patron saint of writers and melancholics. I picked this up from a mention in an early work by Walter Benjamin, a German Jewish Marxist who nevertheless appreciated a figure who linked literary talent with acute depression. There are good sides to Jerome, in fact. He was writing at a time and in a place where women like Paula, Eustochium, Marcella, Melania, Elegia, and Poimenia ran the church. For all his raging ambition, Jerome never attempted to sideline or silence Paula or Eustochium. In their idiosyncratic lives together in Bethlehem, they loved each other as equals.

# CHAPTER 5

# THE EMPEROR'S NEW CHURCH

## *Byzantium*

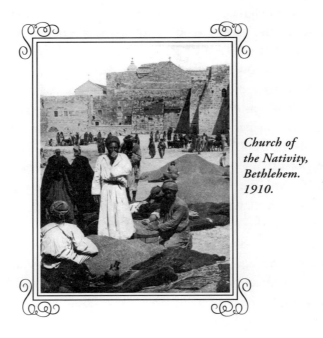

*Church of
the Nativity,
Bethlehem.
1910.*

Herodion is visible from almost everywhere in Bethlehem. On my
daily runs, I would arrive breathless at the top of Beit Jala and
see the flat-topped hill at the edge of desert. It looked as though
a child had overturned a bucketful of sand. I had visited the fortress palace
once, in 1995, and twenty years later it was surely worth a second look.
One unseasonably hot day at the end of October 2016, I asked a local tour
guide named Boulos Aqleh to drive me over.

In Arabic, it is *Jabal al-Fureidis*: the hill of Paradise, derived from the Persian "pardes" and explicitly used to describe the interzone not only between desert and farmland but also between heaven and earth. In certain lights, the body of the hill camouflages with the desert so that the fortress looks like a disc suspended beneath the sky. The fort remained in use until at least the fifth century and was part of the palace complex of the Empress Eudocia when she lived arrived in Bethlehem in 444 CE after the breakdown of her marriage to the Emperor Theodosius II.

I was still using my 1907 Baedeker as a guidebook, or at least those pages that I had photographed and stored on my phone. As Boulos and I drove to Herodion, I tried to follow the route of the aqueduct from Solomon's Pools to Herod's fortress but the settler ringroad that encircles Bethlehem severs the path. Herodion looked very different to my memories. The parking lot held a glass-fronted visitor center, whereas twenty years ago there was a low brick kiosk, which Anton Sansour told me had been closed for years because the army had not authorized anyone to look after the site. There was no one to sell us tickets. There was no one else around at all. We simply parked the car and started walking up the spiral path that surrounds the hill like a helter-skelter slide.

Flagpoles flying both the Israeli flag and the banner of the Israeli Parks Authority flank the present-day parking lot. Herodion underwent massive excavations after 2000, led by Ehud Netzer, an Israeli archaeologist who died on site at the age of seventy-six when some railings gave way and he fell into one of his shafts. I was not prepared for how much his earthworks and shafts had changed the fortress—reconfiguring the site to tell a different and ahistorical story. The sun was beating down, and I was beginning to hover on the verge of hallucinations. I should have worn a hat. I have a lot less hair than I did in 1995, and I sunstroke in a minute. As Boulos and I started up the spiral trail, I remembered my last visit with Anton and Raissa with guilt. I secretly thought we cut a comical party. Raissa Sansour was wearing heels, which did not suit the loose gravel track, while Anton was out of breath almost immediately. Nevertheless, they helped each other to the summit.

This time, Boulos abandoned me. It wasn't out of embarrassment. His wife called saying that their daughter had fallen and hurt her arm. She needed to get to the hospital. I wished Boulos luck, and then wondered what I was going to do. I had been abandoned in the desert, I was not sure how to escape, I had no phone signal and my head was growing very hot.

Netzer proposed that Herodion was a stronghold of the rebels in the Bar Kokhba revolt of the second century CE. He excavated the cisterns beneath the fortress and claimed to have found secret escape tunnels. It is tenuous in the extreme; Netzer ignored any feature built later than the second century, while "reconstructing" features that only existed in his imagination. He also claimed that a large, stone structure jutting from the side of the hill is the tomb of King Herod. A hokey film shown in the visitors' center dramatizes the moment that Herod was laid to rest inside this mausoleum. In fact, few people agree that it is a tomb: my 1907 Baedeker identifies it as church. As I tramped around Netzer's dig, my bad temper increased. The dig seemed a metaphor for Israel: a tough-guy reading of Jewish history that obscured every other story or, worse, erased it entirely. At Herodion, Netzer had literally built over Paradise. Not that the hill felt like the path to paradise as I tramped around the hill on the verge of sunstroke. The view of the surrounding settlements didn't make me any happier. Tekoa, which stands just across the deep valley of Wadi Khreitoun, is four times the size it was in 1995. Moving counterclockwise, Tekoa is at "six o'clock" followed by Nokdim, and then Kfar Eldad, and Sde Bar, peppering the desert with newly built houses and gleaming red roofs, and finally at "eleven" is Har Homa, standing between Bethlehem and distant Jerusalem.

I walked down to the Empress Eudocia's monastery, which unlike Herodion has no ticket office or film show. Eudocia had fallen for Palestine on a short stay in Melania's monastery six years earlier. Now divorced, she returned in exile to build her own palace and monastery in Bethlehem, at Herodion. In the shade of a Roman bathhouse, I took my own tour of the site using the 1907 guidebook. There were rows of columns that would once have made a shady colonnade to the monastery. Eudocia also established a leper colony, the first hospital of its kind. While in Palestine, she commanded a military force, which would have garrisoned the fortress and kept a lookout for Saracen raiders.

Eudocia had been born a pagan in Athens, the daughter of a noted teacher in the Academy. She only converted to Christianity on her marriage. In Palestine, she built her monastery in the Arab style as a remote desert outpost rather than as an urban monastery like Melania and Paula.

She adopted Arab Christianity, the Monophysite view (also known as Miaphysite) that saw the world as broken, and human life as a struggle to reach the divine. She also began writing poetry that recast the gospels in Greek verse. In this, too, Eudocia seemed to be following an Arab model. The successor to Queen Māwiyya's tribe as Rome's foederati were the Salihids, Christians led by a monk king named David/Dawud who ruled from a monastery named Dayr Dawud in Syria. David's scribes invented the flowing Arabic script, and his monastery not only produced Arabic versions of the gospels, but also much Christian poetry from his two court poets, one of whom was his daughter.

The Romans more than doubled the size of Palestine in the fourth and fifth centuries by adding new provinces. Palestine One (*Palaestina Prima*) continued to comprise much of what is now Israel and all of the Palestinian West Bank. The fertile land of Jordan along the Jordan River as well as the Golan Heights became Palestine Two (*Palaestina Secunda*). The desert either side of the Dead Sea became Palestine Three (*Palaestina Salutaris*), comprising the southern halves of both Jordan and Israel as well as Gaza. In Palestine One, the foederati co-commanders were two cousins named Aspebetos and Maris, allies of David's Salihids. In 427 CE, this pair established a semi-permanent city known as a "parembole" beside the Jerusalem-Jericho road, in an area that lies between the Palestinian city of Elazaria and the Jewish settlement of Ma'ale Adumim. The remains of the monastery Maris built to serve the parembole can be found inside the settlement.

The Romans gave Aspebetos the title *phylarch*, a military rank equal to Field Marshall. The bishop of Jerusalem, Juvenal, added another title by ordaining him a bishop. In 431 CE, Aspebetos attended the Church Council at Ephesus, as did many other Palestinian Arab bishops such as Bishop Abdelos of Elusa, Bishop Saida of Phaeno, and Bishop Natiras of Gaza. Juvenal almost certainly overstepped his authority in ordaining new Arab bishops; his intention was to pack the church councils with his supporters. He wished to raise Jerusalem to a patriarchate, and to serve as its first patriarch. Juvenal was tired of being junior to the bishop of Caesarea.

When Eudocia arrived in Bethlehem, she and Juvenal formed an alliance. Bishop and empress built new churches to increase the power and prestige of Jerusalem, and constructed the present-day city walls. In 449 CE, Eudocia's ex-husband convened a second council at Ephesus, which turned into a triumph for Juvenal. The ambitious bishop took a leading role in all the debates, not only cementing his own power within the church, but also ensuring that the Arab Monophysite position was accepted as church doctrine. Yet at the height of this triumph, the Emperor Theodosius was thrown from his horse and died.

Theodosius II had allowed his ex-wife's authority to grow, alongside the Arab and Syriac world that she had embraced. When he died, his older sister, Pulcheria, took over the empire. Like many powerful Roman women, she had taken a vow of celibacy. She remained celibate as empress, though she made a formal marriage of convenience to the General Marcian, anointing him as the emperor. Pulcheria wanted to rein back Eudocia's power, and succeeded in plunging Palestine into a civil war.

Just two years after the Second Council of Ephesus, in 451, Pulcheria and Marcian called for a new council at Nicaea to reaffirm the Nicene Creed. Juvenal believed the bishops would confirm that Monophysitism and the Nicene Creed were compatible, which was the position he had steered through Ephesus. These interminable arguments about the nature of Christ seem distant, but at bottom they are about freedom and authority. Across the Arabic and Syriac-speaking world, Christians believed their faith called them to transcend this hard and barren existence by imitating Christ's struggle. This was a doctrine that appealed to the romantic and heroic Arabic view of the wilderness, but had less appeal in a Greek-speaking milieu. Voices close to the new Empress Pulcheria felt the Arabs emphasized free will at the expense of church authority. A Christian could never truly imitate Christ, because it was impossible for a human to get inside the mind of the divinity. A believer needed to show humility, not heroism. The only way to approach Christ was through obedience to church authority. This was Dyophysitism, a doctrine that emphasized Christ as the "way" between heaven and earth, this life and the hereafter, but in such a mysterious form that one could not hope to understand it without the guidance of the church and its priests.

Juvenal set out for Nicaea in confidence, but the political climate had changed; the Arab doctrine no longer had any powerful champions. The foederati was in chaos. The Salihid king David and his allies Maris and Aspebetos had been weakened fighting the Vandals in North Africa, and were subsequently defeated in intra-tribal conflicts. There was no longer anyone to defend the Monophysites, and Greek-speaking Constantinople saw an opportunity to reclaim authority. At the last minute, the location of the council was changed to Calchedon. This was not the only surprise. The decisions made at the Second Council of Ephesus were set aside, and the council was retrospectively branded a *Latrocinium* or "raiders' council," a term chosen to suggest the delegates had been strong-armed by the Saracen bishops. Juvenal arrived at Calchedon with an entourage of Palestinian monks, all staunch Monophysites. When he saw the way the wind was blowing, he shocked his followers by promptly renouncing his old doctrine. Juvenal was Palestine's Benedict Arnold: overnight he became a passionate Dyophysite, and in return he got the deal on Jerusalem he had craved for so many years. The city would become a patriarchate, and Juvenal its first patriarch. But to claim his seat, he had to join Pulcheria's war against Eudocia—two empresses fighting for the soul of the empire.

A monk named Theodosius escaped Calchedon and rode hard to Palestine to bring the news to Eudocia. When the monks of Palestine learned that they had been betrayed by their own bishop, Eudocia backed them with her own forces and installed the whistleblower, Theodosius, as the new bishop of Jerusalem over Juvenal. She held out for two years, until her ex-sister-in-law sent an imperial army to Palestine, led by Juvenal and swelled by Samaritan forces. Eudocia was defeated and forced into retirement in Bethlehem where she wrote poetry and cared for the lepers at her monastery. Despite her life as a heretic, the church was steered toward recognizing her as an Orthodox saint when she died in 460 CE.

Boulos and his wife Ieva found me sitting in the shade of her monastery. Their three-year-old daughter Trevina had a broken arm inside a plaster cast, which she showed off with wide-eyed seriousness. She was on the path to recovery and so was I. I had found headache tablets in my backpack, and was far less grumpy. My change of mood might also have had something to do with Eudocia's monastery. Herodion has been so dug up and overlaid with dubious history; Eudocia's monastery feels all the more special for having been left alone.

FOR CENTURIES, THE MOST NOTABLE monasteries of Bethlehem had been built and run by women. This changed under Bishop Elias, patriarch of Jerusalem from 494 to 516 CE. Elias was a Roman Arab rather than a Saracen. He was named after a celebrated Palestinian cleric who had been a close friend of Juvenal, which suggests that his family was Jerusalemite. He began his religious life at the monastery of Maris in the parembole, where he forged a lifelong friendship with a Cappadocian monk named Sabbas. When Elias became patriarch, he built the monastery that became known as Mar Saba, after Sabbas who served as its first abbot. The monastery lies a few miles outside Bethlehem in the desert, where the Kidron Valley meets Wadi Khreitoun, but is more easily reached by a winding asphalt road that snakes out of Beit Sahour.

Despite his early life in a Monophysite monastery, Elias became a fierce defender of Constantinople's views. In his day, many Palestinians clung to the old orthodoxies, yet Elias succeeded in turning the country around. Elias's strategy included building new monasteries and renaming older ones. In this way, he erased the last remains of Palestine's Monophysite past, while emphasizing that this was a land that bred ascetic saints. The monasteries also helped in the defense of Palestine, as they were fortified compounds built on the desert approaches. Security was an important consideration when a foederati no longer protected Palestine. Elias was often in need of military help, and even once sent Sabbas as his emissary to Constantinople to lobby for protection from Saracen raiders around Bethlehem.

The church Elias built inside Mar Saba is beautiful, with a high dome in a style that would come to be associated with later Byzantine/Roman architecture. The inside of the golden dome was once covered in mosaics. The monastery is set over a dramatic desert ravine half melting and half merging into the rock face. It is close to Bethlehem, a distance that, before air-conditioned cars, was best made at night because of the heat of the desert, though the paths through the shade of the steep wadis offer some relief from the heat.

I made my first and only visit to Mar Saba in October 2016. A slim, young Russian monk acted as my guide. Though the monastery was rebuilt over and over since the early sixth century, my guide assured me that the basic structure of the church has remained the same. His wispy beard and pale blue eyes gave him an air of fragility, as did the sweet smell of fortified wine on his breath. It was eleven in the morning. I asked how he became a monk, and he told me he had visited on a holiday and soon returned asking to be admitted as a monk. There are twelve monks living in a building that held a hundred and fifty in Sabbas's time. A persistent rumor in Bethlehem is that the church authorities in Athens are so desperate for monks that they allow prisoners serving life sentences to complete their sentences in Mar Saba. I did not ask if this was true.

My eyes wandered toward an ornate glass case, which seemed to contain a robe and a bishop's miter. On closer inspection, I discovered Saint Sabbas himself, or at least his mummified body—sixteen hundred years old, dry as dust, with long, spindly fingers and a translucent, pinched nose. The monk pointed out that the papery corpse was clearly a tall figure, despite the shrinking that comes as a corpse dries. This fits with contemporary descriptions of Sabbas as a powerful man. The saint's body was stolen by relic hunters during the Crusades and only returned by Pope Paul VI in 1965. This was the year I was born, I told my guide. He replied, "That is very significant," in a voice that suggested he found no significance in it at all. When you walk past the mummified body of your patron saint and founder every day, a lot of things become less interesting.

At the dawn of the sixth century, Elias laid the groundwork for an Arabic-speaking church that was nevertheless faithful to the Greek-speaking Orthodox world. This came to be known as the Melkite Church, which translates as Kings' Church, meaning loyal to the emperor. In many ways, the Melkites are the national church of Palestine, at least in the sense that most Melkites are Palestinian, with some communities also in Lebanon. Not all those who adopted Elias's position would have been native Arab speakers—Palestinians also spoke Greek and Aramaic/Syriac at the time. But from the Islamic conquest in the seventh century onwards, the Melkite Church adopted an entirely Arabic liturgy.

The valley walls opposite Mar Saba, on the far side of the Kidron Stream, are peppered with caves that formed the original lauras of the monastery compound. When a party of monks tried to establish new lauras within the monastery's grounds, Elias sent his own men to close up their caves and move the rival monks on. A little later, another sixty monks mutinied, and Sabbas fled into the desert. Once again Elias restored order, dispatching the rebels to Eudocia's monastery beneath Herodion. Elias again showed his formidable political powers. He not only brought the rebels back into line, but also succeeded in installing Sabbas over them as their archabbot.

Elias saw the transfer of Bethlehem's farmland to the church. Mar Saba was given agriculture land in Bethlehem's Beit Sahour, while the monastery of St. George received land then known as Beit Jala (now al-Khader; the current town of Beit Jala is a little further north). The Roman noblewoman Ikelia, responsible for the octagonal Kathisma church outside Bethlehem, was Elias's most important ally. She built at least two monasteries: Mar Elias, named after Bishop Elias, and Mar Theodosius, which lies on the road between Beit Sahour and Mar Saba. Elias had a policy of re-dedicating monasteries, changing their names to erase their heretical Monophysite past. Maris's monastery became St. Martyrius, after the patriarch who succeeded Juvenal, while Eudocia's hospital became an adjunct of Mar Saba. It is likely that Ikelia's monasteries existed in another Monophysite incarnation before Elias took control of them.

There is a reason that this was my first tour of Mar Saba. The monastery forbids women from entering, and I could not see the point of visiting if Leila or Raissa had to sit outside while I took a tour alone. As I emerge from the monastery's small, wooden door into the bright desert sun, a group of women are sitting under an olive tree on a pretty terrace. This is the compromise; women can sit at the doors to the monastery and wait for a monk to come to them. A wiry, pony-tailed monk appears from the doors of a large SUV where he has been giving a blessing to an elderly woman. He bounds over to the women on the terrace, bright and energetic as he takes a seat on the low whitewashed wall. He talks about the history of the church and ends by dispensing blessings.

On the road back to Bethlehem, we pass the Mar Theodosius monastery. The Greek flag flies above the walls of the compound. Ikelia was the last in the long line of women church-builders attracted to Bethlehem, arriving at a time when the church was dividing into Arab and Greek-speaking spheres. She could not have known that the result would see women sidelined, patronized, and locked out of the churches they had built. It is difficult to say quite how the church took such a wrong path. An institution that once offered women so many possibilities ended by locking them out. It is tempting to wonder what kind of church we would have, today, if the Emperor Theodosius had not been thrown off his horse.

ELIAS REESTABLISHED UNITY in Palestine, a generation after the civil war caused by Juvenal's betrayal. In other ways, however, the country was less stable than it had been in a century. The Roman legion in Aqaba could not protect a country with desert borders as wide and sparsely inhabited as Palestine. Inside the original *Palaestina Prima*, the gendarmerie led by the governor in Caesarea proved incapable of dealing with insurrections that broke out in the late fifth and sixth centuries. The Emperor Justin was a military man whose family were pig farmers in the Balkans. He had never learned to read, and foreign policy was set by his nephew, Justinian, a man who was equal parts playboy and politician. Justinian recognized it was time to hire a new foederati and in 516 CE he turned to a tribal alliance known as the Ghassanids, run by two brothers, Al-Hārith ibn Jabala and Abu Karib. As the Ghassanids were Monophysites, this required a more conciliatory approach toward heretics. Justinian was happy to make compromises, but Elias stood in the way. For once, Elias lost a political battle. Justinian sacked him as patriarch and sent him into internal exile in the garrison town of Aqaba.

Justinian did not only want to bolster Palestine. He had a longer-term strategic aim of turning the Red Sea into a Christian Sea. Ethiopian and Egyptian Christian allies controlled the western banks of Africa, but a Jewish-Arab tribe known as the Himyarites menaced the eastern shore. In short order, Abu Karib delivered Justinian's victory by defeating the Himyarites.

In 527 CE, Justinian succeeded his uncle as emperor and immediately faced a series of rebellions, each one seeming to provoke another. In Palestine, the Samaritans numbered somewhere between half a million and 1.2 million people but were treated as second-class citizens in a province that favored Christians. A series of grievances led the Samaritans into a hundred-year revolt, beginning in 484 CE, with each rebellion incurring ever-harsher penalties. The Samaritans were organized on feudal lines, with a landowner acting as the suzerain of a larger number of peasant workers. The landowners were able to deliver forces in each successive rebellion but were

unlikely to have supplied any arms better than scythes and poles. Nevertheless, in 529 CE, a Samaritan named Julian conquered most of Palestine.

Julian began his campaign by hosting rebel games in Nablus, tantamount to declaring his own *Imperium Samaritanum* to rival the Imperium
of Rome. When he discovered that the winner of the chariot race was a
Christian, he beheaded the man on the spot. This would have alarmed the
Christians, and their worst fears were realized as the Samaritans marched
on Bethlehem. Saint Helena's chapel was torched. Nothing remains of her
innovative rotunda, and all that survives of the rest of the complex are
parts of the mosaic floor from the colonnade leading to the chapel, and
the network of subterranean caves that hold the grotto and the burial
chambers of Paul and Eustochium (and, until he was moved, Jerome). The
rest went up in flames.

Justinian responded by reversing the policy that kept Saracens out of
the affairs of Palestine One and ordered the Ghassanids to put down the
Samaritan rebellion. Like their predecessors Maris and Aspebetos, Al-
Ḥārith and Abu Karib ruled as co-regents, a policy that seems to have been
deeply ingrained in the foederati. It is notable that the foederati's patron
saints also came in pairs: Damian and Cosmas, Protus and Hyacinth, and
Sergius and Bacchus, all fourth-century Roman-Arab soldiers. The senior
brother was Al-Harith, otherwise known as Arethas, but Justinian again
turned to Abu Karib. Though the Samaritans had defeated the governor's
police force at Caesarea, they were no match for Abu Karib's heavy cavalry.
The Ghassanids were highly trained horsemen who perfected their skills
with obsessive drilling. A knight had to be able to mount a horse from any
angle, in full armor, in a single leap. For roughly a hundred years, from
the dawn of the sixth century to the early years of the seventh, they gathered a reputation for invincibility. They acted as Rome's shock troops,
capable of punching through enemy lines. Abu Karib is said to have traded
twenty thousand Samaritan women and children south as slaves into Persia, a catastrophic defeat for the Samaritans but also a major problem for
the whole of Palestine as their farmland fed the whole country. Abu Karib's
victory left the wheat fields of Jenin abandoned for a generation, driving
up the price of grain and leading to widespread poverty.

There are two accounts of Abu Karib's campaign. One by John Malalas,
a writer from Antioch who is ultra-loyal to Justinian, and another by a

local, Procopius of Caesarea, who is so hostile that he has been identified as a Samaritan. It is more likely that he was a Christian landowner who bought wheat from the Samaritans. Procopius might have been outraged to see mercenary forces used against Roman citizens, and alarmed that a heretical version of Christianity had returned to Palestine with the Ghassanid forces. But his chief problem seems to have been the rise to the cost of living.

The families of Bethlehem are divided into clans, and two trace their roots back to Abu Karib and the Ghassanids. The thirty-five families of the al-Najajreh are said to be part of Abu Karib's army, which came to oversee the rebuilding of the church. The Sansours are associated with this clan but may have married into it at a later date. The sixty-two families of the al-Farahiyeh clan claim descent from a Ghassanid-era priest named Farah, who lived between 490-570 CE. If these families arrived as Monophysites, however, they did not remain so; rather, they adopted the prevailing orthodoxy in Palestine, which suggests there was a thriving Christian community in Bethlehem capable of influencing the newcomers.

The Ghassanids had far more influence on the church in Syria. The split between Palestinian Melkites and Syrian Monophysites became one of the key cultural markers between Palestine and Syria, serving to underpin the two countries' quite different identities. Indeed, a Monophysite community only arrived in Bethlehem in the twentieth century as refugees from Anatolia, fleeing Turkish persecution. This was the time of the Armenian Holocaust, and Arab Christians were also targeted and chased out of their traditional homelands. A hundred families fled the massacres and settled in the Bethlehem souk area. The refugees formed their own clan and built a new church, known as the Syriac Church, where "Syriac" refers to the language of the liturgy, a dialect of Aramaic. The church still prays in the everyday language of Christ.

In February 2017, Bethlehem's Syriacs became famous when twenty-three-year-old Yaqub Shaheen won Arab Idol, the most popular TV show across the Arab world. Shaheen is the son of a carpenter, and he began his singing career in the church choir. Prior to his victory, the most famous Bethlehem Syriac was his namesake, Father Yaqub. In 2012, Leila Sansour filmed an interview with this redoubtable priest. He was approaching eighty and in poor health, yet he radiated energy. He joked that he would go on forever because he was nuclear-powered, a boast Leila's cameraman caught on film. Sadly, this was over-optimistic. He died shortly afterwards. What I remember best about him is his cracked but warm rendition of a hymn. I listened spellbound, which slowly turned to confusion because the song sounded remarkably similar to "My Country, 'Tis of Thee," more familiar to the English as "God Save the Queen." The complex quarter-tones that give Syriac church music its seductive melodies added a psyche-delic effect, but there was no mistake; it was the same tune. Father Yaqub broke off, laughing. It was a game he often played with English visitors. The tune had been borrowed from a Syriac hymn without ever being cred-ited, or so he said. Though I have never been able to authenticate it, I suspect he was right. The tune is certainly ancient, dating back to before the European Renaissance, so crusaders or merchants trading with An-tioch may have picked it up.

JUSTINIAN SURVIVED ALL the rebellions of his early days and proved to be one of the longest-serving emperors. He had a passion for the grand strategic project, reflected in his determination to control the Red Sea, and for coining the term Holy Land. His lasting monument in Palestine is the Basilica of the Nativity in Bethlehem, built in 565 CE. Unlike the Hagia Sophia, Justinian's innovative domed cathedral in Constantinople, the church in Bethlehem is an old-fashioned design. It is a Roman temple, though it can take a while to see the shape of the temple in the hotchpotch of the current façade, after the rebuilding of the Crusades when it was turned into a fortress. The roof looks like a half-completed garden wall, with an improvised welded cross perched on top. The triangle of the orig-inal gable can be made out, however, and if you continue staring, the lines of the old frontage become visible. The point of the gable sits above the church's main door, which has been bricked up, leaving just a tiny en-trance in the bottom right-hand corner, known as the Door of Humility because visitors must bend low to get inside. The lintel above the original door is still visible, and there are traces of two slightly smaller side en-trances, though a large stone buttress built to support the entire façade hides the left-hand door. A crusader-era extension that juts into Manger Square obscures the door on the right.

Once these elements resolve themselves, the front of Justinian's basilica becomes obvious. The façade would have resembled a triumphal arch, with a large, central entrance flanked by two smaller openings and a high, triangular gable at the top. The crowning glory was a mosaic frieze that covered the entire width of the building. The mosaic told the story of the Nativity and was regarded as so fine that it inspired a legend that it had saved the church from destruction. This was 610 CE, when Persian forces invaded Palestine. The Persians are said to have seen the depiction of the Magi, recognized the likeness of Parthian priests, and decided that they were unable to destroy a church that honored their own people. A Nativity scene from the same period survives in the cathedral at Ravenna, Italy, and shows the Magi wearing the distinctive red headdresses of the Persian priesthood, so maybe there is some truth in the story.

The Ghassanid reputation for invincibility suffered in the wars against the Persians, and though they eventually beat back the invaders in 627 CE, ten years later they were defeated by Muslim forces at the Battle of Yarmuk, 636 CE. This was the battle that brought Palestine under Muslim control, and saw a flood of Christian priests leave for Italy and Constantinople. In 642 CE, six years after the Muslim conquest, one of these priests became Rome's first and only Bethlehem-born pope, Theodore I.

Over the next few hundred years, the papacy would often be filled by Arab clerics who had fled the Roman Oriens after the Muslim conquest. Much like the Cubans of Miami who tirelessly campaign against the island's communists, the Arab exiles colored the church's attitude toward Islam. They were implacable, convinced they alone had the inside track on their enemies; they knew compromise was impossible. Ultimately, this Arab Christian diaspora provided a spark that ignited the Crusades, though it would take a group of hardheaded Norman Vikings to see the Crusades through to victory.

# CHAPTER 6

# TRADERS TO CRUSADERS

## *The Islamic Conquest to the Crusader Town*

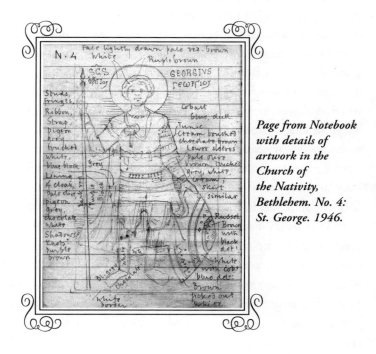

*Page from Notebook with details of artwork in the Church of the Nativity, Bethlehem. No. 4: St. George. 1946.*

I ordered the largest book in the library on Bethlehem's churches and opened it to the Church of the Nativity, convinced there was nothing I did not already know. You can guess what happened. Norman crusaders had left a series of portraits on the double row of columns that line Justinian's basilica. I thought I knew the columns like the back of my hand. How could I have missed a whole series of paintings? Norman paintings? Anyone who's English thinks they know the Normans: the one historical date every child remembers is 1066, the Norman Conquest. The Royal Family is Norman.

The portraits were going to be the first things I checked out on my next visit. That didn't run to plan, either. As of 2014, the Church of the Nativity has been undergoing an extensive restoration program, and when I visited over October and November in 2016, the columns were swaddled in plastic, polystyrene, and wooden battens. No portraits were visible. The closest I got to the portraits was back in London when I consulted annotated illustrations of the portraits, drawn in the 1940s in a survey for the Palestine Exploration Fund.

The portraits are a mix of Norse and Palestinian saints, alongside a few biblical figures. One among them, St. Cathal, appeared to be the odd man out. He was a seventh-century Irish saint from Lismore who visited Bethlehem on pilgrimage thirty years after the Islamic conquest. He had left no obvious trace on Bethlehem, so what made him so special? He might have disappeared from history entirely if he had not run into a Mediterranean storm on his return voyage. He was shipwrecked close to the Italian town of Taranto, where the locals decided that an Irish monk would make the ideal bishop. Cathal remained in Taranto until his death in 685 CE. There are towns, monasteries, and churches named after *San Cataldo* across southern Italy and Sicily, where he is remembered for the many miracles he performed. It is the Italian angle, not the Irish, that connects Cathal to the Normans, as their adventures brought them to Italy at the end of the tenth century. Cathal occupies the space where religious, commercial, and military interests meet, a perfect emblem of the forces that bound Europe and the Middle East together in the four-hundred-year lead-up to the Crusades.

Cathal began his religious life in a monastery at Lismore and rose to become the bishop of nearby Shanrahan. According to his seventeenth-century hagiographer, Bartholomew Moroni, Cathal set out on pilgrimage with a single companion, a monk, Donatus, described as his brother. The two men are likely to have started their journey from Waterford, though the port did not get this name until the Norman Vikings named it *Vedrarfjordr*. His path to Bethlehem followed the old tin trading routes. Cathal would have sailed to St. Michael's Mount in Cornwall and then made the crossing to Bordeaux. From there, the packhorse trail would lead him to Varonne, a river port on the Rhône. Google Maps says the 340-mile journey from Bordeaux to Varonne takes 111 hours on foot, which is faster than the pace of a packhorse. With a full load, a train of packhorses would typically take around three weeks. Travelling on a barque downriver, the fast current would swiftly carry Cathal to Arles, from where he would follow the coast the short distance to the port of Marseilles. He would stay at the monastery John Cassian built in Marseilles after his stay in Bethlehem.

With good winds, at the right time of year, it might take as little as thirty days to sail from Marseille to Palestine. It was no faster to set out from a more southerly port, and an early summer crossing from an Italian port would still take from four to six weeks. Arculf travelled to Bethlehem at much the same time as Cathal, and though the second-hand accounts of his journey do not explain how he got there, he returned via Alexandria and Rome (where Fabiola, the Roman heiress who had stayed with Paula and Jerome in Bethlehem, had built her quayside monastery-guesthouse). The return sea journey was far slower, as the prevailing winds and sea currents force sailors to take a longer anticlockwise path around the Mediterranean. Still, a round trip from Marseilles with a few weeks in Palestine could take as little as ninety days in the summer and still leave time to tour all of the main sites.

Once in Palestine, Cathal is said to have prayed that he could stay forever in the desert:

> With all the love and reverence of a pilgrim [Cathal] sought out the holy places that had been sanctified by the presence of his Heavenly Master; and so great was his joy to live in these solitudes, and dwell on the mysteries of man's salvation, amidst the very scenes in which it had been accomplished, that he earnestly desired and prayed to be relieved of his episcopal burden, and allowed to live and die in the desert in which our Lord had fasted, or in some one of the retreats that had been made sacred for ever by His earthly presence.

Cathal saw the landscape of Bethlehem through the eyes of contemporary Christianity: it was the physical proximity of the wilderness that made Palestine holy, rather than the man-made environment of churches, monasteries, and the temple mount. The desert was where one withdrew from the human needs and desires, to strip away the trappings of this world and get closer to the next. But the focus on the desert may also reflect the fact that there was still not much in the way of a man-made environment in Bethlehem.

At the dawn of the great age of European pilgrimage, a visitor from a colder, darker, and greener country than Palestine might be surprised by the countryside around Bethlehem. The Mediterranean coast of Gaza and Israel is rarely any less than warm and sparkling, but the hills around Bethlehem are gray and bleak in winter. The Bible has a startling number of stories of lions, but the scrub and woodland they need was long gone. Palestine had been deforested by grand construction projects, by the demands of ship-builders working for merchant fleets and the Roman navy, and the creation of terraces for olive oil production. This was a bare-looking land, and a number of earthquakes in 658 CE, 672 CE, the 740s, and 808 CE contributed to a sense that Bethlehem was damaged and perhaps desolate.

Arculf's account describes the long ridge of Bethlehem as sparsely inhabited. The focus of the town lies around the church, and the locals have barely begun to populate the area around today's souk. A pilgrim named Jacinthus arrived seventy years later (in the 750s) to complain that Bethlehem "is destroyed." This may reflect a one-off event like a raid or the ravages of the series of earthquakes of the 740s (though these were centered on the Jordan Valley), but it is likely that Jacinthus simply expected Bethlehem to be a little more impressive. A common refrain with pilgrims, then and now, is that Bethlehem's glory lies in its past. It is revered as David's city and the birthplace of Christ, and so the belief takes hold that it must once have been an imperial stronghold to rival Alexandria, Caesarea, or Jerusalem.

Cathal would have skirted around the ridge to reach the saddle in front of the church, following the pilgrimage route along Star Street associated with the Holy Family and the Magi. In front of him, he would see Justinian's basilica with the mosaic showing the Virgin and Child, the Annunciation to the shepherds, the Adoration of the Magi, the Flight to Egypt, and the Massacre of the Innocents. The Muslim armies captured Palestine through a series of sieges between 636 CE and 640 CE, but Bethlehem was among the first cities to fall. Like all invaders, the Muslim armies attacked Jerusalem through its weakest point, Bethlehem, to cut off the city's water. Jerusalem lasted through a six-month siege between 636-637 CE. A Bethlehem monk named Sophronius had become the patriarch of Jerusalem two years earlier, making him the ruler of the city. He refused to surrender to anyone but the Caliph Umar in person. Sophronius was a gifted canonical lawyer, and the conversations he had with Umar are said to have resulted in the document of understanding known as Umar's Assurances, the code by which Palestine's Christians would be treated. The oldest-existing versions date to the early ninth century, so the code may have been the result of a longer series of understanding than this story suggests.

Cathal entered the church through the grand arch-like entrance. This brought him into a narthex or porch and a second set of doors leading to the basilica. Helena's church had encompassed an open courtyard with a colonnade that led to the small, round rotunda chapel. Now a building with a cedar wood roof enclosed this garden. Like the pantheon in Rome, the roof was clad in copper, and the weight required the large number of columns, which are made from a reddish local marble and stand in two double rows with a wide aisle between them. The apron walls were once covered in mosaics, and the restorers have rediscovered a few of these mosaics beneath layers of plaster. An Italian team from a company named Piacenti won the contract from the Ministry of Antiquities of the State of Palestine, a government department of a country that does not yet exist. The team enters the church at night when the doors are closed to pilgrims and tourists. As I enjoyed late-night coffees and pastries in Manger Square, the church was bright with halogen lamps. The badly leaking roof had not been repaired since the fifteenth century and since then had suffered lead stripping by the Ottomans, the careless removal of additions deemed "inauthentic" by the British, and bullet holes and fire damage from the Israeli soldiers who laid siege to the church in 2002, all stresses that added to the wear and tear of ages. The Italians had erected scaffolding that crisscrossed the basilica. I imagined the young restorers lying on their backs like a pack of youthful Michelangelos, dabbing away at their little pieces of the ceiling. When I checked out the videos on the website, I was alarmed to see them ripping out cedarwood beams with a crowbar. Much like making laws and sausages, I guess it is better not to know how a sixth-century church is restored. The winter of 2015/2016 was the first that the roof had not leaked in living memory.

SOPHRONIUS, BISHOP OF JERUSALEM, and the new Pope Theodore each confronted the Muslim conquerors in their own way. It seems remarkable that these two men were contemporaries and classmates from Bethlehem's monasteries. Evidently, Bethlehem provided one of the best educations available anywhere in the world at the time. Sophronius, the church lawyer, not only bargained for religious freedom with Umar, but also came up with the formula that largely settled the dispute about God's nature, in a doctrine catchily named Dyothelitism. Theodore became pope because of his fluency in Arabic and Greek, which was felt to prepare him for disputing heretics. Bethlehem's monasteries continued to produce brilliant men under Muslim rule, perhaps the greatest being John of Damascus, the eighth-century abbot of Mar Saba, whose arguments against iconoclasm helped save the Orthodox Church from a wave of puritanical destruction—paving the way for the heavily decorated Orthodox churches we know today. John only had the freedom to criticize the Orthodox Church because he was based in Bethlehem, in a Muslim empire, removed from the consequences of his attacks by the Byzantine emperor.

The Arab churchmen who had fled Syria for Sicily after the Islamic conquest did not see any benefits of Muslim rule. When Sicily also fell to the Muslims, this only confirmed their view that Islam represented a dire threat to Christendom. They moved on Rome, where they quickly dominated the papacy. There was an almost-continuous run of nine Syrian popes from 685 CE until 752 CE. Indeed, when Cathal was buried in his cathedral in Taranto, the pope was a Syrian with the emblematic name of Sergius I, named after the patron saint of the Ghassanids. The Syrian legacy built a vehemently anti-Muslim culture in Rome, which was constantly tested by the emerging Italian republics and their enthusiasm for Italian-Muslim trading links.

Arabic ideas spread to the new maritime republics of Italy, like Amalfi, Genoa, Pisa, Gaeta, and Venice. When we think of Europe's Arabic heritage, we look to borrowed words like coffee and cinnamon, and scientific terms like alkali, alembic, and algorithm, but this is only a part of the inheritance. What really shaped the culture and the laws of the Italian republics were the innovative financial tools they adopted from the Arabs. The idea of earning a living through financial speculation is Arabic, as is the word we use to describe it: *rizq* or risk. Other Italian terms borrowed from Arabic include *maone* (*ma'unah*), an association designed to pool risk; a broker, *sensali* (in Arabic, *simsar*); a public auction, *galega* (*halqah*). The contractual term *mukhatarah* entered Italy as a double-exchange contract specifying future payments. This was a tool transparently designed to get around the prohibition on usury by setting a price equivalent to the amount of interest the lender might expect. The pope was not fooled and condemned this kind of contract, which did nothing to halt its spread. It was known as a *mohatra* in Italian and Spanish and became *mofatra* in Portuguese.

The Amalfi merchants traded first with the Aghlabids, a North African dynasty that moved out of Africa to establish satellite kingdoms in Sicily and along southern coastal Italy. The Aghlabids allowed Amalfitans access to bigger local ports and also provided the merchants with muscle for security. The pope tried to pay the Amalfitans to give up their alliance, but they simply took the money and continued to work as closely with the Aghlabids as before. Even excommunication did nothing to deter them.

The ninth and tenth centuries saw the rise of the Fatimid dynasty, which effectively divided the Islamic world into two empires: the Abbasids, controlling the old Arab heartlands from their capital in Baghdad; and the Fatimids—a Mediterranean coastal power based in Egypt—as the new overlords of Aghlabid Sicily and southern Italy. (The older Islamic dynasty, the Ummayads, remained a power in Spain alone.) The Amalfitans continued to grow in parallel with the Fatimids, building a commercial base alongside other Italian trading states in the Rum Market of Cairo. The word Rum is Arabic for Rome, which is to say, Christian.

Trade between East and West went through a blip with the Fatimid Caliph al-Hakim bi-Amr Allah, the first Islamic ruler to go back on the Sophronius-Umar code guaranteeing religious freedom. He destroyed the Holy Sepulchre in Jerusalem in 1009, and even ordered the destruction of the Church of the Nativity, though this command was ignored. Hakim's heirs swiftly rebuilt the Holy Sepulchre and sent emissaries to all their old European friends to reassure and renegotiate their partnerships. The lasting results of Hakim's unhappy rule were new treaties between Roman Byzantium and Cairo, and a Golden Age of pilgrimage that presented a new business opportunity to the shrewd Amalfitans.

Pilgrimage to Palestine was no longer difficult, and the feudal lords of Europe took advantage in their thousands. The new visitors needed to stay somewhere, and institutions evolved to welcome and support the trade. The Fatimids gifted the Amalfitans a Ghassanid-era monastery-guesthouse in Jerusalem known as the Hospital, apparently after the Persian word *bimaristan*. The Amalfitan merchants ran the Hospital in partnership with European Benedictine monks, a partnership that revolutionized pilgrimage by bringing the Arabs' financial tools to the travel industry. The Hospital and its monks are the forerunners of the Hospitallers Order and their success was tied to the banking services they offered pilgrims. The Arabic double-term contract allowed a traveller to make a deposit in one country and withdraw the same sum, minus a consideration, in another: thereby obviating the need to carry large sums on long and hazardous journeys.

Aside from the contract itself, the key innovation that makes banking possible is a trusted currency that can function as a tool of exchange. The coin was the *taris*, or quarter-dinar. The Amalfitans not only used the taris in their own accounts in Italy, but also began minting their own versions of the coins, as did their rival Italian traders, which circulated as the currency of Italy. The Benedictine order allowed the contracts and the taris to spread up into northern Europe where the monastery at Cluny began to create strings of satellite monasteries as staging posts along pilgrimage routes, not only to Palestine but also in northern Spain.

THE NORMANS BEGAN to threaten this comfortable trade by fighting the Fatimids' allies in Sicily and coastal Italy. The Normans were Vikings who had settled in northwest France. From 999 CE, they came to know Italy as a staging post on their regular pilgrimages, which they undertook in their own ships. As they grew familiar with the Italian terrain, they took a leading role in expelling the Aghlabids, which naturally led to a far cooler reception on their visits to the Holy Land. Around the 1060s, the Normans also began fighting as mercenaries in the old Arab-Christian kingdoms of Syria, Edessa, and Cilicia. Norman generals like Robert Crispin and Raimbaud served with Armenian armies who had been driven out of their own Armenian homeland by the Seljuks, a Turkic tribe that had adopted much Persian culture.

Even on the eve of the Crusades, pilgrimage remained strong. Modest townsfolk could contemplate a once-in-a-lifetime pilgrimage, as the land route was both inexpensive and safe. In 1064-1065, a single pilgrimage saw seven thousand pilgrims walk to the Holy Land led by a party of German bishops. However, the encroaching Seljuks threatened this trade; they were everyone's headache, affecting the three great powers: Byzantium, the Fatimids, and the Abbasids.

In 1071, the Seljuks captured Palestine. The Byzantine Emperor appealed to Europe to help expel the Turks. Pope Urban in Rome responded by issuing one of the papacy's regular decrees for a Holy War against the whole of Islam. The pope's message would have been ignored, as it always was, but for an itinerant preacher named Peter the Hermit in France. When Peter took up this call for a global war against Islam, it led to a popular pro-war movement: the People's Crusade. Thousands of peasants armed with little more than gardening implements set out for Palestine, and some even lasted the entire journey. The enthusiasm for war presented the rulers of northern France and Germany with a political issue. The younger sons of the nobility may have joined the clamor purely in the hope of finding glory and wealth. The Dukes of Burgundy, however, had a real interest in war. They controlled the mother abbey of the Benedictines in Cluny, and the Seljuks had killed the Benedictine's lucrative pilgrimage business. This, in turn, damaged Burgundy both financially and politically, as control of the Benedictine Order was the central plank of Burgundy's influence over the papacy.

If we pool these reasons, we could make an argument that a perfect storm was brewing for a Middle Eastern war. Yet this risks over-determining the issue. The effective cause of the Crusades lay with the Normans of southern Italy. They did not see the Crusades as a particularly difficult or adventurous policy. The younger Norman leaders had been successfully fighting Muslim states their entire lives. With their depth of knowledge and their friendship with the Armenians providing allies on the ground, two young Norman knights took control of the Crusades and bent it to their own agenda.

Prince Bohemond and Count Tancred were so closely related that they were cousins as well as uncle and nephew. The Byzantine princess Anna Komnene was overwhelmed at her first sight of Bohemond: "He was so tall in stature that he overtopped the tallest by nearly one cubit, narrow in the waist and loins, with broad shoulders and a deep chest and powerful arms." She added, "[A] certain charm hung about this man but was partly marred by a general air of the horrible."

Bohemond had been christened the less-alarming name Marc in 1054. He earned his *nom de guerre* for the qualities that so impressed and unsettled the Roman princess. Bohemond is a corruption of Bahamut or Behemoth, the mythical monster of what was then the most popular book of the Bible: Job. It was like calling oneself the Terminator. Bohemond was the oldest son of Robert Guiscard but had been all but disinherited when his father repudiated Bohemond's mother in 1058. Bohemond got a title, Prince of Taranto, hence the portrait of St. Cathal in Bethlehem. But he got little else, which made him all the more hungry for land and power.

Bohemond and Tancred's first decision was to enlist their Armenian allies into the crusader forces. The result was that they won Edessa, and in due course Antioch, which may have been Bohemond's real target all along. He became Prince of Antioch. Baldwin, a rival from the Frankish Lorraine dynasty, took Edessa. At the same time, Armenian Cilicia was strengthened as an Armenian crusader state. So far as the Normans and Franks were concerned, with these gains, the mission was over. Bohemond had no intention of stirring from Antioch. Baldwin saw no reason to continue to Palestine once he was ensconced as ruler of Edessa, a position he cemented with a marriage to an Armenian princess. But the chief reason for abandoning the Crusades was that Bethlehem and Jerusalem had already been saved. The Fatimids, allies of many of the crusading forces, had driven out the Seljuks.

THE FATIMID GOVERNOR of Ashkelon, a black African named Iftikhar al-Dawla, had defeated the Seljuks and regained control of Bethlehem and Jerusalem. When he sent word to the crusaders, he fully expected the crusaders to halt. They were all friends, after all. The Fatimids had given the Latin Christians the Jerusalem Hospital and extensively improved Bethlehem to accommodate tourists. They had strengthened Artas to guarantee the water supply to Jerusalem, and developed the urban quarter on the town's long ridge. This period saw the expansion of Bethlehem's Christian merchants, who not only catered for the visitors and exported commemorative trinkets but also ran restaurants and guesthouses. The pilgrimage trade at this time is under-researched, but new work on the distribution of eulogies gives a glimpse of the scale of Bethlehem and Jerusalem's pilgrimage industry. Al-Dawla expected the crusaders to accept the offer to travel to the Holy Land in peace and, no doubt, the leaders would have been happy to agree. However, they faced a rebellion from their junior knights. After much horse-trading, the Council of Nobles reconvened and chose to recommence the Crusades. Now that Bohemond was settled in Antioch, leadership fell to Raymond of Provence, the oldest and wealthiest of the crusaders. His fortune came from the trade that passed through his private port of Marseilles. Raymond was no war general, however, and he soon alienated his forces. By the time the crusaders reached Jerusalem, he had been replaced by Godfrey of Bouillon, the compromise candidate for leader.

As the crusader army approached Jerusalem, al-Dawla expelled the city's Christians fearing they might allow the crusaders in through the porous walls and drainage tunnels of the city. During the siege, the crusaders were approached by a Christian delegation often described as coming from Bethlehem, though perhaps made up of these Jerusalemite refugees. Tancred was told that it would make sense to capture Bethlehem first and the twenty-four-year-old general eagerly seized upon the plan. Within a day, he had conquered Bethlehem and its reservoirs. The water supply for Jerusalem was in crusaders' hands. However, when Tancred raised his banner from the roof of the Church of the Nativity, this caused resentment in the already divided crusader camp. Bethlehem was of clear strategic value, but this did not stop Tancred's rivals portraying him as a glory-hunter.

Tancred changed the face of Bethlehem by turning the area around the church into a fort. The monasteries were commandeered and turned into barracks for his knights who took Holy Orders as Hospitallers. Tancred had conquered Amalfi immediately before the Crusades, so would have regarded the Amalfitan Hospital as his property. The influx of hardened soldiers into the order led to a break with both Amalfi and their partners, the Benedictines. The Hospitallers became self-governing, poaching rules from the Augustinians. The rise of the Hospitallers as a military force reflected its origins in the Roman-era foederati: a brotherhood of knights who embraced codes of chivalry as warmly as religious laws. The order continues to assert its autonomy, challenged in early 2017 by Pope Francis who controversially forced the resignation of its Grand Master.

The Norman's Armenian allies built their own monastery beside the Church of the Nativity, and the crusaders encased the entire campus in thick walls with a large square watchtower at the corner of what is now Milk Grotto Street. Today, it is easy to picture these crusader walls because the backs of the church buildings form a faceless, stone perimeter wall along Milk Grotto Street, while the Armenian monastery makes a massive stone backdrop to Manger Square. The gates to the fortress lay on Milk Grotto Street. A sixteenth-century door halfway along the street marks their likely place, and leads to a central passage that traverses the entire complex. On the few occasions I have walked along it, through the monastery and chapels, I have wondered if it not only marks the entrance to the crusader fortress but perhaps reflects the path of an original high street through the densely packed hillside town.

The crusaders' fortress left no room for the civilian population, and so the last of Bethlehem's civilians spread to the ridge opposite. It is possible that Tancred tore down the mosaic frieze across the face of the church. The Armenians donated elaborately carved doors to the Church of the Nativity and a new carved wooden frieze, perhaps in compensation for their role in Tancred's vandalism. This frieze can still be seen in the narthex, over the inner doors to the basilica. It is an extraordinary work—an intricate tableau of fabulous biblical creatures—currently in the process of being saved by the restoration project.

Inside the basilica, Tancred commissioned portraits for all of Justinian's marble columns. This is where Saint Cathal's portrait can be found, honoring Bohemond's principality in Taranto. Tancred also singled out St. Euthymius, mentor of the foederati general Maris, who founded the Hospital monastery when he succeeded Euthymius as abbot of the parembole. The other portraits are St. Theodosius and St. Sabbas, the abbots of Bethlehem's two most significant monasteries; St. Onophrius, a monastic figure held in such high regard in Norman Sicily that he became the patron saint of Palermo; St. Leo of Catania, another Sicilian saint; the Norse king-saints, Olaf and Canute, representing the Normans' Viking roots; St. Blaise, an Armenian saint to honor the Normans' chief ally; St. George, the knight-saint of Syrian, Armenian and Arab soldiers; and St. Damian and St. Cosmas, the Arab-Christian saints who were also venerated in Armenian-ruled Cilicia. Damian and Cosmas were military doctors, which flattered the Normans' self-image as they rebranded themselves as devout Hospitaller monks.

There are a few pillars spare in the basilica, and Tancred had enough sensitivity to incorporate actual scenes from the Nativity into his remodeling: there are two paintings of the mother and child; a portrait of St. Anne, a relative of Mary; St. Bartholomew and St. Stephen, saints who appear in the New Testament. Finally, there are portraits of John the Baptist and John the Apostle, both irreproachable gospel figures, probably chosen because of the confusion over exactly which St. John was the Hospitallers' patron saint. The patron saint of the Hospitallers is John of Jerusalem, whose thugs had set once fire to Jerome's monastery. Jerome's translation of the bible had made him the most revered saints in the Latin West, and the crusaders no doubt preferred to associate other Johns with their cause rather than Jerome's sworn enemy.

The message of these portraits is clear: this was a church upon which Tancred had stamped his identity, honoring Bohemond and the Normans, with high-fives to the Armenians and a backward glance to the Arab warriors whose mystique and poetry lent a more glamorous air to his gang of monastic knights.

Godfrey, the compromise candidate for leader of the Crusades, refused the grandiose title King of Jerusalem, modestly assuming the governorship instead. He died in 1100, the year after Tancred seized Bethlehem. Godfrey's brother Baldwin hurried from Edessa, abandoning his Armenian wife. He had no scruples about the title "king" and hoped to be crowned in Jerusalem. There was a problem, however. Bohemond might have been happily settled in distant Antioch, but he had managed to install his ally, Bishop Dagobert of Pisa, as the new patriarch of Jerusalem. Pisa was a newish sea power, and Dagobert combined his career as a bishop with a sideline in piracy. Dagobert tried to stall Baldwin's coronation by refusing permission for Baldwin to be crowned in the Holy Sepulchre. A compromise was reached, and the ceremony took place in Bethlehem on the Latin Christmas Day of December 25, 1100 CE.

The crowning of the first crusader king in the Church of the Nativity might be the biggest political event to have taken place in Bethlehem, another of those pivotal moments when world history turns upon the town. The scene captured the imagination of medieval artists, portraying the crowning first as a Byzantine icon of flattened figures in red and gold; it continued to fire the imagination up to Victorian times where artists depicted it like a scene from Ivanhoe or Camelot, with identical-looking knights, tall and slim, wearing the tabards of the Hospitallers and holding their swords like crosses. The church must have been full, but it is unlikely that the gathered knights and nobles looked so European. The crusaders were far from their homelands, and regular supply lines had not yet been established. If they were wearing armor or fresh robes, then these would have been locally made. There would have been a few women, at least, inside the church. Raymond brought his wife with him, others picked up local princesses along the way. The famous conical headdress known as a wimple may have originated in Palestine: it is unclear whether the crusaders brought it to Bethlehem or whether they adopted the dress of the local women. The medieval wimple is still part of the traditional wedding costume in Bethlehem.

Bethlehem was a compromise location for Baldwin's coronation, because it was not under the direct authority of Bishop Dagobert. Baldwin had his big day, but he was never allowed to forget who had gotten there first: Tancred. He accepted the crown of Jerusalem in a chapel customized by his enemy with the portraits of Norman, Armenian, and Arab saints gazing down upon him.

The five crusader kingdoms joined the Middle East at a time when empires were in retreat, once more, and the region had entered a period of No Over-all Control. The unstable coalition of Frankish, Norman, Armenian and Provençal crusaders seemed neither more nor less alien than any of the surrounding garrison states. Everyone came from somewhere else. The Seljuks were Persian-Turks. The Arab Fatimids relied on Berber forces, which they fatally alienated after inviting a tribe named the Banu Hilal to invade Tunisia. The Kurdish Ayyubids began working for the Fatimids before hooking up with the Baghdad-based Abbasids and, in a reverse takeover, taking power for themselves. These were the Islamic parties. The Mongols, a mix of Christian and pagan tribes, were edging their way into Syria. The neighboring Christian states also numbered Georgian and Roman-Byzantine forces, as well as independent Armenians. All competed to establish toeholds and win territory. The crusaders increased the confusion, because each of their five states pursued separate foreign policies. The kingdoms of Jerusalem (later Acre), Antioch, Edessa, Armenian Cilicia, and Cyprus feuded among themselves as often as they bickered with neighboring Turkic, Byzantine, Arab, and Mongol principalities. The monastic military orders evolved into standing armies who took different sides in whatever conflict was brewing; the newly created Knights Templar sided with French forces, while the later Teutonic Knights served the German kings. Once the crusaders succeeded in opening the Palestinian ports of Gaza, Jaffa, Acre, and Caesarea, the Italian states began resupplying the armies, stimulating trade and bringing in new pilgrims. Yet throughout the crusader period, the Italian city-states also traded with the Fatimids and the Ayyubids, even selling war materials like wood and iron.

The greatest change in Bethlehem lay in the kind of Christianity the crusaders bought with them. Despite their internal differences, the crusaders were Latin Christians (aside from the Armenians, who held their own views). As Latins, they had little sympathy for the Greek-speaking Christianity of Constantinople and none for the Arab-speaking churches they found in the lands they conquered. The crusaders effectively nationalized the church in Bethlehem, replacing the Palestinian clerics with foreigners who read the liturgy in the dead language of Latin rather than the everyday language of Arabic. In the five hundred years since the Islamic conquest, the Arab church had become detached from the church in Constantinople. The crusades pushed it into deeper isolation. Arab-speaking priests served the local communities in out-of-the-way small chapels, while the major churches were staffed by Europeans. Since the Crusades, every incoming regime has reserved the right to change the face of the local Christianity.

After the crusaders' defeat, the local church regained authority over the church through their candidate for patriarch, Athanasius. But this measure of autonomy lasted only until the Ottoman Turks captured Constantinople in the sixteenth century with aspirations to recreate the old empire of the *Rum*.

# CHAPTER 7

# MAMLUKS AND OTTOMANS

## *Thirteenth to Nineteenth Century*

*Workers in Mother-of-Pearl, Bethlehem.*

Bethlehem's souk is a noisy, jam-packed place filled with the smells of fresh za'atar and sage, ripening fruit and the sweet-sour smell of lamb fat. The market is the beating heart of the old city, sitting within a ladder of narrow alleys, between two long shopping streets. These two main streets mark the edges of the ridge, running parallel with each other down to Manger Square. On their outside edges, the slope falls away into the maze of passageways and hidden doors of the souk's dense residential areas. The street on the right-hand side of the ridge, if you are facing the square, has the everyday kind of shops: the hardware stores and the shoe repairers, the spice shops with their mounds of dry, powdered cumin and mace, while down at the lower end of this street, hawkers display secondhand goods and, even, junk on plastic sheets on the ground. This is also where my barbers have their shop, a father-and-son team. They work out of a sparsely decorated shop with mismatched furniture. The sparkly melamine surfaces date to the 1960s, a tallboy to the 1930s. The chair has been repaired so many times that it now comprises a car seat welded to the original heavy base. The father is eighty years old, a small man who walks bent over and has the kind of moustache you see in *Asterix* cartoons. When I last got my hair cut, he cooked up coffee in a little two-cup pan on a simmering electric hob as his son finished his work by running a twisted-cotton thread across my cheekbones and the tops of my ears. The smell of coffee distracted from the pain as the thread ripped out the hairs and brought tears to my eyes. An icon of St. Nicholas looked down on me: in sympathy, I thought.

All of Bethlehem's better shops stand on the opposite side of the ridge: the jewelers and money-changers; the tourist shops as well as the crafts shop of the Lutherans' *Dar al-Nadwa* center. Though to be honest, the ridge is so narrow that it is barely fifty yards between the two sides of town. Only the noise and bustle of the souk separates them.

It's a surprise to learn that the souk is less than a hundred years old. The British carved the space from a residential quarter in 1929, after they forced the closure of the market in Manger Square. Moving the stallholders meant demolishing substantial parts of two of the *harats*, or city quarters. These were the homes of the al-Najajreh and the al-Farahiyeh, the two clans that date their arrival to the days of the Ghassanids. The oldest surviving parts of the present town date to the Mamluk period, the Cairo-based regime that succeeded Saladin's Ayyubid dynasty in the thirteenth century. The Mamluks were technically slaves, though it would be better to view them as a guild of soldiers, a profession that required a long apprenticeship. The Mamluks were recruited—or stolen—from people living on the eastern coast of the Black Sea, often referred to as Circassians but including Georgians and Chechen, too. The hope was that by recruiting boys and moving them thousands of miles from their families, they would have no local distractions and their first loyalty would be to the sultan who paid their wages. In fact, their chief loyalty was to their corps. The Mamluks seized control of Egypt in 1250 and ten years later took over Palestine. They are said to have destroyed Bethlehem's city walls in 1260, but this probably refers to the fortress walls that the crusaders had built around the church. The Mamluks tended to improve, not destroy, the cities they held. It is likely that the Mamluks constructed the first walls around Bethlehem's ridge. The long, tunnel-like arch at the end of Star Street, al-Zarrara Arch, marks part of these original walls.

Bethlehem was becoming increasingly autonomous thanks to the networks provided by the extended family clans, as well as private land-ownership. The al-Farahiyeh, in particular, held extensive holdings around the monastery of St. George according to sixteenth-century tax records. As the families trace their roots back to a Ghassanid priest, perhaps their wealth was acquired as the descendants of priests inherited church property.

The next two clans to build homes in Bethlehem, the al-Tarajmeh and the al-Fawaghreh, arrived around the fourteenth century and marked a new stage in Bethlehem's evolution. The al-Tarajmeh clan, whose name means "the translators," appeared in parallel with the adventurous Venetians. These Italian newcomers settled with the permission of the Mamluks, who were always responsive to diplomatic and commercial approaches. In 1347 they allowed the Franciscans to take over and rebuild the crusader monastery, where they created the peaceful cloister that lies in the heart of the Catholic section of the Church of the Nativity. Unlike the previous crusader tenants, the Franciscan friars were not interested in confrontation; they came as emissaries, eager to win the favor of the new Muslim rulers. This was diplomatic soft power, a strategy that the Franciscans pretty much invented. But though they were careful to imitate St. Francis in poverty and humility, they retained a steely resolve to keep a Latin presence in the Holy Land. It helped that they were happy to help enrich others. They worked closely with the Venetians, who were undergoing something of a rebirth in the post-crusader world: in fact, an actual Renaissance. Together, the Franciscans and Venetians brought European pilgrims into the town, repaired the roof of the church in 1480 (with funds they raised from Edward IV of England and Mary of Burgundy), and exported souvenir goods from Bethlehem. The partnership not only led to the rise of the al-Tarajmeh as emissaries and translators, but also to an increase in the number of craftsmen making religious icons and mementoes. Bethlehem earned an international reputation for carving miniature three-dimensional scenes on oyster shells, reviving the skills that had once made the carved shells of the goddess Astarte so popular around the Mediterranean.

The al-Tarajmeh clan may have been the agents of Venetian trading firms, or of the Franciscan Friars, or a mix of both. Despite arriving in Bethlehem under the Mamluks, the individual family names do not appear in the sixteenth-century tax records which focus purely on agriculture products. The taxes of the al-Tarajmeh were paid directly by the Venetians as "capitulation"; that is, as the right to enjoy a trading monopoly. Even today, many of the al-Tarajmeh families are still associated with trade and tourism. I found a passage in a nineteenth-century Baedeker describing a hotelier named Dabdoub as a huge, welcoming figure, an image that immediately recalls the gigantic figure of Andre Dabdoub, the husband of a cousin, Carol Sansour, and one of my closest Bethlehem friends. Andre is enormously tall and heavily built. He bends over as he makes conversation, blinking warmly through his spectacles like a bear inspecting a delicacy. This is what Dabdoub means, baby bear, and it is tempting to think of a long line of bear-like Dabdoubs stretching back seven hundred years. Andre has a more self-deprecating theory, however, suggesting that Dabdoub is a play on a similar sounding Arabic word that means "two-faced." Perhaps he is right. His family rose to prominence in Bethlehem society as emissaries of Europeans, so it easy to imagine they were pulled in two directions trying to please both.

The pilgrim and trinket trade boosted the wealth of Bethlehem, but it was only a small part of the Venetian operations in Palestine. The trade added new products to the familiar list of spices and incense. The Venetians had bought the island of Crete off the crusaders, renamed it the Kingdom of Candia, and turned the island into a wine-producing factory. They also leased space in Lebanon from the Mamluks to build sugar refineries. Wherever they went, they sought out monopolies. They bought all of the available Egyptian coral, for instance, and turned it into jewelry and ornaments, which were sold back to Egypt.

Venice traded two things above all others: soap and glass. Both products use alkalines like potassium or soda, derived from materials found in quantities along Bethlehem's Dead Sea coast. The chemicals act as reacting agents, which make molten glass flow and soap produce froth. The Dead

Sea is a potassium-rich lake, while soda could be extracted from the burnt ashes of plants grown in the region's limestone soil. Liquid detergent, or soft soap, had long been a staple industrial product in Palestine's wool industry, but now the region started producing lathering soap. Nablus became a center of soap production, while smaller quantities were also manufactured in Bethlehem. It was a high quality product that competed with Marseilles and Venetian soap on the world market. However, the Mamluks afforded the Venetians an unfair advantage by selling them a monopoly in soda ash. Venice also bought the raw materials for glassmaking from Dead Sea sources and sold luxury finished goods—Murano glassware and mirrors, for instance—back to customers in Syria and Egypt.

The al-Tarajmeh brought a dash of international mystery to Bethlehem. The al-Fawaghreh, in contrast, emerged as a result of mundane improvements in local government. They were a rural family from the hills close to the Hebron Road. They were farmers, but also levied a toll charge from travellers, which might be termed a service but is rather closer to a protection racket. Their rise to prominence came with their custodianship of the Ain Faghour springs, which gave the clan its name. These became the headsprings of Bethlehem's reservoirs after 1461, when the Mamluk sultan Qaitbay renovated Jerusalem's water supply. The Sultan entrusted his chief architect Murad al-Nasrani with the job. The high-level Herodian aqueduct had long ago crumbled into disuse, and now only the lower Greek aqueduct supplied Jerusalem. Al-Nasrani re-laid the Greek pipeline and reconstructed the two lower pools to make the single giant pool we see today. The al-Fawaghreh were hired to safeguard the pipeline and keep the water flowing to Jerusalem.

Al-Nasrani's masterpiece is said to be the Fountain of Qayt Bay, which brings Bethlehem's spring water directly to the al-Aqsa Mosque in Jerusalem. The architect of a Muslim monument, Murad al-Nasrani was actually a Christian; his name means Nazarene. The small Murad fortress overlooking the reservoirs seems to have been named after him, though it dates to the early sixteenth century, after the Ottoman Turks had taken over Palestine. Al-Nasrani may have started the project, or perhaps it was named after him in tribute. The twilight years of the Mamluks rule were recorded by the contemporary writer Mujir al-Din, a judge in Jerusalem who writes with endless fascination about a land he alternately calls

"Filastin" and the "Holy Land," an indication of how Palestinians saw their homeland.


THE OTTOMANS SEIZED PALESTINE in 1517, replacing the Circassian and Chechen Mamluks with their own forces: the Circassian and Chechen Janissaries. In practice, it was no great change at all. The Ottomans formally made the al-Fawaghreh family responsible for Jerusalem's water supply, and the family—the only Muslims among Bethlehem's Christian families—rose to prominence in Bethlehem society, building their own quarter inside the town.

The Ottomans allowed other European nations a slice of the Palestinian trade. Elizabethan England was particularly energetic, lobbying at the Ottoman court, the *Sublime Porte*, for the right to bid against the Venetians. The English were early allies of the Ottomans, who they regarded as a friendly bulwark against the rising Catholic Hapsburg Empire. Queen Elizabeth established a new joint stock company named the Levant Company to underwrite business in the Ottoman eastern Mediterranean. The Levant Company brought its own innovations, in particular a new, faster cargo ship: the Dutch *fluyt* (Mediterranean shipping had seen little real innovation to its galleys since the days of Greece and Rome). The English came bearing new hi-tech fabrics, worsted wool and a material called kersey, which resembles sweatshirt material, smooth on one side and cozy on the other. English woolen merchants made unimaginable fortunes.

The English traded their wool for everything from chemicals to camel hair, but they could not get enough of wine and raisins. This was the age when alcohol-soused puddings, stuffed with raisins, were becoming ever-more affordable. One of the Dutch fluyts of the Levant Company was the *Mayflower*, and though there were twenty-five *Mayflower*s sailing out of England around this time, judging by its weight, crew numbers, and age, this is the *Mayflower* that later transported the Pilgrim Fathers to the New World at the end of its grape-running life. Of course, until the American Revolution, the Levant Company handled all of America's exotic-goods needs.

The great European grape rush, and the English love of wine and pudding, reshaped the Bethlehem landscape. The hills around al-Makhrour,

Battir, and Wadi Fuqin, all to the west of Bethlehem, are truly startling, filled with valleys carved into ziggurats that rival any Chinese tea plantation. The landscape can be tied to Bethlehem's Christian character. Grapes have many uses, of course. They can be dried to make raisins; carpets of grapes are left to dry on sheets between the vines at harvest time in al-Khader. Bethlehem's grapes are also used for molasses, a kitchen staple known as *dibis*. (Outside of Palestine, dibis is made from pomegranates or dates.) But above all, grapes are great for alcohol. What remains of Bethlehem's wine industry is now in the hands of the monks of the Cremisan Monastery, but there is a long domestic tradition of wine production. Bethlehemites my age can remember trampling grapes in the tub as children to make farm wine. The association between grapes and wine led to a taboo against vineyards in Muslim towns, and as a consequence Bethlehem became a center for large-scale grape farming. When European demand for raisins and wine continued to grow, there were no barriers to families like the al-Farahiyeh clan turning every available square of the surrounding hills over to grapevines. Unlike the olive terraces that date back to antiquity, these terraces are relatively remote from the urban population centers, and are dotted with circular stone watchtowers along the crests of the hills to guard the crops.

Life under the Ottomans continued much as it had under the Mamluks, as Circassian, Chechen, and later Albanian and Bosnian soldiers continued to secure the borders and enforced the laws. But for Christians, Ottoman rule meant far less say over their religious life. The Ottomans stripped the local priests and bishops of their power, favoring Constantinople's Greek-speaking clerics, which led to Arab-speaking Christians once more being pushed out of the cathedrals and parish churches. This was partly greed. The Ottomans were happy to sell honors, and there were periods where the Bishop of Jerusalem changed every year. But it was also in part because the Ottomans saw their 1517 conquest of Palestine as a restitution of the Roman Oriens, painting themselves as the successors of Imperial Rome. They centralized power in Constantinople, but this was certainly not a return to the old Roman days in any meaningful sense. The Greek Orthodox Church had changed dramatically over the past thousand years, and the Greek clerics brought in customs and liturgy that bore little relation to the church nine hundred years earlier.

Over time, Bethlehem's Christians adapted, and local clerics began to rise through the Greek-dominated Palestinian church, recognized as Arab Orthodox clerics. However, there was a ceiling on their progress, as there still is today, with a Greek-speaking hierarchy running the Orthodox churches of Palestine and—crucially—operating the church's rich property portfolio. The Greek Orthodox Church has its own priorities, focused on church politics as well as power struggles in Greece. Palestine is merely a source of wealth, through property deals and rent, and of prestige. The rights of Palestinians come far down the Greeks' agenda. The church is mired in property scandals and condemned for its failure to promote Palestinian clerics, and is often seen as an accomplice of the hostile occupation.

The situation for the Melkite Church under the Ottomans was even worse, at least at first. The crusaders had placed all the Oriental churches—the Maronite, Syriac, and, in Palestine, the Melkite communities—under the authority of their Armenian allies. The Ottomans continued this arrangement, which pushed the Melkite Church one rung down the pecking order, reliant on Armenian clerics who owed them no particular allegiance. Over the course of the seventeenth and eighteenth centuries, this injustice led the Melkites and other Oriental churches to look toward Rome, and in 1729 the Melkite joined the Latin communion as a self-governing Uniate church. It is now officially known as the Melkite Greek Catholic Church, an odd name for a church that is stateless, so has no King or *Melek* to obey; has Arabic liturgy not Greek; and is Uniate or self-governing so is free to adopt positions that the Catholic world would not recognize.

The idea that the local churches should turn to the West for protection was all the more daring because the Ottomans began to see the Western Latin Church as the tool of the Habsburg Holy Roman Emperors, their closest enemy. In the seventeenth century, the counter-reformation unleashed a new energy among Latin clerics. The Franciscan community in Bethlehem grew, swelled by evangelical friars who hoped to make converts. From the seventeenth century, the Vatican allowed local Latin Christians to use Arabic liturgy, which helped attract disaffected Orthodox Christians. The Ottomans responded by restricting clerics entering the country and regulating pilgrimage as jealously as they regulated trade. It was a situation that engendered paranoia. Bethlehem was an outward-looking city with strong international connections and ties to the Latin Church, while the Ottoman Empire was only growing more inward-looking and centralizing.

IN THE EARLY 1980S, Anton Sansour built a villa close to Bab al-Zqaq, the border between Beit Jala and Bethlehem. This has always been my home in Bethlehem, but I had never experienced life in the heart of the old town, in one of the traditional Palestinian stone houses. After meeting Boulos, my tour guide to Herodion, I rented a room from him, moving into the house he shares with Ieva, and Trevina, his daughter with the broken arm. The bedroom at the back of their home is a cave-like cube with a slightly domed roof. Imagine a stone igloo, with the roof formed from two transverse arches that intersect at the apex. Traditionally, the inside of the arches is plastered, but Bethlehem has recently gotten the bug for raw brick; so as I lay in my bed, I found I was staring at a ceiling of several tons of stones of all different shapes and sizes. I spent quite some time wondering why they did not come crashing down on my head.

The whole of Bethlehem's old city is constructed from these boxy units, known as *hoshes*. There is something childlike about a town of identical square units, as though it is made out of shoeboxes. The units are so flexible that they can be used to make a single hole-in-the-wall shop in the market, or they can become the basis of a rambling mansion arranged across multiple floors around a hidden courtyard garden. The hosh gets around the single great construction problem in Palestine: the lack of trees. It is a unique style, characteristic of the high country in Palestine and especially Bethlehem, where stone is as plentiful as wood is non-existent.

As Bethlehem grew throughout the eighteenth century, the old town organized itself around the clan-based *harats*. By the end of the eighteenth century, there were seven (with an eighth formed in the twentieth century by the influx of Syriac refugees fleeing the Turkish massacres). The Ghassanid-era al-Najajreh and al-Farahiyeh clans, and the Muslim al-Fawaghreh, all built their quarters on the top of the ridge, while the al-Tarajmeh sit off to the side around the base of Star Street. These four clans were joined by the al-Kwawseh and al-Anatreh, Christian families from the desert borders of Tuqu' who found room above Wadi Ma'ali and the southern side of Milk Grotto Street. The final clan, al-Hreizat, has its home village just north of Bethlehem, below the monastery Mar Elias.

Boulos's family is from the al-Hreizat, but though their harat lies high on the ridge, he and Ieva live on Wadi Ma'ali Street, a few yards from Al Ain, the fountain. These days, families are no longer strongly identified with their historical quarters. The al-Anatreh quarter has been home to families from almost all of the clans at one time or another. A friend, Darine Flefel, who moved into a house on Milk Grotto Street as a young child tells the sweetest romance I know. The house had belonged to a family named Hazboun, and Darine saw a series of pencil lines on a doorway marking the growth of two boys, alongside their names. She stared at the lines every day and began to invent stories about Johnny, the boy who started off her size and grew tall. As time passed, she decided she was in love with him. When they finally met, he fell in love with her. They are now married.

Boulos's home becomes my base for a week as I roam the quarters, working out how they fit together. Few Christian families still live inside the densest parts of the souk. Where they can afford to, they have moved to more modern homes, and the hoshes have been let to villagers who have moved from remote farmlands. The Ottoman-era laws of inheritance still apply in Bethlehem, which requires that assets be scrupulously divided among all the heirs. The result is that the ownership of some of the older houses has become murky. Quite a few are simply squatted; others are abandoned. Only a handful of the most splendid have been restored. There is a constant struggle to try and make them economically viable as hotels or shops. For instance, one of the hoshes on Star Street is now a school for icon painters and is run by an English artist. Another is a boutique hotel and restaurant. On the day I dine there, the chef is cooking an ambitious dinner for the daughter of the Italian President, who has joined her father on a tour of the restoration of the church.

ITINERANT PUPPET SHOWS telling tales of past heroism often provided entertainment in the seventeenth and eighteenth centuries. These shows took place under lamps in the nighttime marketplaces of Manger Square, where the puppets would enact stories recounted in sinuously rhyming couplets. One of the most popular was the epic poem of the Banu Hilal and their chivalrous leader, Abu Zeid. The poem is based on what might be the worst political decision in world history, when the Fatimids invited an Arabian tribe to attack their own Berber allies. It not only weakened the Fatimid hold on North Africa, but also led directly to the loss of Sicily to the Normans. Reworked in poetry, however, a tale of woeful incompetence became a stirring tale of romance and fellowship. This and other epic poems were the mass entertainments of their day. They also had a political function, as they helped foster the idea that speakers of Arabic might share a political identity, just as Greek speakers in Ottoman lands were beginning to wonder if sharing a Greek tongue might also constitute a new kind of national identity.

The idea of a shared Arab culture helped foster cooperation across class and social divides, which had a more decisive impact on Bethlehem than abstract notions of pan-Arabism. Bethlehem grew up around three distinct groups: townsfolk, peasants, and Bedouin. This has always led to divisions within society, which the emergence of political parties in the eighteenth century helped to bridge. The two parties, the Yamani and the Qais, take their names from a semi-mythical feud between tribes of the Arabian Peninsula but are "fictive" political identities: they have no more connection to the real Qais and Yamani than the Whigs and Tories of eighteenth-century England have to Scottish cattle-drivers and Irish outlaws. The Qais and Yamani also resemble the Whigs and Tories in that the Yamanis emphasized localism, autonomy, and breaks from tradition, making it a kind of "people's party," while the Qais erred toward the side of authority and ancestral wisdom. Bethlehem was solidly Yamani, reflecting a multi-faith city with no single sense of authority or tradition, whose wealth depended on the many international connections that the Ottomans were trying to limit. This was an age of emerging political nationalism in Palestine. When a revolution broke out in 1834, Bethlehem's al-Fawaghreh families were at its heart.

BETWEEN 1798 AND 1801, Napoleon set up camp in Egypt. He was only passing through, stranded under a British blockade. In Alexandria, he enjoyed the admiration of some Egyptian intellectuals, just as he did among contemporary Europeans. To many, Napoleon appeared the height of modernity, and certainly he championed distinctly modern ideas, such as an aggressive secularism that questioned religious authority. But Napoleon combined these ideas with a very old concept: the military strongman. You could argue that he represented a kind of futuristic militarism. He was a technocrat and a soldier, who had risen from a modest Corsican background to the summit of the French army. He certainly led a better-equipped army. His trousers caused particular excitement. The French wore tight trousers, rather than the loose balloons of the Mamluks and Janissaries, though Napoleon said he would have happily dressed his troops in baggy trousers to escape Palestine and march on Constantinople.

Napoleon's attempt to break out through Palestine ended in failure and a peevish scorched earth policy as he retreated to Egypt. He finally slipped back to France leaving much of his army behind. The Ottomans had been embarrassed by Napoleon's antics and, once he was gone, sought to strengthen Egypt. A force of Janissaries were sent to Cairo, led by an Albanian named Muhammad Ali who hired some of Napoleon's ex-commanders. He cleared out the existing ruling caste, the aristocratic Mamluks, by the simple strategy of inviting them for a meal and then butchering them. Though notionally a slave, Ali had never lost touch with his Greek-Albanian Christian family. His officers included close relatives such as his nephews Ibrahim and Tusun, who were also either his real or his adopted sons. (The Janissaries are not supposed to have had families, so historians are unable to be clear on the connection.) Once in Egypt, Ali showed his modernizing credentials by dressing his soldiers in tight trousers. He ruled Egypt as his own kingdom, backed by European powers who were allowed access to Egyptian markets and flattered with gifts: Ali gave Louis-Philippe of France the Luxor Obelisk, or Cleopatra's Needle, in 1826. The Ottomans suffered the rise of Ali and his family. It was not until 1831 that Ali directly confronted the Ottomans, invading Palestine and occupying Jerusalem.

The Yamani factions in Palestine initially welcomed the Egyptians. A soap magnate from Nablus, Qasim al-Ahmad, sent men to bolster Egyptian forces fighting in Damascus. The Yamani support flowed from an opposition to Ottoman taxes, and to Ottoman control of the borders: Yamani entrepreneurs wanted free trade, while Yamani city dwellers wanted lower taxes. Bethlehem's support for the Egyptians paid off as wealthy Europeans began to arrive in Bethlehem via Alexandria. Palestine was suddenly accessible without the entanglements of Ottoman bureaucracy. In a more general sense, too, Palestine was suddenly a European issue, part of the so-called "Middle Eastern question," though some Europeans had the oddest answers to this question, such as the London Society for Promoting Christianity Among the Jews. The Europeans also came to measure and detail the land, using new techniques and equipment. In 1833, the English draughtsman Frederick Catherwood accurately measured and surveyed the Dome of the Rock using a world-inverting camera lucida.

The sudden opening of Palestine coincided with the rise of mass circulation magazines, filled with new lithographic pictures, quickly followed by the invention of photography. Bethlehem was no longer a fairy tale, depicted inaccurately in paintings of Nativity scenes. It was real, drawn by draughtsmen and architects, and soon photographed and sold as postcards or as 3-D stereoscopic pictures. The Europeans came in large numbers and spent money, and their stories stimulated new travellers to follow them.

Within two years, however, support for the Egyptians had soured. The fellahin had been roused because the Egyptians began to conscript the peasants for their continuing war against the Ottomans. By Easter 1834, the countryside was in open revolt. Once again, the Yamani were at the forefront, and for the much the same reasons that they had supported Egypt in the first place: it was all about autonomy and taxation.

Details of the war preparations come from a Greek priest named Neophytus who was present at a meeting in Jerusalem when the city's notables—the local aristocrats—discussed the rebellion. Ali's son, Ibrahim, the governor of Palestine, had left the city, and though his reasons for leaving were obscure, it was likely that he was bringing back fresh troops. Now was the time to seize Jerusalem. The notables held back, though they discussed the tight trousers of Ibrahim's troops with disapproval.

Sheikh Shokeh, the clan leader of Bethlehem's al-Fawaghreh, seized Jerusalem. His force included both Fellahin and Ta'amareh Bedouin, crossing the traditional divisions of Palestine. Indeed, the wider Yamani coalition included a clan called the Abu Gosh, Chechen Janissaries who had gone native and settled on the road between Jerusalem and Jaffa, where they levied tolls on passing trade. Shokeh's rebel forces laid siege to the city but, as Neophytus reports, the notables were still reluctant to commit their support.

Neophytus's report is augmented by a much-later account—claimed to come "from native sources"—by an Irish archaeologist, R. A. Stewart Macalister. Written in 1900, Macalister adopts a jokey tone, claiming that Shokeh's forces entered the city through the drain that carried Jerusalem's sewage into Silwan below; and when Shokeh was shot in the feet while looting a thirty-pound sack of coffee, he ordered his men to carry him while he continued to hold on to the coffee. Macalister later gained a name back home in Ireland retelling Celtic fairy stories.

The contemporary Neophytus provides a more sober version of the war. The first day of the siege coincided with an earthquake that delayed reinforcement from Nablus. Shokeh was able to enter the city when locals opened the Dung Gate in Jerusalem's wall. As his forces swept in, the notables, who had previously stated they owned no weapons, appeared heavily armed and joined the Bethlehem fighters. Whereas Macalister claims Shokeh was interested only in looting the city, Neophytus does not mention looting at all; indeed, the owners of the stores joined in the fighting. The battle for Jerusalem was soon reinforced by troops arriving from Nablus, and the city was taken.

The rebels remained in power across Palestine until midsummer, when the peasants returned home to the harvests. Egyptian forces led by Muhammad Ali mounted a counterattack and recaptured Jerusalem. Neophytus reports the notables claimed a few young hotheads had joined Shokeh, but the majority had only taken up arms to protect their property.

The Christians of Bethlehem had tried to remain neutral, unlike forces from Beit Jala that had joined the attack on Jerusalem. The three old towns that make up the core of the Bethlehem conurbation have quite distinct personalities. Bethlehem is a free-trade town, all about tourism and global ties. Beit Sahour is more socialist; it is all about NGOs and social activism, which makes the organic cafes of the old town a lively hotspot of argument, dancing, and romance. The focus in Beit Jala is on local industry and its customers, who live close by in both Palestine and

Israel. This makes its concerns more parochial and its people hardheaded and skeptical. It is capable of extraordinary bravery and belligerence. The town was on the frontline in the 1948 war, and Beit Jalans mobilized to defend their homes from Israeli forces. But it comes with an innate conservatism, and this made Beit Jala a Qais stronghold. In the nineteenth century, the crossroads by the Sansours' home at Bab al-Zqaq saw scenes of Qais-Yamani fighting between Beit Jala and Bethlehem. When the Latin minority in Beit Jala wanted to build their own church in the mid-nineteenth century, the Orthodox majority tried to prevent it and it took years of negotiations before a Catholic church was allowed to stand opposite the two older Orthodox churches. A photograph taken to celebrate repairs to the church in the early twentieth century shows Anton Sansour's father on the rooftop with another fifty men, their work completed. The photograph is a clue to Beit Jala's prime industry. This was a city formed by stonemasons. Though there are twelfth-century accounts of visits to Beit Jala, these reports refer to the church of St. George and al-Khader. The current town is relatively new, emerging in Ottoman times around an existing sixth-century chapel to St. Nicholas. The remains of this primitive building can be seen in the crypt below the present gleaming-white church. Many of Beit Jala's families arrived from Christian towns across the Jordan, attracted by the proximity of Bethlehem and the lure of work building the beautiful Ottoman-era city of Jerusalem found within Eudocia's walls today.

Beit Jala may have joined an alliance with Yamani forces against the Egyptians out of loyalty to the Ottomans, their chief clients and paymasters. However, the 1830s marked a change of political direction in the entire country: another Qais stronghold, Hebron, also joined the rebellion. By this time, the war was already lost. Egyptian forces had regained control of Jerusalem, and punished the rebels with a massacre in Beit Jala. The Ta'amareh Bedouin responded by rushing to defend the al-Fawaghreh harat in Bethlehem, while the Christian clans took sanctuary in the Church of the Nativity. The Egyptians defeated the Ta'amareh and al-Fawaghreh and razed the al-Fawaghreh homes.

The leader of the Nablus forces, the soap manufacturer Qasim al-Ahmad, was pursued to Hebron, where the Egyptian victory was accompanied by massacres and rapes. Children were kidnapped and handed as rewards to the Egyptian soldiers. Hebron had a small Jewish population that had remained neutral through the rebellion and believed they had assurances from the Egyptians that they would not be harmed. They were betrayed, massacred in the streets with the other Hebronites.

The failed rebellion strengthened Palestinians' self-identity. When the Ottomans regained control of Palestine eight years later, in 1841, they immediately began to address the complaints that had tempted the Yamanis into revolt. From the middle of the nineteenth century, the Ottomans delivered a series of reforms that offered Palestinians political representation in Constantinople, increased autonomy at home, and also opened the country to foreign trade. These reforms greatly improved life in Bethlehem, yet proved double-edged. European governments competed to stamp their own identity on the Holy Land, chief among them the British, who would eventually gain control of the entire country.

# CHAPTER 8

# THE BRITISH

## *The Victorian Age to the Second World War*

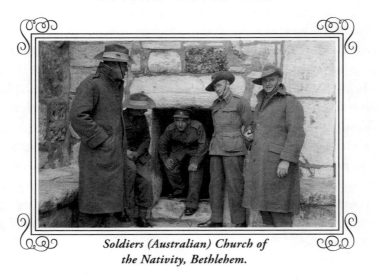

*Soldiers (Australian) Church of the Nativity, Bethlehem.*

The old city of Bethlehem is at its best first thing in the morning. The schoolgirls hurry to the convent schools in their smocks and backpacks. The shopkeepers fold back the heavy turquoise metal shutters that cover their storefronts. The market traders struggle to push barrows laden with ripe tomatoes and earthy potatoes up the hill to the souk. The monks and nuns appear shortly after morning prayers, padding around the marble streets in socks and Jesus sandals. Breakfast is sold on the street. A brightly painted blue cart sells simit rings, the sweetened bread circles dusted with sesame seeds. A coffee seller in Ottoman dress and a large, brass pot tied to his back sells single shots of cardamom-flavored coffee, performing a quick bow to fill a cup from the spout above his shoulder. One of Bethlehem's most unusual institutions is a communal oven that stands at the edge of the souk, among the hardware stores of the poorer side of town. The heat hits you at the doorway, which opens onto a flight of steps leading to basement level. The oven has a cast-iron door set into a brickwork face, and the oven is fed with stacks of olive wood. The bulk of the oven is dug straight into the side of the hill, and the oven master uses a long paddle to push in the stewpots or to hook them out. Neighborhood women place orders for evening stews and return the iron pots from the night before. They also bring their own prepared dishes to be cooked alongside the day's menu. A communal oven not only makes life easier, but also spares you using your own oven in the heat of summer.

Stews of one kind or another are the staples of Palestinian home cooking, soaked up with maftoul, flat bread, or rice that is toasted lightly in the pan before being boiled. Palestinian stews tend to be heavy on vegetables and sparing on meat, though I once had a dark rich stew of the songbirds that pass over Palestine on migration. Leila remembered a story about her father's prowess with a catapult as a boy, when he would hunt these birds. Anton died of a heart attack the year after we married, a loss that was so unexpected it seemed to pull the world off its hinges. Somehow, we got the idea that we might commemorate him by eating a dish from his childhood, though we had no idea how to catch the birds, let alone cook them. In the end, I think, it was Mustafa—the taxi driver—who volunteered to sort it out. The birds were slow-cooked in a cast-iron pot from the communal oven and eaten whole as part of a gluey-rich stew. They had a dark, liver-ish quality but what made them so strange was the crunch as the hollow bones splintered into shards in my mouth. I now know that the birds are endangered migrants, eaten in secrecy by the late president Francois Mitterrand, who knew full well that they were protected in France, and the object of campaigns by wildlife activists like the novelist Jonathan Franzen. I will never eat them again, but I do not need to: once is unforgettable. The experience will always be associated with an act of mourning.

IN 1837, AN IRISH DOCTOR named William Wilde visited Bethlehem and noted how much the grotto beneath the Church of the Nativity resembled one of Bethlehem's communal ovens. A curving staircase enters the cave below the church. The curve means the cave remains hidden almost until your feet touch its floor. At basement level, you find a kind of low cubbyhole cut into the side of the cave, lined with marble and hung with golden incense burners. A silver plate in the shape of a star marks the spot where Mary gave birth to Christ inside this nook, which does indeed look like the mouth of an oven. It may simply be coincidence, in the way that the mouth of a platypus resembles a duck's beak, but Wilde took the resemblance seriously. He saw it as evidence that the grotto could not be the site of the original caravanserai in Bethlehem but it is as easy to argue the opposite. Travellers have to eat, and inns serve food.

Oil lamps hanging from chains light the cave, and their smoke has blackened the tapestries and paintings that hide the raw stone walls. The walls are black, too, from a fire that broke out in the grotto in 1869, destroying the attractive paintings that Wilde saw and described. (The Franciscan website says the walls are covered with asbestos, a gift from France, but I saw no evidence: I believe the asbestos has been removed.) The cave actually has two staircases, either side of the nook, which curve away in opposite directions like mirror images. At the busiest times of day, one flight becomes the entrance to the grotto and the other the exit as pilgrims queue above. The cave is lozenge shaped. In diagram it resembles a uterus, and the two staircases look rather like the fallopian tubes. I am certain that this resemblance really is coincidental but having once made this association I cannot un-think it. Maybe it's a subliminal reminder that Bethlehem was built by women.

Wilde was the father of Oscar Wilde. When he visited Bethlehem, he was travelling as the personal physician of an elderly invalid who owned a private yacht. His account of his journey, *Narrative of a Voyage*, was first published in 1840 but revised in 1844 after the British helped the Ottomans recapture the country from the Egyptians. The second edition carries the subtitle: *Observations on the present state of Egypt and Palestine and their prospects*, a sign that the Middle East Question had begun to impinge on the British public conscience. The Holy Land had been a remote place for so long that it was a world that few people knew. Just a decade earlier, anyone visiting Bethlehem without Ottoman papers had to sneak across the border in disguise, as another Irish doctor, Richard Robert Madden, did in the 1820s.

Wilde's observations on the state and prospects of the country turn out to be quite random. He notes that the Muslim clan al-Fawaghreh have recently been expelled from Bethlehem, but when the Egyptian authorities tell him it was because they feuded with the Christians, Wilde accepts it without learning anything of the recent rebellion or the massacres in Beit Jala and Hebron. Wilde is only in his twenties and devotes far more pages to the young women at the fountain on Wadi Ma'ali Street than to religion or politics. Their beauty entrances him, and soon he heads into a lengthy digression, recommending that all women carry water jars on their heads to improve posture, strength, and gracefulness. The notes are so sexualized that one wonders if Wilde is even aware of it. By the time he married Oscar's mother, he had three children by two different women. His family seem to have packed him off on his Mediterranean voyage so that he would avoid the birth of his first son, Oscar's illegitimate half-brother.

LUNCH IS OFTEN FALAFEL; my favorite choice is always Efteem in Manger Square. It has photographs of passing celebrities on the wall, if international politicians such as ex-Prime Minister David Cameron are your idea of celebrities. I also like a modest place tucked behind Beit Jala souk. For years, the only photographs on its walls were a fading picture of Yasser Arafat shaking hands with Saddam Hussein and a calendar of Orthodox saints. I don't know whom the owner hoped to appeal to with that particular mix, though his sandwiches are so good that he could have put a picture of an Israeli politician on the wall and people would still stop by for lunch. As he opens out the pouch of the pita bread, he runs a hand over the salads: "What do you want? Everything?" I always want everything: salad, hot sauce, tahini, pickles. Food historians seem to agree that dishes of pulses and chickpeas, like foule and falafel, probably came from Egypt in the long distant past.

The Ottoman influence on Bethlehem lives on in grills, the food of nomadic horsemen. *Shawarma* is Arabic for doner kebab, which like the Greek *gyros* refers to the circular turning of the meat. The days when I don't feel like falafel, I might go to Shawarma King on New Road, or the place halfway up the hill in Beit Jala, next to the fish shop. The choice is either chicken or meat, which means lamb, though these days, beef is often substituted. Beef is factory farmed in big sheds in the nearby Migdal Oz settlement, while lamb has become prohibitively expensive because the settlements have driven the shepherds off the grazing land. Butchers in Bethlehem only ever specialize in one kind of meat, so in Beit Jala's tiny souk, the chicken butcher, the beef butcher, the lamb butcher, and (because it is a Christian town) the pork butcher sit facing each at the four points of a crossroad.

The Ottomans recaptured Palestine from the Egyptians in 1841, with dubious help from the Royal Navy. British gunships bombarded Acre on November 3, and the exploding shells hit an ammunitions dump, taking half the city with it as it blew sky high. The British acted in the hope that a stable Ottoman Empire could act as a buffer against Russia at a time when tensions were growing over Afghanistan. The intervention backfired, and war came anyway thanks to an incident in Bethlehem, as France and Russia competed to be appointed the custodians of the Church of the Nativity. The French had close ties to Bethlehem's Franciscans, while the Russians were trying to stake a claim to the Orthodox chapel above the grotto. There was no way of pleasing both parties.

In 1847, the original star marking the site of Christ's birth was jimmied off the floor and disappeared. The Latin script on the silver plate was seen as a territorial mark by the Catholics. No one doubted that the thieves were Orthodox monks. France and Russia escalated their campaigns for ownership of the cave, and this time both sides brought out their gunboats. The French sent a naval force to the Dardanelles, south of Constantinople: the Russians menaced the city from the north in the Black Sea. As tensions escalated, the French and British became convinced that the Russians would invade Constantinople and remove the Sultan. An ultimatum to Russia in February 1854 went unanswered. The next month, Britain and France declared war. The Crimean War had started, thanks to a silver star in Bethlehem.

The Ottoman Empire was characterized as the "sick man of Europe" in the run-up to the Crimean War, serving as part of the *casus belli* that allowed Britain to declare war on Russia. The tag stuck, but was never accurate. It was not essentially infirm, and neither was it more immoral or decadent than western nations. The empire was in a constant process of modernization from the mid-nineteenth century. The *Tanzimat-I Hayriye* (Auspicious Reordering) began in 1839 with the abolition of tax farming. The government also guaranteed Ottoman subjects security of life and property and accepted the principle of equality before the law. This was positively enlightened by contrast with Britain's attitude toward the non-British subjects of its empire, or with America's reliance on the industrial slavery of Africans. By 1908, the Ottomans recognized the need for representative government, which saw Palestinians taking seats in the Ottoman parliament in Constantinople.

The Ottoman Empire's embrace of free trade had an enormous impact on Bethlehem's icon and souvenir business, run by families like the Dabdoubs, the Giacamettis, the Jacirs, the Hazbouns, the Handals, the Mikels, the Zoughbis, the Kattans, and even the Muslim Shokehs. (The Shokehs rebuilt their quarter in Bethlehem after the defeat of the Egyptians. The great-great-great grandson of the rebel leader, Khalil Shokeh, is a teacher at Bethlehem University and a notable historian.) These families established trading empires that stretched from the Philippines and Australia to the Ukraine and Russia, and from France to the United States and Latin America, with the families exhibiting at international trade shows; Bethlehemites are listed as exhibitors in Philadelphia (1876), Chicago (1893), and St. Louis (1903). Bethlehem families followed pilgrims back to their homes; the Kattans, for instance, built outposts in Kiev. They also scoured the world looking for raw materials, opening offices in the Philippines after discovering a new species of oyster with thicker shells that allowed for more detail in the carvings.

The global connections led to a Bethlehem diaspora, as families sent emissaries to their overseas offices. Toward the end of the nineteenth century, the Ottomans began to conscript Palestinians to help put down national rebellions in the Balkans. Bethlehem's families countered by keeping their sons abroad to avoid the draft. Even so, the emigrants would often return, and Bethlehemites became used to moving backward and forward. This remains the case today, as military occupation limits work opportunities and freedom of movement, as well as the freedom to marry: Israeli Palestinians who marry Palestinians from the occupied territories lose their right to live in Israel. In a single generation of Sansours, there are cousins living in Dubai, North Carolina, London, Jordan, San Diego, and Denmark, while retaining homes and property in Bethlehem.

The Bethlehem diaspora is more than a century old and has had a particularly great impact in Latin America. Bethlehemites and Beit Jalans founded the great Chilean Premier League football team, Palestino, in the 1920s. The 2004 El Salvadorian presidential election was contested by opposing candidates from the al-Najajreh clan: the left-wing Shafik Handal, and the winner, Antonio Saca, a Christian evangelical running on a Conservative platform. The al-Tarajmeh includes one family, the Comandari, who were involved in the darker side of Latin American life: a branch of the family were major cocaine narcos in the 1980s.

If the Ottoman reforms opened up the world for Palestinians, it also opened Palestine to the world. The scramble continued, even after it provoked the Crimean War. British influence was initially restricted to individuals and charities. As early as 1841, the English philanthropist Moses Montefiore obtained a leasehold on Rachel's Tomb. The shrine had been an object of Christian pilgrimage since at least the fourth century, as St. Jerome mentions in a letter to Rome. In Montefiore's day, the shrine was part of a Muslim cemetery, on a stretch of the Hebron Road that was already growing into a place of souvenir sellers and restaurants. The shrine was an open-sided pavilion with a domed roof, in some disrepair. Montefiore filled in the sides to create a structure that more closely resembles a sepulchre. (When Montefiore died at one hundred years of age, he was buried in a replica tomb at his home in England.) When I first visited Bethlehem in 1994, the shrine was still an attractive, two-roomed, single-story building, shaded by trees and facing a row of restaurants. The tomb stood within the tree-lined cemetery, and beyond it lay the Aida refugee camp. Today, it is surrounded by a high, concrete wall and can only be seen from the top floor of some of the nearby hotels (including the one that English artist Banksy opened in early 2017). All that can be glimpsed is the curve of its domed roof. The Israeli-built wall is designed to carve the tomb out of Bethlehem. It slithers down Hebron Road, looping around the building like an amoeba stretching a tendril to absorb an alien organism. I first visited the tomb twenty years ago, when it attracted Israeli and foreign tourists, as well as local Christian and Muslim women who prayed to Rachel to intercede in family problems. I have only returned once since the tomb was stolen, and found a very different place, bustling with Yiddish-speaking Hasidim who arrive on coaches and divide the shrine into male and female sections.

The British were determined and strenuous meddlers in Palestine, which is perhaps why they ended up exerting the strongest influence. The future British Prime Minister Benjamin Disraeli visited Palestine hot on the heels of the Egyptians. As Palestine became a national obsession in Britain, Disraeli followed Wilde in writing about his experiences in the novel *Tancred* (1847). Disraeli was a Sephardic Jew whose father had fallen out with his local synagogue and taken his whole family over to Christianity. Disraeli's novel takes up the theme of Jewish-Christian reconciliation: "I commend my soul to Jesus Christ, and to the God of Sinai, in whose cause I perish." So says this Victorian-era Tancred, just before he shoots a hostile Bedouin between the eyes.

Disraeli's novel joined an astonishing wealth of magazine articles, lithographs, photographs, and books on Palestine that flooded Britain and America through the Victorian Age. The interest was never greater than at Christmas, when Bethlehem was the focus. The month that British gunships helped liberate Palestine, the diminutive twenty-one-year-old Queen Victoria gave birth to her first child. That Christmas, she and Prince Albert celebrated as a family—a mother, father, and child—like the original Holy Family. In 1848, the Royal Family was depicted gathered around their tree in a lithograph in the *Illustrated London News*, with three of their children. As England was reshaped by the royal couple, Christmas became the great British holiday, with all the trappings we know today: the pudding, the tree that Albert introduced from his native Germany, and carved-wood Nativity scenes that were often manufactured in Bethlehem. Christmas became a celebration of domesticity, and even had its own poet laureate in Charles Dickens, who wrote a Christmas story each year from 1843 as a gift to the nation. Dickens made Christmas into the great moral litmus test of the day: a good man was a man who knew how to keep Christmas.

Victoria and Albert's Anglo-German union was the inspiration for a joint project between the Anglican Church and the German Lutherans: a new bishop in Jerusalem. The idea was far from universally popular, and even required an act of parliament. John Henry Newman converted to Catholicism in protest. Nevertheless, in January 1842, the first Anglo-German Bishop arrived in Jerusalem. He was Michael Alexander Wolff, a German-born Jew and ex-rabbi who had converted to Anglicanism as a twenty-six-year-old living in Dublin. Bishop Michael Alexander, as he was known, worked closely with the London Society for Promoting Christianity Among the Jews (known as The Jews' Society). The society had already opened an infirmary in Jerusalem under Egyptian rule in 1836, and this was expanded into a twenty-four-bed hospital. The society's most ambitious project, however, was underwriting a scheme by two young Jewish converts to Christianity, the couple John and Mary Meshullam. The Meshullams hoped to open a farm in Bethlehem, making them, in effect, Palestine's first Jewish settlers.

The Meshullams were converted by a Swiss cleric named Samuel Gobat, who in 1846 succeeded Michael Alexander as the second Bishop of Jerusalem. The Meshullams ran a small hotel in Jerusalem, the first European-owned in the city. One day, John Meshullam was taking a horse ride through Bethlehem when he came upon Artas. The village was deserted, and Meshullam was mystified that anyone should abandon such a beautiful spot. He was even more bewildered when he discovered the entire displaced village living inside the cramped Murad Fortress above Solomon's Pools. The Artas villagers had been living as refugees in the fortress for four years and were poverty-stricken and desperate. Meshullam learned there was a blood feud with the Ta'amareh Bedouin, who were demanding a large payment in settlement. The roots of the dispute lay in the war with Egypt a decade earlier. After the Egyptians drove the Ta'amareh and al-Fawaghreh out of Bethlehem, the Artas villagers were hired to replace the al-Fawaghreh as protectors of the Jerusalem aqueduct. With the defeat of the Egyptians, the villagers found themselves branded as traitors. They were in a desperate situation.

Meshullam decided to raise the money to pay the Ta'amareh and lease the farmland himself. He hatched a plan in collaboration with another two members of the Jews' Society, James Finn, British Consul in Jerusalem since 1846, and his wife Elizabeth, who raised the money for the project. The Ta'amareh were bought off, the Artas's land was leased for a new farming settlement, and the villagers of Artas rehired as laborers. The Meshullams were joined in their settlement by other members of the Jews' Society, including John Steinbeck's grandfather and a German family called the Baldenspergers, who continued to live in Artas until well into the twentieth century.

John Meshullam's story took a dark turn after Finn employed his son Peter at the British consulate. Peter was an angry young man, and his job brought him into conflict with local Palestinians. One night on the road to Bethlehem, he was ambushed and murdered. Meshullam blamed Finn for putting his son in danger's way. The argument escalated and began to hinge on the ownership of Artas. Did it belong to Meshullam, who founded the farm? Or to Elizabeth Finn, who continued to fund the settlement through her charity work? One major donor was Queen Victoria's young son, Prince Arthur. In 1863, Meshullam brought a civil case against Elizabeth, and when the case was heard in the Consular Court, Finn ruled in his wife's favor. The British Foreign Office overturned the biased judgment and Finn was dismissed. The couple moved to Brook Green, London, where Finn died in poverty, and Elizabeth established the Distressed Gentlefolk's Aid Association.

THERE IS A NEW GELATERIA at the top of New Road, by the entrance to Manger Square. It is owned by the Franciscans and has a unique attraction: Pope Francis's popemobile is parked in the terrace, where anyone can try the seat out for size. Sitting in the pope's leatherette chair, having my afternoon ice cream cone, the tourists trudge past, up the hill toward the church. They arrive in coaches from Jerusalem. Twenty years ago, the coaches would park in Manger Square but are now directed to a multistory parking lot on New Road. The idea is that the tourists will see a little more of the town if they have to walk. The tourists blink and sweat in the full glare of the sun, kept in line by their Israeli tour guides with dire warnings about the town's safety. The church is the main stop, one hour maximum, followed by a visit to Beit Sahour and one of the two rival Shepherds' Fields, either the Orthodox site or the Catholic. The journey from Bethlehem to Beit Sahour takes the tourists from the highest to the lowest point in the district, inadvertently revealing what is so unusual about Bethlehem town. It is in the worst possible spot for a town: perched on top of a hill, with no natural water.

The oldest clusters of homes in the wider Bethlehem district can always be found halfway up the shadiest side of hills, not at the summit in the full glare of the mid-day sun. The alluvium soil in the bottom of the wadis is turned over to market crops like cabbages and lettuces, as at Artas and Wadi Fuqin. The sunny south-facing hills hold vineyards, like the now-abandoned terraces in Cremisan Valley, below Gilo settlement. The orchards and olive groves fill the upper slopes of the hills. The position of Bethlehem on a hilltop marks it out as a military lookout, not a village. It is a garrison far removed from the farming life of the valleys it commands.

One early Victorian visitor to Bethlehem made something of a cult out of hilltop sites. Arthur Stanley, the Dean of Westminster Cathedral, was already an author and celebrity when he made his pilgrimage over Christmas 1852-53. His account of this journey became a best seller when it was published as *Sinai and Palestine* (1856). Stanley hoped to bring a new rigor to Bible studies by blowing away the dusty, misguided views that had accumulated over the centuries. Like Jerome, he wanted to get "back to the Hebrews," not by returning to the texts, but by touring the land the scriptures described. Stanley wanted to see Palestine through the eyes of a biblical patriarch. He did this, chiefly, by climbing every available hill and soaking up the view.

Stanley imagined he stood in the spot where Moab was defeated, or where Joshua crossed the Jordan, or where Moses sat to behold "all the land of Gilead unto Dan, and all Naphtali, and all the land of Ephraim and Manasseh, and all the land of Judah to the utmost Sea, and the south, and the valley of the plain of Jericho, the city of palm trees, to Zoar." Every vista seemed to confirm the truth of the Bible, or would if he only looked harder. These hill-climbing expeditions were, to borrow Derrida's phrase, "detours in sight of the truth." Stanley prided himself on being a progressive Victorian: a man of science. Yet his method was a kind of parody of the scientific method. He came to Palestine believing he would find the truth of the Bible, and each time he hauled himself up a hill, he made the vista fit both with the Bible texts and his preexisting beliefs.

Despite his preconceptions, Stanley was scathing about older explorers. He was particularly critical of the traditions of the rival Latin and Orthodox churches whose mistakes he traced to St. Helena. Stanley mocked the fact that Helena had discovered a cave for every aspect of Christ's life, from the annunciation to the shepherds, the nursing of the infant, to the flight to Egypt. He writes: "The moment the religion of Palestine fell into the hands of Europeans it is hardly too much to say that it became a religion of caves." Even the murder of the innocents has its cave beneath the Church of the Nativity. It is startling to come across a pile of skulls and bones in a gloomy cell. It takes a moment as the chill clears and the eyes adjust, and you realize these human remains are too large to be infants; they are actually the unsorted contents of an old Bethlehem cemetery.

Stanley opposed Helena's religion of caves with his own religion of the hills. This was his big idea. Stanley noted the number of times that biblical prophets ascended mountains. He was also aware from the nascent field of biblical archaeology that a large number of pagan shrines lay on top of hills. Most of these shrines were extant in the Victorian era and were still venerated by locals Muslims, having been rededicated to Islamic saints. The likelihood—as Stanley and others surmised—was that these shrines marked the location of more ancient temples to Iron Age gods, such as the Philistines' Marduk, the Phoenicians' Baal or Yehu and El. If the ancient gods were worshipped in the high places, as the Bible suggests, then Stanley would, too. But he was mistaken in believing that these hilltop shrines were more indigenous—more redolent of the land—than Helena's caves. The hilltops might have contained shrines, but this reflected the culture of highly mobile warlords, who established fortresses to hold back rivals and to subjugate peasants. The farmers in the valleys had their own shrines, as the discovery of so many hundreds of domestic Astarte pillar statues shows. The statues to the goddess have a stronger claim to reflect the indigenous people than Stanley's hilltop shrines.

Stanley returned to Britain to lobby to set up a fund to explore Palestine in detail. With an act of parliament and a generous grant, the Palestine Exploration Fund (PEF) came into existence in 1865. The fund employed military engineers who eventually mapped the whole of Palestine, taking Stanley's high spots as triangulation points. The British Army, under the guise of the PEF, mapped every hilltop and wadi, every road and packhorse track. These are the maps used by General Allenby's forces when they invaded Palestine in 1917. The military instinctively saw what Stanley had missed: the high places are about control. Anything that you can see, you can target, control, or kill.

A large plaster relief map is bolted to a wall on a landing in the PEF offices in London. The PEF received its initial funding from the government and help from the army, yet it has been funded ever since by private members—including me—as well as by renting out the large Marylebone townhouse it bought in its heyday. Today, the PEF lives like a poor relation, squeezed into the old servant quarters. Every available corner is given over to books and boxes: cartons of files are even stacked in the fireplace of the old kitchen. The relief map of Palestine is the color of a Brown Betty teapot, possibly even browner. Labels attached to the plasterwork hills and valleys are falling off, but even so I can trace my journeys through the desert. As a symbol of the PEF, the map is both splendid and ramshackle, and probably fatally compromised by its past: a clergyman's vanity project that paved the way for a military invasion.

WELSH INFANTRYMEN CAPTURED Bethlehem's reservoirs in early December 1917, as a prelude to the battle for Jerusalem. The Prime Minister Lloyd George, also Welsh and a devout Baptist in public, declared the invasion "a Christmas gift to the British people." Bethlehemites did not know what British rule might portend, but in 1919 they learned that Lloyd George's cabinet had issued a secret document, the Balfour Declaration, dated November 2, 1917, written while the Ottomans were still in control and British and Anzac forces were mired in the Negev. The document took the unusual form of a letter from the Foreign Secretary James Arthur Balfour to Walter Rothschild, a leading figure in Britain's Jewish community. The letter caused immediate controversy when it became public, because the promise to establish a Jewish homeland in Palestine appeared to contradict specific promises made by Britain to its Palestinian and Arab allies during the war. The declaration does not specify what a "Jewish homeland" might mean, or where in Palestine it might be located, but the letter became the founding document behind the creation of Israel. (Incidentally, Foreign Secretary James Balfour is the man who inspired the phrase "Bob's your uncle," because his Uncle Robert Balfour is said to have ensured James always got good jobs.)

My former university professor, Rick Gekoski, amazed me when he announced he had the earliest extant version of the Balfour Declaration. Rick is responsible for introducing me to philosophers like Jacques Derrida, though he claims his students' enthusiasm for French theorists was the reason he quit teaching. He went on to become a rare book dealer. The draft copy of the Balfour declaration passed through his hands after it was discovered in the records of a London synagogue. It was sold at auction in New York in June 2005. Rick's draft version was composed by a man named Leon Simon, an English civil servant who was simultaneously a member of the World Zionist Organization (WZO), the Jewish activist group pressing for a homeland in Palestine. Though the document takes the form of a letter, in effect Simon was both the sender and the addressee. Yet it should not be thought that this letter was imposed upon the government: it was fully in line with the Christian-Zionism favored by the British establishment. From the PEF, to the Anglo-German Bishop of Jerusalem, to the Jews' Society, Christian-Zionism was a popular movement in Britain. It was backed not only by the church and government, but also by the armed forces. Even apparently benign organizations like the travel company Thomas Cook were military contractors. The Holy Land tours that Thomas Cook organized to Palestine from 1869 onwards were only a sideline to the company's real business, transporting military mail and equipment to British troops based in Egypt and the Sudan.

In Britain, Christian-Zionism has its roots in the divisions between "High Church" Anglicans, who emphasize continuity with Rome, and "Low Church" Protestants, such as the Methodists, Baptists, Unitarians, and others, who focus on the break. This division was exacerbated by the nineteenth-century conflict between London and the new factory cities in the provinces, especially in northern England, home to antiestablishment industrialists and a devoutly Christian working class. Finally, Christian-Zionism was a feature of Britain's Celtic fringes: Scotland, Wales, and especially Ireland where Christian-Zionism comforted a Protestant minority placed in authority over a hostile Catholic majority. An unusual number of the London Jews' Society were Irish Protestants. Michael Alexander converted to Christianity in Ireland; James Finn's father was an Irish Catholic convert to Protestantism; Reverend Barclay, not only Jerusalem's bishop but also the first translator of the Talmud into English, was Irish.

Lloyd George's cabinet was founded by Low Church Christians who held a strong emotional investment to Christian-Zionism. They represented a rising provincial class whose enthusiasm for a literal reading of the Bible reflected their identification with the Jews of the Bible. Like the Israelites under Egypt, they felt that they had been held back too long by the old establishment. As they assumed power, they began to bare their teeth. Christian-Zionism continues to form an important political current today in support of Israel, though its center has migrated from the UK to the United States. The idea that the Bible ought to be taken literally is surely one of history's strangest ideas: when Jesus speaks almost exclusively in parables, even God is warning us not to take the written word at face value.

EACH EVENING DURING MY STAY in Boulos's home, I wander into town to drink a late-night coffee and eat something sweet at the café in the corner of the Peace Center. The church buzzes through the night as young Italian restorers work on saving the roof built by the Venetians in 1480 with Lebanese cedar and English lead. The lead was stolen by the Ottomans to help fight the British.

The British ruled Palestine between 1917 and 1948. There are many reminders of their stay. The Bethlehem Arab Orthodox Club has a Scout troop with a pipe band. It is quite a sight at Christmas to see Palestinian pipers march into Manger Square. Outside the post office in Beit Jala is an English postbox with the initials GR, George Rex, standing proud of the cast metal. There are plenty of other examples of infrastructure and major works if one cares to look. The British army refurbished Bethlehem's reservoirs with a new pumping station and repaired the Ottoman pipeline. Yet what stands out about British rule is its sheer destructive nature, both to the landscape and the people. The British closed down the millennia-old market in Manger Square, moving the Ta'amareh livestock traders to the foot of Wadi Ma'ali and the local stallholders to the present site on the ridge, pulling down three blocks of the oldest part of the city to accommodate the stalls. The Peace Center on Manger Square is also a reminder of British violence: it stands on the old police station. I remember it well from the 1990s, a squat building with iron bars on the windows.

The most damaging effects of the British occupation are hidden in legal phrases of official papers. The document outlining the British Mandate in Palestine states: "The Administration may arrange with the Jewish Agency mentioned in Article 4 to construct or operate, on fair and equitable terms, any public works, services and utilities." There is no mention of the Palestinian Arab community. The terms that establish the extent and purpose of the British Mandate see no role for the indigenous Palestinian population: fairness does not apply to them, and they will have no say in the public sphere or the bodies and infrastructure that shape it.

The Jewish Agency was a body created by the WZO expressly to partner with the British in Palestine. Chaim Weizmann, a leader of the WZO and a key figure behind the Balfour Declaration, headed the agency. The High Commissioner Herbert Samuels, an early proponent of establishing a Jewish homeland, headed the British administration. The mandate envisaged that Samuels and Weizmann, High Commissioner and director of the Jewish Agency, would work in concert; indeed, it was a legal requirement. Samuels' job was to pave the way for a Jewish homeland and accustom the Palestinian population to this new reality. The Jewish community was small when the British arrived in 1917, but as the terms of the mandate so favored Jewish business and industries, the population grew rapidly through the 1920s, and the administration expropriated land for their settlement and granted monopolies in utility companies to the Jewish entrepreneurs.

The story of a Bethlehem businessman, Ibrahim Hazboun, illustrates how the British discrimination against indigenous communities worked in practice. Hazboun hoped to win the franchise to exploit mineral rights in the Dead Sea. He bought land around the sea and operated a ferry company to defray costs, transporting livestock and agricultural products from the Jordan to the Palestinian side. Hazboun's ferry operated with the encouragement of the British administration, yet they held off awarding mineral rights. Hazboun's debts mounted, and the British authorities negotiated refinancing for Hazboun from the Anglo-Egyptian Bank, an overseas British bank owned by Barclays whose Jerusalem branch opened in the wake of the British invasion.

Hazboun sought out his own partners, hoping to go into business with the wealthy Palestinian financiers, the Kattans. The British vetoed the deal. Their preferred partner was a Jewish Russian entrepreneur, Moshe Novomeysky, who had already been granted a license to conduct surveys in the Dead Sea, undertaken by British geologists. Hazboun was under both financial and political pressure, and so he agreed a deal with Novomeysky. The Russian disappeared abroad without honoring the agreement, and on his return a second deal was negotiated, again under British pressure, at a reduced price with stocks replacing cash. Hazboun was despondent, but again felt he had no choice but to agree. Once more, the deal was not honored. This time, the British bank foreclosed. Hazboun went bankrupt, and Novomeysky bought his Dead Sea holdings from the receivers. The British administration and

Jewish Agency then granted Novomeysky monopoly rights to exploit the Dead Sea resources for seventy-five years, a deal regarded as a scandal and debated in the Westminster parliament at the time. Novomeysky's company, the Palestine Potash Company, was immensely profitable.

The make-up of Jewish Palestine changed through the 1920s. The numbers of middle European Jewish emigrants brought a more hostile and skeptical attitude to British rule than the generation embodied by "Establishment" British Jews like Herbert Samuels and Chaim Weizmann, who were at ease doing business within the British corridors of power. The situation changed, too, as the 1920s shaded into the 1930s. The British faced a Palestinian uprising in 1929, which prompted the British to introduce some distance between the administration and the Jewish Agency. This in turn stoked Jewish militancy and the beginnings of an explicitly anti-British mood among the *New Yishuv*, the name adopted by the European Jewish community in Palestine. The leaders who emerged from the late 1920s reflected the Polish and Russian character of the Yishuv, preeminent among them David Ben-Gurion. He was not even five feet tall, yet he combined implacable stubbornness with a strong pragmatic streak. Throughout the 1930s, Ben-Gurion dominated every aspect of the New Yishuv. He was the General Secretary of *Histadrut*, the Jewish Trade Union; he was the leader of the dominant party, *Mapai* (an acronym of the Workers Party of the Land of Israel); he was the Commander-in-Chief of the *Haganah*, a Jewish militia; and he was even Weizmann's replacement as the head of the Jewish Agency. He held most of these posts simultaneously. The concentration of Jewish power in a single hierarchical organization, and even a single figure, contrasted with the situation among the Palestinians. The politics of Jerusalem were riven by rivalries between the notables. On a national level, Palestinian strategies reflected either a top-down approach, which favored appeals between ruling elites, or a more populist or bottom-up approach that emphasized building institutions and preparing for statehood, such as the establishment of a sovereign wealth fund to underwrite civil society, and the creation of banks like the Arab Bank and the Arab National Bank to support the businessmen like Ibrahim Hazboun who were exploited by British imperial bankers. The soldier and banker Ahmed Hilmi Pasha exemplified this more popular approach.

The British administration may have distanced itself from the Jewish community over the course of the mandate, but it was entirely hostile to the Palestinians. It was imperial policy to favor new settlers over the indigenous population, regarding the one group as economic migrants who could help a colony to thrive, and the other as a source of potential nationalism that would challenge the imperial project. When the Jerusalem notables settled their rivalries and formed the Higher Arab Committee, the British arrested all the committee members and exiled them to the Seychelles in the Indian Ocean. During the Palestinian Arab Revolt of 1936 to 1939, the British closed every Arab organization, whether these were social groups, sporting clubs, or political parties. The army sealed the buildings, confiscated records and property, and arrested and expelled leaders. Any attempt at organizing Palestinians in preparation for either war or for statehood became impossible.

Where communal violence broke out, it was in cities with the most competition over the public sphere, such as Jerusalem, Jaffa, or Hebron. Bethlehem had no Jewish population, then or now, as the British censuses show (there was a single Jew living in Beit Jala in the early 1930s). There was, however, a small Jewish community living at the Ain Faghour springs, the ancestral home of the al-Fawaghreh clan. This settlement was named Kfar Etzion: Village of the Zion Woodland, and at its peak numbered some twenty young couples. The Kfar Etzion community lasted through a number of incarnations, beginning life as a religious back-to-the-land project in the 1920s, which was shortly abandoned. It was then revived by a small Haredi community and abandoned again. In the late 1930s, Kfar Etzion was taken over by the Kibbutz Movement, a left-wing organization inspired by anarcho-communist ideas about cooperation, and industrial and military self-sufficiency. The kibbutzim supplied the New Yishuv with its commando units known as the *Palmach*. Despite their military proficiency, Ben-Gurion regarded the Palmach with suspicion. The kibbutzim militia remained proudly independent of his Haganah forces, even after war broke out in May 1948.

Kfar Etzion straddles the al-Arrub and al-Biyar aqueducts, and encompasses the headspring at Ain Faghour. Like every invading force, the kibbutzim commandos recognized that controlling the water in the Bethlehem hills meant controlling Jerusalem. When war broke out in 1948, the battle at Kfar Etzion was the only battle in the Bethlehem region. It was also one of the most controversial in the entire war.

# CHAPTER 9

# JORDAN

## *1948–1967*

*Landscape and trainline between Jerusalem and Jaffa.*

ethlehem may have been shaped by its position between desert and hills, and its size determined by the web of aqueducts that connect the surrounding villages. But since the 1948 war, the Jerusalem-Jaffa railway has defined Bethlehem's western edge. This is a single-line track that meanders south through a series of valleys before looping west toward the coast, through Beit Shemesh and Ramle. French investors funded it under license from the Ottomans. When it opened in 1892, the journey to the coast took between three-and-a-half and six hours, which was comparable to the speed of a horse-drawn carriage. Today, there is a train every hour, and it takes ninety minutes to reach Tel Aviv. The coach from Jerusalem Central Bus Station runs every quarter of an hour and does the journey in fifty minutes. It is easy to see why the railway has never been popular with travellers.

The best vantage point to see the railway track is on the far side of the Cremisan Monastery at a village called al-Walajeh. It's a good walk uphill through Beit Jala. About a quarter of a mile past the little square in front of the Arab Orthodox Boys Club, the road peels to the right. Gilo settlement sits opposite, on the south-facing side of Cremisan Valley. Here you have a perfect view of the flyover that forms the most startling part of the settler bypass around Bethlehem. The flyover emerges from a tunnel directly below Gilo, crossing the valley on tall stilts, and disappearing into a second tunnel below Beit Jala. To the right of the tunnel beneath Gilo, an odd assortment of houses clings to the abandoned terraces. The houses are clearly Palestinian, not only because they look so improvised, but also because each has a couple of water tanks on the roof. Palestinians need emergency tanks to cope with sudden shortages, because the water company prioritizes Israeli homes. This hamlet is New Malha. The original Malha lies at the end of the valley and is now a shopping mall.

The road continues through the monastery's vineyards and a shady pine forest. You emerge from the trees on a hillside promontory, with the railway tracks below, and Malha Mall to your right, next to Jerusalem's Teddy Kollek Stadium. The removal of the original Malha village was part of the deal between Israel and Jordan when they chose the railway tracks as the route of the armistice line that ended the war of 1948.

Al-Walajeh has a similar story to Malha. A few years ago, Leila and I visited a seventy-year-old farmer, Ahmed Barghouth, who keeps bees for honey and grows fruit and herbs. Barghouth told us that the original al-Walajeh, like Malha, once lay on the other side of the valley. The present village is built on their orchards. We took a tour of his terraces, which hold the al-Badawi variety of olive from a tree that has been dated to 4-5,000 years old. In the shady grove we look at the remains of his beehives, recently smashed by the army, and the handmade mausoleum he built for his parents. Down in the valley, a northbound train pulled out of Malha Station. Next to the station, there is a new zoo, and Barghouth told us he could see the giraffe in the mornings when its keeper takes it for a walk. He could also hear the Beitar Jerusalem fans at soccer matches in Teddy Stadium. Beitar Jerusalem was founded by immigrants from Poland in the

1930s who belonged to Betar Youth, an extreme right-wing Jewish "brown shirt" movement. The team is now popular with Jerusalem's blue-collar workers, and strongly supported by immigrants from Middle Eastern Mizrahi Jewish communities. The Betar fans' chant is: "Death to Arabs."

The post-war British plan to partition Palestine between Jewish and Palestinian communities was rejected by the Palestinians and the neighboring states. The British declared that they would unilaterally renounce their mandate in May 1948 and hand responsibility for Palestine to the UN. The day before the set date, Ben-Gurion declared the State of Israel. The United States recognized the new state, and the declaration became a *fait accompli*. Israel was born. However, in the months before this, the British had hosted secret negotiations to revive the partition plan between the Yishuv and the Hashemite Kingdom of Jordan, led by King Abdullah. The details still excite controversy, but it is widely agreed that, before the war at least, Britain's shuttle diplomacy resulted in Jordan and Israel agreeing on their future borders. The more controversial claim is that this deal remained in place, despite pressure, and throughout the worst of the fighting. Yet in Bethlehem, this is certainly what happened. Both sides knew the agreed route of the borders before they were fighting, and quickly ceased hostilities along this line.

BETWEEN DECEMBER 1947 AND JANUARY 1948, Jewish Haganah forces defeated the sole Palestinian army, a force based in Jerusalem. The British were still in control of the country, and oversaw this defeat. As the May deadline approached, the British were confident that Jewish forces were in control of the country. The Palestinians were in poor shape. With no military force, most of its leaders exiled, and all of its civil institutions shattered, there was little in the way of a state-in-waiting on the Palestinian side. This was the background as British intelligence organized secret negotiations between Jordan and Ben-Gurion's administration. The British wanted to see Jordanian control over the areas designated for the Palestinian population in the original partition plan. Jordan was a known quantity: the British had not only created and trained Jordan's army in 1920, it had even chosen the force's name, the Arab Legion. The Legion had been intended as a gendarmerie. By 1948 it numbered 4,500 fighting men (ten thousand by the end of the war), trained and led by Lieutenant-General John Bagot Glubb, a British officer. In March 1948, Glubb handed field responsibility to the senior British intelligence officer in Palestine, Norman Lash, code-named "The Lion" by his counterpart in the Haganah's intelligence services, Ezra Danin. Lash and Danin were old colleagues who had worked together on counter-insurgency ten years earlier during the Arab Revolt, when the fluent Arab-speaker Danin interrogated prisoners for the British police. In 1948, Lash was transferred from the colonial police to the Arab legion with the rank of Brigadier, despite the complaints of his more junior Arab officers that he was a politician, rather than a soldier. Lash and his deputy, Colonel Desmond Goldie, took responsibility for Jordan's negotiations with Israel, in coordination with Danin.

Ben-Gurion's declaration of the State of Israel brought an immediate reaction from the neighboring countries. King Farouk of Egypt crossed into Palestine from the Sinai, against the advice of his own military. The Arab Legion entered Jerusalem under the command of a junior Arab officer, Abdullah el-Tell, stationed in Jericho, who had received his orders directly from King Abullah. The British command under Lash in Ramallah was caught off-guard, but by evening sent forces to back el-Tell and secure what would become the armistice lines in Jerusalem. The Arab Legion was joined by limited forces from Iraq, Jordan's sister kingdom, notionally ruled by Abdullah's thirteen-year-old great nephew. Meanwhile, Lebanon and Syria moved to defend their existing international borders. Despite the apparent superiority of these five Arab forces, there were always more Israeli troops in the field: by the end of the war, they numbered some one hundred thousand. Moreover, after just a month of fighting, a ceasefire was declared in June 1948, and Israel succeeded in re-arming by sea. From June until the end of the war, Israel had heavy weapons superior to all of the Arab forces combined, and was the only combatant with air power. In addition, Israel had shorter supply lines and coherent war aims. Finally, Israel had the unique advantage of a unified command structure under Ben-Gurion, which gave the Israeli forces their discipline. However, Ben-Gurion did not achieve this unity until the June ceasefire. He used the cover of the ceasefire not simply to acquire heavy artillery, but also to stamp out dissent among the Jewish forces and bring all of them under his command.

The fact that Ben-Gurion did not have complete control over the kibbutzim forces in May 1948 casts a light on the events in Bethlehem at the Kfar Etzion. The Kibbutz Movement assumed responsibility for the abandoned Kfar Etzion settlement in 1943. Palmach commandoes reenforced the settlement, and from November 1947 were involved in defeating the Jerusalem-based Palestinian forces. The Palmach remained in Kfar Etzion as the deadline for the May 1948 British withdrawal approached, fully aware of how vulnerable they were. Kfar Etzion lay in a highly advanced position, far from Jewish centers of population and power. Yet the Palmach continued to believe it had strategic worth. The settlement not only controlled Jerusalem's water, but also commanded the Hebron Road, breaking lines communication between the two largest Palestinian cities: Hebron and Jerusalem. The settlement remained a flashpoint through to May 1948 and the beginning of the war. It was an obvious target for Palestinian irregulars because its situation made travel around Bethlehem so dangerous. The settlement was also a target for the British-controlled Arab Legion, as it lay so far on the "wrong" side of the British partition plan. Given these factors, Ben-Gurion's military leadership regularly discussed evacuating Kfar Etzion. Women and children were moved out with British help in January 1948, but the Palmach remained.

Kfar Etzion was never evacuated. One widely cited reason is that the Haganah made a cold-blooded decision to keep forces in Kfar Etzion. The intention was to draw the Arab Legion into a fight in Bethlehem, drain resources, and buy further time for Israeli troops to mobilize. On this view, Kfar Etzion was deliberately sacrificed. It seems unlikely that the army would sacrifice their best commandos, in a debacle they were certain to lose. It also overlooks the fact that the Palmach was not under Haganah command: and you cannot sacrifice troops that you do not control. In fact, when one considers the number of times that the settlement was almost evacuated, it is likely that the simple truth was that the defenders did not wish to go. The Palmach had taken the decision to occupy this abandoned settlement, five years earlier. They were too stubborn to change their minds as the war started. Ben-Gurion would have little say in the matter, as he did not control Palmach forces until June 1948.

In early May 1948, Palestinian irregulars from both Bethlehem and Hebron, later joined by el-Tell's Jerusalem forces, attacked Kfar Etzion.

The fighting took two days, and when the Palmach surrendered, the death toll inside Kfar Etzion numbered around a hundred and thirty. A further fifteen fighters were killed in cold blood after the surrender. Kfar Etzion has become a *cause celebre* because of the execution of these prisoners. Though the details are murky, evidence from both the Israeli and Palestinian sides suggests that the killings were a response to a massacre one month earlier at Deir Yassin, a village outside Jerusalem. The *mukhtar* of Deir Yassin had received written guarantees from the Haganah High Command that his village could remain neutral. However, these guarantees were rescinded under pressure from irregulars belonging to the Betar Youth Movement. The Haganah gave the green light to Betar to attack Deir Yassin, and also did nothing to warn the villagers that they were at risk. Six hundred unarmed people were murdered, including women and children. Israeli accounts also describe mutilations and rapes. The official Israeli report into the incident remains a state secret.

In the June ceasefire, Ben-Gurion cemented his control over both the Palmach and Betar. In the process, he faced a revolt from his own generals, yet he won out. His victory ensured that he could determine the war aims, rather than allowing them to be decided in the field by freelance commanders, as had happened at Kfar Etzion. In the immediate aftermath of the June ceasefire, the fighting between Israel and Jordan briefly grew fierce as Israel attacked with its new heavy weapons. There was a concerted attempt to seize the Latrun Benedictine monastery that overlooks much of western Jerusalem. For many Israeli soldiers, seizing the mythical city of Zion was the heart and soul of the conflict. After all, this had been the attraction of Kfar Etzion: it was the source of Jerusalem's water. Nevertheless, the Jerusalem-centric period of the 1948 war was short-lived, and both the Israeli and Jordanian forces returned to their agreed lines. The Israeli cabinet debated launching a second assault on Jerusalem in September. The idea was rejected, and the cited reason was an agreement with Abdullah of Jordan. In any case, there was no point seizing Jerusalem without first holding Bethlehem's springs.

Twice, in October and December 1948, Israel led offenses against Egypt on the far side of the country, and both times Jordan held to its lines in the hills of Bethlehem. There was no attempt by Jordan to acquire new territory, nor to aid Egypt. Jordanian forces never strayed outside of the original

UN plan for the partition of Palestine, except for a few extremely minor exceptions. The Israeli forces had more troops, secure supply lines, better equipment, air power, and more unity of purpose than the forces ranged against them. Yet their greatest resource was surely the knowledge that the British-commanded Arab Legion would never press an advantage and attack.

The 1949 armistice agreement between Israel and Jordan reiterated the prewar agreement and resulted in a negotiated border between Israeli and Palestinian territory. It is known as the Green Line or the 1949 Armistice Line. In Bethlehem, the line is marked by the railway tracks along the valley floor. As the track follows a geographical feature, it might be classed as a natural border, even though it cuts across privately owned land. The decision to relocate the residents of Malha and al-Walajeh, two villages that blurred the armistice line, shows that both negotiators believed they had settled upon a defensible border. Indeed, the joint document states that it is a border for military purposes: Israel and Jordan legally agreed it was defensible. Despite a long list of infractions, the Green Line held without major hostilities until 1967. The Jordanian/Israeli deal states that the line could not be seen as a political solution to the question of Palestine. Here, the phrase "question of Palestine" refers back to the original British plan to partition Palestine. However, from their future actions, it became clear that both Jordan and Israel saw the term "Palestine" as an empty tag: it was the name of a piece of real estate rather than the home of people demanding self-representation.

The Jordanian army carted the villagers from al-Walajeh to Bethlehem in trucks, before turning their terraces into a militarized border zone of barbed wire, tank traps, and gunnery posts. It was a similar story all down the line, through the valley. The next village, Battir, lost much of their land as the Green Line separated the village from its fields. The villagers of Wadi Fuqin were expelled from their village by the Israelis, and had to fight a campaign with the UN to return, only to discover that the Israeli army had already blown up their houses. The villagers were deported again, fought again, and with persistence were eventually allowed to rebuild their homes. Their stubbornness apparently scuppered a secret detail in the agreement between Jordan and Israel.

The Israeli practice of dynamiting Palestinian villages means there are many stories of villages forming night-watches with birding rifles and muskets, as happened in Beit Jala, and even more poignant stories of elderly people remaining behind in all-but abandoned villages and fooling the Israelis by going around the houses lighting lamps and moving animals. Bethlehem's monasteries, like Saint Mariam's Carmelite convent, were filled with refugees whose homes were only a few miles distant, on the other side of the Green Line.

Three refugee camps were established in Bethlehem. Deheisha stands in an old quarry on the Hebron Road. Aida lies behind the cemetery at Rachel's Tomb. Azar is a single winding street in the exact place there would be a tail, if Bethlehem really were a sleeping cat. Jordanian rule did little to build infrastructure in Bethlehem and certainly not in the camps, which had no drainage or sewage systems until the Oslo Accords in 1993. The Jordanians followed the British example of demolishing blocks of Bethlehem's ancient city quarters, this time to enlarge Manger Square. They also took over the British police station. In 1955, soldiers from the Arab League shot into a Bethlehem crowd that was demonstrating against the army. Four people were killed.

I remember, back in the 1990s, visiting a hotel at Everest, as the summit of Beit Jala is known. I was shown a room and told it was the Royal Suite. It was modest, painted blue with a double bed filling much of the space. A sliding window creaked back to reveal stunning views of al-Makhrour as well as the water tanks on the hotel roof. It was the Royal Suite because Abdullah had stayed there on a visit to Bethlehem. The fact that the owner could claim a connection to Abdullah suggests that the Jordanian royals were not universally hated. Nevertheless, for many, the shooting of protesters in Bethlehem was a turning point. By this point, King Abdullah was dead. A Palestinian gunman in Jerusalem had assassinated him in 1951. To suppress the story of local antipathy to Jordanian rule, the investigation blamed a conspiracy between Abdullah el-Tell and a group of Palestinian aristocrats living in exile in Egypt. In the aftermath of the shooting, Colonel Glubb's Arab Legion swiftly deposed the king's son and heir, Talal, claiming he was mentally unstable. As in Iraq, a child was placed on the throne and controlled by appointed officers: the new king was Hussein, Abdullah's fifteen-year-old grandson. Hussein was abroad at Harrow School which he followed with a course of study at Sandringham Military Academy.

As a young man, Barghouth was bitterly opposed to Jordanian rule. He joined the Communist Party and took part in demonstrations. He was angry to have been made a refugee: he had never abandoned his home. Barghouth describes how he would sneak up to the Green Line to see what had become of his land, now covered in barbed wire and trenches. A Jordanian army post stood across from old al-Walajeh, opposite another post built by the Israelis.

Barghouth is living on his land again. Not the actual village, but the orchards where the Jordanian army had its lookout posts. We sit on his terrace, eating biscuits flavored with sage and drinking strong mint tea: black tea, fresh mint, sugar. He returned after the Israelis' invasion of 1967, when the army cleared out the Jordanian barbed wire and tank traps. The villagers took the decision to build new homes on the abandoned terraces, without waiting to ask or be told they couldn't. The Israelis were slow to react, and because the villagers could prove they owned the land, the houses were allowed to stand. The army frequently demolishes structures they claim have no building permit, such as Barghouth's beehives. He fought a court case to keep his parents' mausoleum from being destroyed. The army has restricted vehicle access, and so despite its proximity to Beit Jala—not to mention football stadiums, malls, and zoos—al-Walajeh actually feels remote and inaccessible. If it is a kind of triumph, it is a fragile one. Israel has published plans to confiscate all of al-Walajeh on both sides of the tracks and extend the zoo to make a country park.

IF ONE FIGURE EMBODIES the complex relation with Jordan, it is Asad Sulayman Abd al-Qadir, known by his *nom de guerre* Salah Taamari. He was just thirteen when he witnessed the Jordanian soldiers shoot the four protesters in Bethlehem. He left Bethlehem a few years later to attend university in Cairo. There were no universities in either Jordan or Palestine in the 1950s and bright young men and, more rarely, women had to go abroad to study. Anton Sansour attended university in both Cairo and Baghdad before his post-graduate work in Moscow. Taamari also went to Cairo. He is a handsome man even in his seventies; tall and broad, with icy blue eyes and gray hair that he wears swept back from his high forehead. He must have cut a dash at Cairo University, quoting T. S. Eliot, his favorite poet. He was politicized by the army shootings in Bethlehem, and he was an early member of Fatah, the political party formed by Yasser Arafat in the 1960s. He soon became a militant or *fedayeen*, the Arabic word for a guerrilla fighter. He is from the Ta'amareh Bedouin, which is how he chose his distinctive name.

The war of 1967 that saw the invasion of Bethlehem began with a series of Israeli air strikes code-named Operation Focus. Egyptian troop movements in the Sinai had alarmed Israel. Claiming fears of a possible invasion, Israel bombed airfields across Egypt, Jordan, and Syria, the first actions in what became known as the Six-Day War. As the scale of the Israeli victory became apparent, Israel launched a preemptive attack on the West Bank, later citing infractions of the armistice line as justification. Bethlehem was captured in an afternoon, and Israeli flags were raised over the Church of the Nativity and Rachel's Tomb. The year afterwards, 1968, forces associated with Yasser Arafat's Fatah Party established training bases along the Jordan River, despite opposition from the Jordanians. Taamari's new home was a camp in the border town of Karameh, from where the fedayeen conducted regular missions into Israel and the West Bank.

In March 1968, Israel launched an attack against Karameh. Contemporary accounts suggest the Israelis were overconfident of success. They had encountered little opposition when they captured Jerusalem the previous year, and appear to have assumed the Jordanian army would melt away, leaving them free to destroy Fatah's forces and kill or capture Arafat. However, when the Jordanians saw the dust cloud across the Jordan River, they thought it was the beginning of an invasion. Rather than retreat, they chose to fight. Taamari and the other Palestinian fighters had no choice but to hold their ground. The battle lasted only fifteen hours, and out of an estimated thousand fedayeen, 156 were killed, 100 wounded, and 140 captured. It should have been remembered as a debacle but instead it built a legend. The famous quote from King Hussein, "I think we may reach the point where we are all fedayeen," set the tone for how the battle is remembered. Arafat survived the battle unharmed. The next year, he became leader of the Palestinian Liberation Organization (PLO), ultimately becoming synonymous with the organization. Under his leadership, the PLO became the face of Palestine, internationally recognized as the representative of the Palestinian people.

From the mid-1960s, the Palestinian cause was seen as a revolution. Palestine became a popular cause among Arabs not only because it opposed Israel, but also because it represented a call to popular self-determination, and against unaccountable elites. But a revolution needs a battle, which is what the Battle of Karameh supplied. It remains a defining moment, giving every Palestinian the cachet of being a fighter for liberty. One of the shocks of a tour of Bethlehem's refugee camps, even today, is how often the image of Che Guevara can be seen painted on the walls, his face alongside the Palestinian heroes.

As much as any fedayeen, Salah Taamari embodied the image of a romantic revolutionary. It was not simply that he was handsome, or loved poetry, or even that he had fought at Karameh. He was also the lover of a princess. Around the same time as the Battle of Karameh, Taamari had met and fallen in love with King Hussein's first wife, the beautiful Dina bint 'Abdu'l-Hamid, a genuine princess who could trace her lineage back to the earliest caliphs on one side, and to Mamluk aristocrats on the other. Hussein and Dina had divorced in 1957 after only two years of marriage, but had one child together, the Princess Alia of Jordan, which made it particularly sensitive that Dina was the lover of a Palestinian freedom fighter. Nevertheless Taamari and Dina married in 1970 and are still together.

THE YEAR TAAMARI AND DINA married saw a conflict between the Jordanian Armed Forces and the PLO. The large number of Palestinian revolutionaries in the kingdom undermined Hussein's authority. The PLO operated as a state within a state, controlling roads and checking identity cards as they ran their own security operations. But the event that precipitated the 1970 war known as Black September was an aircraft hijacking organized by one of the smaller political parties within the PLO, the Popular Front for the Liberation of Palestine (PFLP). This was a militantly secular socialist party led by a charismatic intellectual named George Habash. King Hussein later claimed that Black September was forced upon him: a matter of "law and order and chaos and anarchy . . . an experience that was a very sad one for all concerned." The experience was worse for the Palestinians, as the Jordanian Army had heavy weapons and tanks. The 1970 war saw many thousands of the lightly armed Palestinians killed, before they were driven out of Jordan. They regrouped in Lebanon, which really did no one any good.

One image often seen beside Che Guevara in Bethlehem is the iconic Leila Khaled, one of the PFLP hijackers. The pairing of Che and Leila makes them appear like a sacred couple. It is difficult to know if the spirit of revolution has had a positive or negative effect on Palestine and its politics, but it has left an indelible mark. It tempts one to believe, if pushed hard enough, anyone might be a fedayeen. Leila Khaled was the most famous of the hijackers. She was young and beautiful, but what made her so remarkable was her commitment: the 1970 hijacking was the second time she had seized a plane. The name Leila sounds just as romantic to Arabs as it does to westerners. It is not particularly common, yet women with the name are often charismatic. It is commonly associated with a homonym meaning "night," as in the stories of *Kitāb 'alf layla wa-layla,* or *The Book of the Thousand and One Nights.* In fact, it derives from a more archaic word meaning the feeling of wooziness that comes with intoxication. The name suggests a dangerous power. Leila Sansour's theory is that it gives its holders a confidence that they can make a difference, and is a sign their fathers loved them very much.

# CHAPTER 10

# ISRAEL

## *From 1967 to Oslo*

*Mitzpe Shalem settlement, and the Ahava factory.*

One of the last events I attended with Anton was a reception for Suha Arafat, Yasser Arafat's wife. This was Christmas in 1995. The next morning, Arafat gave a speech from the roof of the Church of the Nativity to announce his return from exile. It was the period of the Oslo Accords, and there was a spirit of optimism, especially among the younger men and women who filled Manger Square waving flags as he spoke, or who raced along Hebron Road beeping their car horns. Arafat was the new president of the Palestinian Authority (PA), and it seemed that Palestinians were on the verge of getting a state. Anton was less optimistic. He had turned down an offer to run the PA Ministry of Higher Education, just as he had turned down an offer to join the Madrid Peace

Conference a few years earlier. Perhaps he was feeling tired or unwell, as he died five months later. But he was wonderful that Christmas, and he was delighted to see his family, especially Leila.

The reception was in one of the hotels that line New Road with names like Nativity, or Three Kings. I forget which. The reception was upstairs, in a hall that was already filled with Bethlehem society. Suha Arafat has always complained that she was the object of too much Palestinian gossip, but being the large and flamboyant blond Christian wife of a tiny, elderly, abstemious Muslim revolutionary, she might have expected some gossip. There was plenty of gossip that night. Suha Arafat was thirty-two years old, two years older than me. She had married Arafat in secret in Tunis when she was twenty-seven and Arafat was in his early sixties. In 1995, she gave birth to a daughter, their only child. Anton greeted Suha and introduced me as his son-in-law. Suha was my height in her heels. I remember she was wearing a silk blouse in a bright orange color that was fashionable that year. She was warm toward me, and even more so toward Anton, a friend of her mother, Raymonda Tawil. Leila had been talking to a friend across the room but now appeared at her father's side. The moment Anton introduced Leila, Suha's warmth turned up a notch. She kissed and embraced Leila, talking excitedly. I did not understand Arabic, but I could see that Anton and Leila were growing uncomfortable. When I got a chance to ask what it had been about, Leila told me that Suha wanted to fix her up with her brother, who was looking for a wife.

"But she met me two seconds earlier."

"Yes. That was awkward."

I met someone else that night, Elias Freij, the mayor of Bethlehem. He was standing on a dais when Anton introduced me. As I shook his hand, he stumbled. I somehow managed to lift him in the air and set him down on solid ground. He weighed nothing. I thought he was the most fragile person I had ever met. I was later told that he had been the target of a car bombing less than ten years earlier.

Bethlehem has had a mayor and city council since the Ottoman reforms of the late nineteenth century. The institution survived through British and Jordanian rule, into Israeli control. Elias Freij had won an election in 1972, when the PLO had demanded a boycott. He won again in 1976 when the PLO lifted their objections. This was the last time the

Israelis allowed elections, so Freij had been mayor for twenty-five years. He was not a PLO member, but he was a pragmatic man. Unlike Anton Sansour, Freij had joined the negotiating team at the Madrid Conference, that precursor to Oslo.

AFTER THE ISRAELI TAKEOVER of the West Bank in 1967, a military governor ruled Bethlehem. The new regime brought checkpoints, raids, curfews, and arrests, but also one advantage. It reunited Bethlehem with Palestinian communities in cities like Gaza, Haifa, Nazareth, and Tiberias. In the early 1970s, there was considerable freedom of movement. Anton had been working in the math department of Moscow State University, but in 1973 he took a teaching job at Birzeit University. From there, he joined the founding committee of Bethlehem University. Israel had tried to impose the Israeli curriculum on the West Bank, but had relented in the face of protests. The 1970s became a boom time for education in Palestine. Israel collected Palestinians' taxes and tried to claim responsibility for the burst of new schools and universities. In fact, the initial funding for Bethlehem University came from the Vatican, and when Anton and the other teachers insisted that it would be a secular institution with Muslim and Christian students, funds were also gathered from the Arab world. In many ways, men like Anton Sansour and Elias Freij were international bagmen: they went out looking for money to bring back to Palestine. Bethlehem University was part of the Catholic *Frères* group of universities, and Anton used his connections to win recognition for Bethlehem's degree courses. Bethlehem was the first internationally recognized university, paving the way for Birzeit and Al-Quds. Freij helped build high schools in Bethlehem, seeking donors in both the Arab world and even the American Evangelical community. Freij was born in 1918 and had attended a Protestant school in Jerusalem established by Bishop Gobat, which gave him an insight into Protestant and Evangelical circles.

The bodies created to run Palestine's schools, hospitals, welfare societies, and all the other elements of the welfare state that emerged in the 1970s and '80s are self-consciously termed "civil society." Bethlehem is run by committees, with every decision slowly inched forward through endless votes. The term civil society is both a description and a concept, drawing upon left-wing traditions of cooperation and mutualism. Bethlehem comes close to showing how such a society might work—and, at times, how it does not. When Leila made her award-winning documentary "Open Bethlehem," an early rough cut ran for three and a half hours and seemed to consist of nothing but people sitting around conference tables, debating finer points of process. Even researching this history, the books I found in Bethlehem pointedly omitted the names of individual authors, and rather listed the members of the committees involved in their production. Bethlehem's civil society includes unique institutions that are a product of a long occupation. The Palestinian Prisoners Society (PPS), for instance, provides welfare and legal help for prisoners inside Israeli jails, and for their families. The PPS is a powerful factor in Palestinian life because sixty percent of Palestinian men have been imprisoned, meaning that every family is affected, and the society exists to reflect their views. In the mid-seventies, Anton was arrested for membership of the Communist Party, then regarded as a particular threat by Israel because it was the only party to operate across Israel and occupied Palestine. Anton was only released after frantic appeals by his family to the Jordanians, who in turn lobbied the Israeli authorities, stressing that his communism was social and had no political dimension.

Even with the arrests and military controls, the seventies are regarded as a Golden Age, at least compared with what came next. The 1977 Israeli election saw the collapse of the once dominant Labor party. Menachem Begin, the one-time leader of Betar in Poland, headed the new government. Begin came to Palestine in the early 1940s after defecting from General Anders' Polish Army of the Middle East. He went underground in Palestine, where he led terrorist attacks against the British army. Although settlements existed before 1977, Begin's victory marks the great sea change, the moment when Israel's politics and energy became almost entirely focused on colonizing new land at the expense of the Palestinians. Bethlehem was always a major focus of the settlement program. The first two—Gilo and Kfar Etzion—were built in Bethlehem and, today, almost a quarter of the 800,000 settlers live within the Bethlehem governorate. There are settlements and factories on the Dead Sea shore, including the Ahava cosmetics plant, straddling the outlet of the Kidron Stream which brings the raw sewage from East Jerusalem. But most of the settlements lie on the ringroad around the city.

Begin might have been Israel's prime minister, but he was not the founder of the winning party, Likud. This was the brainchild of an Israeli soldier-turned-politician named Ariel Sharon, who negotiated an alliance between squabbling right-wing parties in the mid-1960s. Sharon was well known by the Palestinians of the West Bank. In 1953, he had led a massacre by three hundred Israeli troops in Qibya, a Palestinian city then under Jordanian rule. Sharon's written orders to his troops stated they were to "carry out the maximal killing and damage to property." His forces blew up fifty homes and killed at least sixty-nine unarmed civilians. In return for masterminding Likud's victory in 1977, Sharon demanded a free hand in the West Bank. His master plan was to bypass Palestinian civil society, especially the mayors, which he regarded as PLO operatives. He divided the West Bank into seven districts and set up a new body called the Village Leagues, staffed by Palestinian collaborators. The head of the Bethlehem League was Bishara Qumsiyeh, who in addition was appointed Deputy Head of the Leagues in the West Bank. Although Qumsiyeh was answerable to the Israeli military, he had unique powers to issue building and travel permits. Selling the permits became a considerable source of revenue. In November 1981, the leader of the Ramallah district Village League, Yousef Khatib, was ambushed and murdered by Palestinian militants. Sharon responded by authorizing the arming of the Village Leagues as a paramilitary force. At its peak, four hundred Palestinian collaborators were trained by the Israeli army and permitted to carry guns. The Bethlehem force was led by Qumsiyeh's four sons, who were notorious for handing out beatings, as well as destroying cars and property.

The period saw a war against the Palestinian mayors, who were arrested, deposed, and murdered. A Jewish terror group led by an American named Meir Kahane carried out coordinated attacks on three West Bank mayors in May 1980. Two of the mayors were severely injured; the third bomb injured an Israeli soldier who was checking the mayor's car. A bomb was planted beneath Freij's car, though it was discovered before it exploded: this was not why Freij was so fragile, I later learned. When I met him he was almost eighty, and was unused to strangers manhandling him while shaking his hand.

Qumsiyeh and his sons were arrested by the Israelis and charged with planting the bomb, and ultimately convicted of violent offenses. Qumsiyeh received a two-year sentence while his sons' sentences ranged from three to eighteen months. Qumsiyeh did not serve the full sentence, and was soon promoted to head the West Bank Village League. His eldest son took over as boss of the Bethlehem League. They were still in their positions when the Village Leagues were wound up in 1988 during the Palestinian revolt known as the Intifada.

The army took direct control of Bethlehem during the Intifada. The revolt began in 1987 with a strike by students in Bethlehem. In 1988, the Israelis shut the universities, and they remained closed for five years, to Anton's acute personal pain. The Intifada saw Palestinian civil society organize strikes and demonstrations and create militant organizations, while also continuing to run the basics of a Palestinian welfare state. The Intifada led directly to the Oslo Accords and ultimately the establishment of the Palestinian Authority.


AS FAR BACK AS THE 1980S, Ronald Reagan proposed a deal for Palestinian self-government. Prime Minister Begin rejected the suggestion without discussing it with his cabinet or even the US president. In 1991, Begin's heir, the Likud prime minister, Yitzhak Shamir, announced the creation of a new settlement around Har Gilo, a military listening post above the Cremisan Monastery. In a letter, President George Bush asked Shamir to either cease settlements or make other substantive offers that would underpin serious negotiations. Shamir, like his predecessor Begin, dismissed the president's letter. It was, he said, "merely the expression of a wish." Bush responded by turning up the heat. He threatened Shamir that the US would withhold guarantees for $10 billion worth of loans that Israel was seeking to raise from banks and the international markets. Bush cited the fact that such loans were likely to be used for settlements, and this was contrary to US policy. Shamir relented, allowed Israeli negotiators to attend the Madrid Conference, but lost the subsequent election. The elections brought Labor back to power under Prime Minister Yitzhak Rabin, one of the men responsible for signing the Oslo Accords.

Oslo had rejectionists on both sides, but the rejectionists came with different agendas and ideas, while the dealmakers were clear about what peace meant: two states based on the Jordanian-Israel Armistice Line of 1949. It was likely that territorial concessions would be made, and the granting of these would encompass concessions on other issues, such as the Right of Return of stateless Palestinian families living as refugees around the world. All these issues could expect to be met with help and aid from the international community, if a deal was made.

No deal was made.

Any assessment of the failure of Oslo has to reckon with the killing of its chief Israeli architect, Yitzhak Rabin, in November 1995. The murderer, Yigal Amir, was part of organized right-wing circles and had not acted alone: his accomplices were also convicted. The view of rejectionists like Amir—that the Palestinian territory can never be negotiated away—was fully reflected in the anti-Oslo rallies staged in Israel. It is a position that shuts down any possibility of Palestinians' autonomy and statehood.

The fact that the murderer of Rabin was neither a loner nor a fantasist reflects the political reality in Israel: the rejectionists may not be a majority, and may not agree when violence is appropriate, but they are part of the mainstream. And because they are part of the mainstream, no Israeli politician will ever make a deal with the Palestinians. I am not saying that Israeli politicians lack personal courage. They are scared in another sense: they do not believe that there is any possible deal that can be put before the Israeli public, without further fracturing the society and punishing the party and the politician responsible. In recognition of this, international politicians have retreated from making the kind of substantive threats that Bush used to push Shamir into negotiations. Instead, Israeli politicians have been treated with kid gloves, which can seem tantamount to rewarding the people responsible for the collapse of Oslo.

The knowledge that no Israeli politician will support negotiations has become part of the framework of the problem. There are only so many possible responses. In fact, there are probably only three. The first is that the international community can find a way to cajole Israel into making a deal, a position that is always portrayed as saving Israel from itself (which is as patronizing as it sounds, yet true). Or an Israeli politician can offer an alternative solution that does not require speaking to the Palestinians, which was Ariel Sharon's tactic through the Village Leagues of the seventies and eighties, and continued with his unilateral actions during his premiership of 2000-2006. The third strategy is to do nothing, which the present Prime Minister Benjamin Netanyahu has perfected into a highly aggressive art form.

# CHAPTER 11

# PALESTINE

## *After Oslo*

*Bethlehem wall with graffiti depicting
Leila Khaled.*

I ask Boulos if we can use his wife's car to tour the villages around Bethlehem. Ieva bought the car in Israel, and with Israeli plates it can be driven on settler roads—though not with Boulos at the wheel. He asks if I know how to drive a stick shift. I assure him that I can handle his wife's car. Then once I take the wheel, I grind the gears so badly that the smile freezes on his face.

As lunchtime approaches, we are outside the village of Beit Fajjar wondering about the quality of their bakeries. The huge tin sheds of Migdal Oz settlement, a factory farm specializing in turkeys and cattle, dominate the high ground above the village. The road descends in a gentle curve with Beit Fajjar on one side and a series of stone quarries on the other. I get out of the car to take a photograph. The wind feels different, less dry, changeable. The breeze is strong enough to swirl the fine particles of stone dust in the air. The previous day, I had visited a stonemason on the outskirts of al-Khader, and I wanted to see where the ten-tonne cubes of limestone came from. Stone from Bethlehem in the form of paving slabs and tile cladding pretty much covers the entire built environment of Jerusalem. The quarries are deep welts that look white against the desert. The quarry conveyor belts are shrouded in dust. Living in Beit Fajjar would be a kind of hell, I think, but I wear contact lenses. There is clearly work here. The average unemployment rate in the Bethlehem district is 27 percent, and in the most remote villages, such as Nahalin, youth unemployment runs at ninety percent. In comparison, Beit Fajjar feels like a comparatively wealthy town.

We reach the center of the village to find the streets have filled with schoolkids on their lunch break. They walk three and five abreast, so we have to crawl along the main street. The girls are wearing the distinctive blue and white striped smocks with white cotton collars.

The PA runs Palestinian schools. Oslo brought the exiled PLO leaders back to Palestine, all of them veterans of wars in Jordan and Lebanon. They had little familiarity with the administration of hospitals, schools, and social welfare. Unlike Palestinian civil society, which had previously run so much of the country, they were less sensitive to democracy, less keen on committees, more used to giving and receiving orders. They were now charged with creating a government that would sit above civil society, and in many ways supplant it. The friction began immediately, and was always portrayed as "insiders" versus "outsiders." The conflict flared around issues of corruption by the men from abroad.

The most spectacular example of government corruption I came across was in the summer of 1996. We were in the kitchen of the Sansour home when Leila's cousin Carol arrived in a temper. A story had broken that the new education minister had ruled that every child in Palestine had to buy uniforms from a single manufacturer in Greece. Anton's brother, Tawfik, Carol's father, ran a small sock factory in a single-storey cinder-block building behind his home in Beit Jala, and there were other textile factories across Palestine. There was no reason to source school uniforms from elsewhere. It made no sense. Then it was discovered that the schools' min-

ister actually owned the Greek factory. The scandal was the talk of Bethlehem but when the directive was overturned, the story fizzled out and I
forgot about it. Only the sight of the Beit Fajjar schoolgirls brings it back.
The children remind me of photographs of Leila, her sister Larissa, and her
cousins, Carol, Vivien, and Nadira when they were schoolchildren, wearing these same uniforms. Writing about the scandal twenty years later, I
wish I could find the damning paper trail. I know that the PA commissioned a report into government corruption in 1996, and this was delivered in July 1997. The report pointed to $326 million that appeared to be
missing from the PA's overall budget of $800 million, and also identified
three ministers as corrupt. President Arafat sat on the report for a year,
until 1998, and then he chose to retain the three criticized ministers, PLO
veterans. He also demoted the two ministers who had agitated most
strongly for the report: Hanan Ashrawi and Abdul Jawad Saleh, both insiders. Ashrawi and Saleh resigned in protest. Though I find nothing about
the school uniform scandal, I discover, tellingly, that the president only
sacked one minister: the minister for schools.

Arafat's 1998 cabinet reshuffle represented an irreparable rupture between civil society and the PA. The ill feeling has barely diminished, a
quarter of a century later. Yet the issue of insiders and outsiders is not as
cut and dried as it is often portrayed. The returning PLO officers were not
necessarily uncritical of Arafat. They often had their own agendas and
power base. Bethlehem's Saleh Taamari had been captured and imprisoned
in the Israeli invasion of Lebanon in 1982, and became the leader of all the
prisoners in South Lebanon's Israeli jails. He arrived back in Palestine in
1996, several years after other PLO leaders because Israel had dragged out
the process of permitting his return. He forged his own base, both in the
Ta'amareh and in the Prisoners' Society. Taamari was critical of many as-
pects of the PA, and even critical of Arafat. He won a seat as a Legislative
Council member, and in 2004, became the governor of Bethlehem.

If Arafat had rivals among the returning outsiders, he also had close
associates among the insiders. Indeed, his cabinet was equally split between PLO officers and local representatives. However, his choices were
rarely drawn from the circles of civil society. Arafat preferred to appoint
businessmen. The fact that he turned to financiers and technocrats over
social organizers may have seemed like a betrayal, but he is not the only

political leader to favor businessmen over activists. His cabinet picks no doubt reflected Arafat's belief that money was power. While he was alive, the entire Palestinian budget went through his hands.

The PA income derives largely from foreign aid, and from Palestinian tax revenues gathered by Israel. Withholding the tax revenues has become a tool Israel uses to exert pressure on Palestine. The irregularity of the payments is part of the reason that the PA is always in financial straits and struggles to pay the wages of state employees like teachers and municipal workers, the security forces, and its own officers. Since the creation of the PA, the term civil society tends to be reserved for non-governmental organizations (NGOs), and while these bodies also often face funding crises, their money comes from charitable organizations, or is won by applying for niche foreign aid funds. This gives the NGOs a source of money independent of the PA, and means that they exert a kind of internal "brain drain" on the Palestinian state. NGOs can offer bright graduates more secure wages, more autonomy and varied work, and less political oversight than the PA ministries.

The PA is often charged with being a tool of the occupation, as well as being corrupt. These charges are particularly strong in Bethlehem, a dissenting town. Bethlehem's NGOs are filled with capable men and women from a generation that, thanks to the closure of Palestinian universities, were largely educated abroad. In a sense, of course, they are right: the PA is nothing but a tool of the occupation. The Oslo Accords led to the creation of the Palestinian Authority specifically to offer limited self government to a people under hostile military occupation, a unique situation. I doubt there is a worse job in politics than being the president of Palestine.

Stories of flagrant corruption, like the school uniform affair, are rare. Palestinian government accounts are now transparent and published online. A culture of secrecy has ended. When anyone speaks about corruption today, they really mean nepotism, not embezzlement or theft. Jobs for loyalty is an ever-present feature of Palestinian political life. As the PA loses popularity, it must buy support with jobs. By the late 1990s, Arafat's problem was that his administration was tied to the peace process and the process was over. There was no longer the kind of optimism that would allow the PA to issue government bonds, lure investors, and even remotely dream of one day raising money through income tax. Arafat could no longer hope to please all the people, and so his reaction was to please those closest to him. He shored up his base, the Fatah party.

The process of turning the PLO into the PA had always encouraged nepotism. The pre-Oslo PLO was an international talking shop, an unwieldy pseudo-parliament riddled with placemen who were sponsored by unsavory Arab regimes like Syria and Iraq. After Oslo, it seemed like smart politics to supplant the PLO with the PA, but this inevitably led to the promotion of a single core party. As state income in Palestine declined, and the hope of delivering peace stretched further away, Fatah's habit of rewarding loyalists became something else: a sign of desperation. Fatah is by far the largest political organization in Palestine; but its popularity is fragile, and patronage is the only way it can reward members and instill discipline. However, giving jobs to family members diminishes the quality of government, increases resentment, and fuels the brain drain to the NGOs. Fatah is also constrained to employ loyalists for another, knottier reason. The party controls the security forces, which provide a police force for Palestinians, as well as offering security guarantees to Israel. The government needs to know that these forces are loyal, especially in the bad times when the government's appeal is at its weakest.

Palestinians have an ingrained anti-elitist streak. This may be the result of a long history of dealing with foreigners who are not as smart as they think they are, or it may be another legacy of the Palestinian Revolution, where everyone is equal and decisions are made by consensus. Either way, anyone in authority is likely to see intense and sustained criticism. The irony is that Fatah represents this popular leftist attitude as much as any other organization: it is the party of the fedayeen, after all! Yet because Fatah actually is in authority, it can never hope to satisfy the popular demands it encourages. A free and equal society is out of reach, partly because of poverty, partly from incompetence and nepotism, but always chiefly because it is running against the weight of the Israeli occupation. This track record of failure makes Fatah's left-wing populism vulnerable to a new populism from the right, from its Islamist rival Hamas.

Everything Fatah does, it does with an eye on Hamas. The Islamic Party is an offshoot of Egypt's Muslim Brotherhood. It was formed as a charity in Gaza in 1974 by the cleric Sheikh Ahmed Yassin. Israel endorsed Yassin's charity in 1979, funding it directly through Palestinian tax receipts.

This happened in parallel with Ariel Sharon's Village Leagues, and the principle was the same. Rather than hand tax receipts to the existing mayors and town councils to fund municipal schools, Israel chose to hand money to Yassin's group to fund religious schools and welfare charities. When the Intifada broke out in 1987, Yassin formed Hamas as a militant anti-Israel organization. Yassin authored the notoriously anti-Semitic Hamas charter that repudiates his once-close links to Israel.

Hamas began a terror campaign in the mid-nineties now best remembered for suicide bombings. There were four bombings in the run-up to the Israeli elections of 1996, between the end of February and the beginning of March. The elections were called after Rabin's murder, and Labor started out with a twenty-point lead. The bombings soon cut it down. Netanyahu had become Likud leader in 1993, and he led the party to a surprise victory with a single-seat lead. Once in government, he resisted any movement in the peace process, failed to implement the few deals he signed up to, and devised a policy of refusing to negotiate with preconditions, which effectively suspended the Oslo Accords. His administration lasted three years, falling in 1999 when Netanyahu faced corruption charges for influence peddling.

Labor returned to power under a new prime minister, Ehud Barak. He governed at the head of an unstable coalition, but adopted a proactive, swaggering approach to the peace process, which resulted in fresh negotiations at Camp David in 2000. These talks failed. Although Barak's coalition government was falling apart, the Camp David talks were followed in January 2001 by new talks at the Red Sea resort of Taba, in Egypt. These also failed: this time because a looming general election meant that the Israeli negotiators had to abruptly pull out. US President Clinton, the sponsor of the talks, was also running out of time as he made way for his successor, President George W. Bush.

In the Israel elections of 2001, Barak went on the offensive by rehashing the negotiations at Camp David, absolving himself of blame for their failure. He campaigned on the basis that Arafat had rejected all offers, thereby killing the peace process. Clinton was edging out of the White House, but issued a statement backing Barak's false story in the hope that this would improve Barak's fortunes at the polls. Arafat was branded a rejectionist, and though other negotiators from both the Israeli and the

American teams would later strongly refute the Barak/Clinton account, in the heat of an Israeli election campaign a narrative was framed that Arafat had rejected the best deal Palestine could ever expect, and instead had chosen to embrace terror. This narrative did nothing to help Barak, but more than suited the Likud leader, a revitalized Ariel Sharon. He had returned after twenty years in the political cold and was also campaigning on the basis that the peace process was bogus. With both sides agreeing that the peace process was a fraud, the Israeli public naturally chose the candidate who had never believed in it, over the self-confessed dupe Barak. Sharon won by a landslide.

Barak's account of the peace process has colored opinion about Arafat ever since. One of the most interesting and dynamic political leaders of the twentieth century is remembered for a story cooked up by a desperate politician in an election he could not hope to win. But worse than tainting Arafat's reputation, the story killed the peace process. By painting the Palestinian leadership as untrustworthy and violent, Barak and Clinton absolved any future Israeli politician of taking negotiations seriously again. Sharon never had any intention of negotiating. He became prime minister as the Second Intifada was growing in intensity, bringing protests and violence from the Palestinians, and crackdowns and shootings from the army.

If any single event was responsible for kick-starting the Second Intifada, it was Sharon's visit to the al-Aqsa Mosque in Jerusalem, the previous September 2000. Any visit by an Israeli leader to the compound of the al-Aqsa Mosque is sensitive and is strictly controlled by Israeli law. Sharon did not enter alone: a security force numbering a thousand policemen accompanied him. The visuals were everything: it looked like Sharon was bringing an army to invade the mosque compound. In case anyone missed the point, Sharon gave a triumphal speech declaring the site would remain forever in Israeli hands. A few years previously, the decision to open a tunnel beneath the mosque had led to three days of rioting in Jerusalem. Sharon knew his mini-invasion would lead to violence, and this became his route to becoming prime minister.

The Second Intifada was a dark and violent disaster. My mother-in-law, Raissa Sansour, was a widow, living alone in the family home in Bethlehem. In October 2001, Israelis shelled the nearby Deheisha refugee camp. On March 5, 2002, an Israeli F-16 warplane bombed Bethlehem's government buildings, across the road from her home. The force of the explosion ripped the roof off the house and buckled all of the metal roll-down shutters. The shutters on the side of the house facing the explosion were blown inwards, while those on the far side were buckled outwards, as the force of the explosion passed through the entire building. I have no idea how Raissa coped. She was a Russian from the war generation and would never think of sharing fears or anxieties.

Leila and I came to Bethlehem and lived there through most of that year. The Israeli bombings and invasions were punctuated by suicide attacks. Since the 1990s, the real target of Hamas's suicide bombing was Fatah; or so I felt. Hamas did not believe they could effect any change in Israel, they were only competing to represent populist discontent in Palestine. As the situation descended in to out-and-out violence, militant leaders associated with Fatah responded. In Bethlehem, cadres established by Fatah militants took up positions on the hillside above Beit Jala and shot at Gilo across the valley. They even posed for Bethlehem TV. In Bethlehem's tiny TV station, in a studio above a lingerie shop, I saw footage of a beefy kid holding the kind of chain gun that is usually mounted on an armored personnel carrier. He was showing off that he could wield the gun like a rifle. The nightly shootings brought return fire, helicopter attacks, and army incursions.

A militant Fatah leader in Bethlehem's Deheisha refugee camp crossed a line and began recruiting suicide bombers. I remember the shock around Bethlehem on March 29, 2002, when we learned that a girl from the camp, eighteen years old and an "A" student, had blown herself up close to the Malha mall. This seemed to me proof that the terror campaign had become an exercise in arms escalation between Fatah's militias and Hamas. It was emotional blackmail, waged on Palestinian society to win popular support. The point of the deaths was not to intimidate Israel. It was all about the posters commemorating the dead boys and girls that were plastered around town after each death. As the Israeli revenge attacks increased in savagery, the status of the dead youth rose. The mood was that they had responded to Israel's violence with sacrifice. It was an arms race that only Hamas could win, because it had no social or international responsibilities, unlike the governing Fatah, which was being pulled toward its destruction.

Against a backdrop of a United Nations Security Council (UNSC) resolution asking Israel to show restraint, and a conference of Arab ministers that produced a widely praised document—The Arab Peace Initiative—offering full recognition to Israel, the Israeli army invaded the West Bank. On the eve of the invasion, Arafat offered an immediate and unconditional ceasefire. The Israeli government responded by declaring Arafat an enemy, and surrounding his compound in Ramallah. Clinton and Barak's false claims that Arafat was the man who had killed the peace process led to this: an elderly man imprisoned in squalid unsanitary conditions, the water and heating cut off, surrounded by his closest cadre. He survived for two years, dying on November 11, 2004.

The invasion of Ramallah took place on Good Friday. On Easter Monday, I attended a demonstration in Bethlehem among a mixed crowd of foreigners and Palestinians. An Israeli gunner perched on his APC fired shots. People around me in the crowd began to fall as shrapnel, which hit the road in front of us, began to ricochet into bodies. I saw the BBC war correspondent cowering behind her car as bullets raked the asphalt around her. I went to the hospital with one of the most badly wounded demonstrators, where shrapnel was removed from her abdomen.

That evening, Bethlehem was invaded. We were woken by Apache helicopters swooping over the house and the sound of shelling in the direction of the Deheisha refugee camp. A wire-guided missile punched a large hole in the side of Bethlehem University, and further missiles were used in the souk area. The fighting was concentrated around the Church of the Nativity, as we learned two days later: a hundred and fifty men, which included fighters, neighborhood locals, and Bethlehem policemen, had taken refuge inside the church. The Israeli army sat in for a long siege.

During those weeks, I twice tried to approach the church with a group of the same foreigners who had been shot at. The souk area smelled of rotting food. Meat and vegetables had been locked in cold stores before the electricity was shut off. In the windows of the hoshes above me, children peeked to see who was on the street. They were confined to their houses for weeks. Both of my attempts to bring food to the church ended with the army turning us back. I thought I would do my bit by volunteering to ride on ambulances, because there was nothing I could do for the people in the church. After I had given up, a small group of foreigners not only made it to the church, they also entered and stayed inside for the entire siege.

The Israelis suspended a shipping container over the Church of the Nativity, using a crane. This became a sniper post. Shots were fired through the roof, and the snipers also covered the open space between the basilica and the only cistern in the complex. At least one person was shot trying to get water. Arafat appointed Saleh Taamari as the lead negotiator, as the senior PA figure in Bethlehem and a leader of the PPS. Taamari set out an uncompromising position, refusing to countenance exile for anyone in the church. As a result, he was swiftly deposed by Arafat. The eventual deal was brokered at an international level. Thirteen Palestinian militants were taken by British transporter plane to Cyprus to be resettled in third-party countries. Another twenty-six were sent into internal exile in Gaza, and eighty-four civilians were freed.

The first Palestinian parliamentary elections following the Israeli invasions only came in 2006 and were a disaster for Fatah. The party was so disorganized and so incapable of instilling discipline in its local committees that it often ran competing candidates against each other. As Fatah split its own vote, it opened the way for a Hamas victory. In Gaza, Hamas was emboldened by winning an election, and there was a military standoff over who had the right to control the security forces. Hamas defeated Fatah's military forces, and it has ruled Gaza ever since. In the West Bank, Hamas is largely underground. Mayor Elias Freij had retired in 1997, replaced by the tall and courtly Hana Nasser: "Hana" is Arabic for John. Nasser chose not to contest the Bethlehem municipal elections of 2004, in which Hamas members ran as independents. Fatah hoped for a win, but the results delivered a divided council, and the combined independents chose the non-Fatah candidate, Dr. Victor Batarseh, a precise and dapper seventy-one-year-old GP. Batarseh had run for council with the backing of the PFLP and its supporters. During his time in office, the foreign aid needed to rebuild Bethlehem after the invasion was frozen because of the role of Hamas in his elevation to mayor. A Fatah mayor, Vera Baboun, was finally returned in the elections of 2012. She is the first woman to run Bethlehem since St. Paula.

# CHAPTER 12

# THE FUTURE FOR
# THE SETTLERS

*Tunnel Road, seen from Gilo
settlement looking towards Beit Jala.*

Bethlehem sits within a doughnut of Israeli settlements called the Gush Etzion block. The name comes from Kfar Etzion, the first West Bank settlement, established in the wake of the 1967 war to secure Jerusalem's water supply. The Israeli engineers chose to bypass the two-thousand-year-old aqueduct through Bethlehem by drawing water straight from the Ain Faghour spring. Although the settlement was a civil engineering project, it was claimed to be an act of memorial and vengeance for the May 1948 deaths at Kfar Etzion. The principle of revenge has been a key feature of Israeli policy in Palestine. To claim the right to avenge an event a generation earlier suggests that wrongs never fade. The more so as a massacre carried out in the Hebron village of al-Dawayima in October 1948 was also justified on the basis of the killings at Kfar Etzion. The same Betar forces responsible for the Deir Yassin massacre carried out al-Dawayima, after they were folded into the Haganah's 8th Battalion. To recommit to revenge endlessly like this suggests that every injury is an open wound that must be repaid indefinitely, wherever possible, by as many people as possible, in a constantly growing crescendo. Is this the future for the settlers?

In 1967, Kfar Etzion contained a few homes adjacent to an army base. It began to grow after the 1977 victory by Betar's veteran commander, Menachem Begin, at the head of the Likud party. It now makes up thirty-four of the forty-two settlements around Bethlehem (See Appendix for the full list). In practice, Gush Etzion comprises two separate blocks: Gush Etzion West and Gush Etzion East—or, to put it more plainly, hills and desert. The older and larger settlements in the western area lie close to the Green Line. The communities here have seen their homes increasingly integrated into Israel by new roads, public works, and improvements to the train line, which they live along. The settlers on the eastern, desert side of Bethlehem, by contrast, were always somewhat less integrated, and the desert and the remoteness has attracted more ideological settlers. By building their homes on the far side of two hundred thousand Palestinians, the settlers have calculated that there is no easy way of absorbing their homes into Israel. To live in these settlements, you have already gambled that the whole of Palestine will one day be annexed to a single Jewish state with a permanent Palestinian underclass.

The Gush Etzion settlements, east and west, are joined by a ringroad that hugs the last houses in Bethlehem's built-up areas and effectively separates the city from its villages, farmland, and the desert. Pinned behind this road, Bethlehem is an open-air prison. To the west, the ringroad is reinforced by an eight-meter-high concrete wall. To the south and east, there are double rows of chainlink fences and stretches of gravel no-man's land.

By 1999, the Bethlehem area had fifty thousand settlers against a Palestinian population of 137,286. By 2008, Bethlehem's population had grown to 176,235, while settlers' numbers had leapt to between a hundred and twenty and a hundred and thirty thousand. These figures suggested the settlers could soon overtake the Palestinian community. This proved illusory. By 2016, the settler numbers stood at a hundred and forty-two thousand while Bethlehem had grown to two hundred and ten thousand.

The settlements continue to expand. There are plans to build more, but it is certain that Jewish Israelis will never form a significant majority in the West Bank. Living in Gush Etzion East remains a political gamble. The Israeli government is committed to expanding settlements, but the areas marked for expansion are close to the Green Line and Jerusalem, with easy access to Israel's infrastructure and without the militant "settlement feel" of Gush Etzion East with its armed guards, gate houses, and Palestinian workers who, by law, must be supervised by armed Jewish overseers. The government plans mark out lands around Wadi Fuqin and al-Walajeh for expansion, for instance. They are also currently building close to Jerusalem, in Givat Hamatos and Gilo, which, so far as many Israelis are concerned, are already a part of the city's sprawl. The historian and one-time deputy mayor of Jerusalem Meron Benvenisti argues that what seems like ideologically driven movement is nothing of the sort. As he succinctly puts it: the settlements are a "commercial real estate project that conscripts Zionist rhetoric for profit."

The land on which the new homes stand costs nothing, making the developers' overheads the lowest in the world. The new homes are offered with generous mortgage subsidies, which benefit Israel's domestic banking sector. The cheap homes underpin a troubled sector rather more effectively than the quantitative easing recently practiced in the UK and America. The settlement project eases the money supply in the domestic banking sector, to the benefit of Israel's blue-collar families, the people who missed out on the boom years in hi-tech weaponry, software, and computer systems that enriched Israel's elite. As long as the domestic economy is propped up by real estate and cheap mortgages, any attempt to cut the supply of new homes risks a financial crisis that would rebound on the government.

Which is to say, the settlements are very much an old-fashioned colonial project. The committed settlers may not see it in those terms, but for Israel as a whole, the West Bank is a credit bank: it supplies the juice that keeps the economy just about working for the poorer citizens, also often core Likud voters. The West Bank is all about natural resources: vacant lots rather than the diamonds or petroleum of more familiar colonial projects. This is why real estate millionaires are so well represented among donors to Israeli political parties. This is not limited to Israeli businessmen—it includes French and American donors, including US President Donald Trump. Trump may be derided as an inexperienced politician, yet it is possible that he sees the occupation more clearly than his predecessors.

THE OCCUPATION IS unbelievably baroque. It is governed by a civil authority that answers to a military authority, both of which coexist with a council of settlers (known as the Yesha Council). It operates according to various contradictory legal codes (Ottoman, British, Israeli civil, and Israeli military), and it is all subject to military secrecy. This complexity is nowhere more apparent than in Bethlehem, with its bypasses, tunnels, and fly-overs designed to keep Jewish settlers and Bethlehemites apart. There are different water and electric pipes to ensure that only Palestinians suffer outages. Even the microwave bands that fill the air are segregated, keeping the telecommunications separate so the listening post at Har Gilo can tune into everything Bethlehem says.

At every level, from deep underground to high above our heads, this system of separation delivers a comfortable lifestyle to the Jewish community, and a harsher and crueler life to the Palestinians. The Dutch South African word "apartheid" means "separation," and Israel has always described the system of control in the West Bank as separation; the official Israeli term for the wall, for instance, is "separation barrier." Using the term apartheid is often regarded as provocative, which means that it is difficult to compare what is happening in the West Bank to anything similar. If it cannot be described, the problem is that no one ever quite understands what it is—and we become more willing to say: *ah, well, yes, but I've heard it's complex.*

Yet the complexity masks a basic simplicity. As the Christmas 2016 United Nations Security Council resolution reaffirmed, the West Bank is under a hostile military occupation. This is as simple a situation as one can imagine: an army occupies territory as a result of a war. It is not even illegal: it is simply a description of a situation. However, an occupation is governed by the rules of war, currently the Geneva Conventions. These conventions forbid a state from acquiring territory as a result of war, as well as from taking actions or profiting in ways that amount to ownership of the territory. The agreement between Israel and Jordan that established the Green Armistice Line, for instance, states that any decision on the Palestine question must be taken peaceably. In this document, Israel agreed not to preempt peaceful negotiations through warfare. Everything it is doing in the West Bank contradicts this agreement and others it has signed. Israel cannot build homes, it cannot move civilians into occupied territory, it cannot run businesses, organize holidays and tours, sell cosmetics, run call centers, breed turkeys, milk dairy cows, or sell tickets to archaeological sites. And this is before one considers the responsibilities of an occupying power toward the civilian population: it cannot deport them, demolish their homes, or use collective punishments.

The Fourth Geneva Convention was developed in response to Germany's conduct in the Second World War, in particular the invasion of Czechoslovakia. We often remember that the British Prime Minister Neville Chamberlain appeased the German invasion of Czechoslovakia, but we remember it without context and overlook that Chamberlain was far from alone in believing appeasement was acceptable. As Simon Winder details in his book *Germania*, the emergence of ethnic nationalism in nineteenth-century Europe led to a keen interest in ethnography. The idea that the cradle of German life lay in northern Czechoslovakia was embraced by practically all Germans, irrespective of their political allegiances, long before the Nazis came to power. In consequence, it was not only the Nazis who supported the annexation of the Sudetenland. It was a widely popular measure that felt like part of Germany was being brought home. Little wonder that Chamberlain was swayed into believing that annexing a largely German-speaking Czechoslovakian territory was a historical inevitability rather than a war crime.

More recently, we have seen Serbia declare that Kosovo is the cradle of Serbian ethnicity and nationhood, a belief that stretches back to the twelfth century. Russia has annexed Crimea on the grounds that it has a Russian speaking population and that it was an integral part of Russia from 1783 to 1954. The Serbian claim on Kosovo was rejected, and the Russian actions in Crimea continue to be condemned.

Many Israelis, and probably most settlers, feel their claim to the West Bank is not comparable to these cases. The claim takes three forms. The first is that Palestine is not occupied territory because it has never been independent and so has never been "owned." This is akin to claiming a penny found on the ground has no owner and so finders-keepers. Whether there is an owner or not, however, makes no difference to the situation: if the territory was acquired through war, then the civilian population is under a hostile military occupation; taking any steps that change the facts on the ground is illegal.

The second tack has been to claim that the legal situation has evolved over the course of the occupation; that the Balfour Declaration gave the Jewish state an interest in the West Bank as part of historic Palestine; that the decision by Jordan in 1988 to relinquish the mandate over the West Bank left the country without any competing claim other than the Palestinians; and that the 1993 Oslo Accords give legal validity to Israel's claims that the territory is disputed rather than occupied. This is a fancier version of the first argument, made more complex only because it is left vague as to what Israel is disputing. If Israel is disputing ownership of the territory with the Palestinians, this makes no difference: it is still a hostile occupation, the Palestinians are still civilians, and the Fourth Geneva Convention still holds. If they are only disputing a point of law as to whether Palestine is occupied or not, the dispute is one-sided: every member of the UN that has ever been canvassed agrees that Israel is a hostile occupying power. This is why the Christmas 2016 UNSC resolution was greeted with shock in Israel. The judgement cut the legs away from Israel's argument that the situation had evolved over time. The vote reminds Israel that nothing has changed and that the Fourth Geneva Convention will apply for as long as Israel fails to make peace.

Israel's third claim is that God gave the land to Jews alone. Whether this claim is supernatural or merely ancient, it constitutes an ancestral attachment to the land similar to the German claim to the Sudetenland, or to Serbia's claim to Kosovo. Again, this is not the view in Israel, where such comparisons are deemed offensive. The chief consequence of viewing the Israeli claim as unique, of course, is that the Palestinians are forbidden, *a priori*, from making the same claim. The Palestinian claim to the land is as ancient and as deep as any connection to any homeland, by any people, anywhere, but it is all but impossible to make this claim within Israel.

I AM NOT SURE THAT ANYONE has ever changed their minds by recognizing points of legality or logic. No one, at least, when it comes to the Israeli Palestinian conflict. Nevertheless, I had long felt that I needed to hear a settler's point of view.

The opportunity comes unexpectedly.

I am driving Boulos along a stretch of the settler ringroad, colloquially known as the Lieberman Highway after Avigdor Lieberman, an Israeli minister who lives in Nokdim, one of the settlements arranged around Herodion like numbers on a clockface. An Israeli joke goes that the road was built to shave a half hour off Lieberman's journey to work, but in fact the highway plugged these desert settlements into Jerusalem's infrastructure for the first time, increasing the confidence of the settlers that they would never be forced to leave. Another minister, Ze'ev Elkin, lives in another Herodion settlement, Kfar Eldad. Elkin's name is prominent in lists of politicians who are funded by real estate developers.

This is a week after I visited Mount Herodion, and I have returned because I want a second look at Wadi Khreitoun, the valley where the Ain Sakhri lovers were found. I can see the mouth of the wadi, but not how to enter. Neither can Boulos. A road sign directs sightseers to the settlement of Tekoa. The settlers' homes are laid out in a series of concentric rings, as though the hill has been squeezed in the coils of a dragon. As I park at the settlement gatehouse, I assume Boulos is as nervous as I am. Although Israelis can be wonderful friends, all my dealings with settlers have been horrible. In Hebron, a woman rushed across a street to spit in my face and scream "Nazi"; a pistol was pushed against my forehead when I was trying to calm a boy at a demonstration. So I am worried when I see a young man with a gun emerge from the gatehouse.

Of course, he is the nicest guy you could imagine.

He examines my passport and Boulos's ID. After asking if Boulos has a permit to enter the settlement, he tells us he doubts we will be allowed in. Yet he says he will talk to his boss. In the meantime, he invites us for coffee. We stand beneath a canopy outside his hut while he heats the kettle and waits for his boss to return his call. He examines our clothes and suggests we aren't dressed for caving. I am wearing jeans and a shirt; Boulos is in shorts and sandals. Apparently we need boots, flashlights, and helmets, because the caves run for miles underground. The guard is in his mid-twenties and was born in Tekoa, so he has been exploring the caves all his life.

I ask if it is possible to reach the Dead Sea through the wadi. It is not easy, he tells me, and as it will soon be night, I will need to read the stars because the GPS is unreliable. I ask how he learned to navigate by the stars.

"Five years in the fucking army."

He has a scar on his neck, the legacy of the last invasion of Gaza in 2014. I don't ask how it happened. Perhaps I ought to, but I prefer to self-censor. The war was purportedly a crackdown on Hamas after the kidnapping and murder of three Israeli teenagers by two men from Hebron, aged twenty-nine and thirty-two. The connection between the kidnappers and the Hamas organization in Gaza was never satisfactorily established, and the war left two thousand Palestinians dead, of which at least a quarter were civilians. The spirit of revenge saw a variety of responses to the killings. A group of settlers set up two new outposts close to Ma'ale Adumim. Six fans of Betar Jerusalem Football Club tortured and murdered a sixteen-year-old Palestinian boy. A government ministry instructed the army to seize 1.54 square miles of land by the Gevaot settlement, privately owned by Bethlehem families around Wadi Fuqin. The Minister of Industry Naftali Bennett stated this was "an appropriate Zionist response to murder," though the land was not owned by family of the kidnappers, nor by Hamas supporters, and was in Bethlehem rather than the kidnappers' hometown of Hebron. All these separate acts of vengeance came from different parts of Israeli society; none had any connection to the original crime, nor was there any coordination between the responses. It was all a kind of freelance activism, justified because rage and vengeance have no end. Except for Bennett's confiscation of the private land—that was just business.

I did not ask the guard about his part in the war. My ears prick up when he states the war "was shit: a piece of shit." He is disillusioned and intends to immigrate to the States. He is not sure for how long, perhaps forever, perhaps not.

I never ask his name, which is not very friendly of me. The truth is that I am taken by his openness, his warmth, his confidence, the fact that he looks rather like the French film star Romain Duris. Snarkily, I note in my head that it is easy to be confident with a Heckler & Koch submachine gun hanging from your shoulder. Boulos also has a bro-crush. He comes right out and tells the guard he has never met a settler like him before.

Later, Ieva reminds us that the late rabbi at Tekoa, Menachem Froman, was famous for his efforts to speak to Palestinian groups. He had a reputation as the sole eccentric liberal settler rabbi, and having decided that neither he nor the Palestinians were going anywhere, chose to open dialogue on his own. He died in March 2013. Our guard is acting in Froman's spirit.

As we finish the coffees, we get word back from his boss. We cannot enter the settlement. The guard is sorry, asks if we are hungry, and suggests we eat at his friend's restaurant in a nearby settlement, Sde Bar. He praises the view: "It's just clean, straight across the desert."

He uses the word clean another couple of times, I notice. He says that the desert is clean, and makes a gesture with his hands as though wiping crumbs off a table. He next uses the word when I ask if he believes that Tekoa settlement is on the site of the biblical site. He tells me, certainly. He has seen photographs from the 1930s, and the land was clean; he makes the gesture again. What he means is that the village currently named Tuqu' cannot be the original as it did not exist until recently. Where we stand, we are looking down on the village roofs, a mess of washing lines, water tanks, satellite dishes, and solar panels. The guard is right: the Ta'amareh Bedouin built the present-day Tuqu' quite recently. The village is a bit messy, true, but the settlement of Tekoa is in even less sympathy with the landscape, thanks to the snake coil of asphalt, and bright red roofs. Not to mention that it is built on the top of a hill in the middle of a fucking desert, rather than in the shade of a wadi like any sane town.

I might have told the guard that I believe the original Tuqu' lies under the remains of Eudocia's monastery. But Tekoa settlement is not about authenticity. It is about the view, the clean view. Settlers think about the physical space of Palestine in terms of the heights. The idea of "running to seize the hilltops," as Ariel Sharon instructed Israelis to do during the time of the Oslo Accords, is an old one in Israel. Militant settlers call themselves "hilltop youth." But this love of the heights is not an ancient tradition or even a Jewish tradition: it was invented by an English Christian, Dean Arthur Stanley who sought out the high spots to admire the scenery. Looking down from a height, Stanley was able to ignore the distractions of a living landscape and imagine that he was seeing a land that corresponded to the one described in his pocket Bible. He was deluded, yet his search never led him to actually destroy the real archaeology of Palestine. This is what has happened at Herodion, where layers of history have been wiped away to provide a blank slate on which a new archaeology can be written; in effect, a brand-new version of the past.

The settlements also destroy an exisiting landscape, and with even less sophistication than shown at Herodion. In his interviews, Menachem Froman always insisted that he loved the land. I don't want to second-guess what that meant to him, but I know that the land is never an abstract, empty concept. It is concrete, and the desert around Bethlehem was never clean or empty. From the earliest Natufian people, through shepherds, merchants, and bitumen traders, to boskoi, monks, and the desert fathers, to the people of Bethlehem's al-Anatreh quarter who came from Tuqu' in the eighteenth century, right up to the present-day Ta'amareh and settlers, the wilderness is always surprisingly busy. It is a place that people live. Palestine was never "clean." The urge to wish everything away reflects the desire of an immigrant to make a fresh start in a new landscape. History is an inconvenience when you are focused on starting over. This might be the unique attraction of the desert—the fact that it is bare enough to support our imaginary plans. The desert allows the settlers to reinvent themselves, and also to reinvent what it means to be a Jew.

One of the great ideas motivating Jewish migration to Palestine and Israel is the idea that life in the diaspora is demeaning. Prime Minister Netanyahu made play of this in his attack on the 2016 UNSC vote condemning the settlements. He said: "Enough of this exile mentality. There is no political wisdom to groveling . . . Other countries respect strong nations that stand up for themselves, and they do not respect weak countries that grovel and bow their heads." The old Jews in their exile will swallow the insults of the United Nations Security Council, Netanyahu is saying, but not so the new Jews of Israel. The problem is, if you reject history, even Jewish history, what exactly are you replacing the old ideas with? It often seems that the settlers are going crazy because they need to find an *unprecedented* project: that one act of vengeance that will leave an indelible mark. Among a people who were so recently at risk of extermination, that may feel like motivation enough to some.

Boulos asks our new friend to come visit Bethlehem. This is not a straightforward request. Sharon's 2000 government made it illegal for Israelis to enter Palestinian towns. There are large signs at the entrances telling Israelis that the law is for their own safety. Nevertheless, I tend to be angry if any of my Israeli friends refuse to visit me in Bethlehem. I tell them foreign Jews visit Bethlehem all the time: the Nativity Hotel hosted a conference of US Jewish peaceniks. And of course thousands of visitors pass through Bethlehem every day, so it is easy enough to blend in. However, while no Israeli has ever been kidnapped in Bethlehem, it is impossible to say it could never happen, at least because of the three teenagers who were murdered in Hebron in 2014.

Boulos must be thinking this, because he suggests that the guard pretend he is Spanish. After all, he *does* looks Spanish.

The guard says, "But I don't want to go as a Spaniard. I want to go as myself."

Of course he should go as himself. This is what the peace process should be about: freedom for everyone. But in another act of self-censorship, I don't ask what he means, exactly. Does he want to go as a Jew, or as an Israeli, or as a settler? Presumably, he means as a neighbor from Tekoa. Boulos can only enter Tekoa with a work permit, supervised by a man with a gun and I doubt our new friend would enter Bethlehem under those conditions. But the chief problem of talking in terms of neighbors is that it is impossible to imagine a neighborly relation with the settlements, because they are conceived as violent acts, as acts of vengeance. They only exist as part of a hostile government project to seize land and build apartments with no reference to anyone, least of all the legal owners. How do you begin to talk about neighbors and neighborhoods in that context?

# CHAPTER 13

# THE FUTURE FOR BETHLEHEM

*Nation Estate*

Until recently, villagers in Husan, Beit Fajjar, Nahalin and Wadi Fuqin would gravitate toward Jerusalem rather than Bethlehem. This is where they shopped after attending al-Aqsa mosque on the religious holidays. The villages may be part of the Bethlehem district, but no one necessarily saw Bethlehem as a center. For almost twenty years, however, Jerusalem has been closed to the West Bank, and a generation has grown up that has rarely visited Jerusalem—in many cases, has never visited it at all. Bethlehem is a substitute and its shops and mosques a new focal point. On weekends and feast days, the town is packed with rural villagers, which has left Bethlehemites feeling squeezed and complaining that they no longer recognize their town.

Over the past seven centuries, Bethlehem has developed its own culture, somewhat in a bubble. It is a bit posh, quite Christian, and filled with impossible-seeming contradictions. It is insular yet international, educated and open yet capable of the worst small-town snobbery. It is a town of shopkeepers, natural conservatives, yet it sympathizes with the populism and anti-elitism of the radical left. The city has embraced the nationalist struggle, while keeping aloof from the political mainstream, favoring smaller parties like the PFLP and Communists rather than Fatah.

The influx of refugees in 1948 presented a challenge. It was resolved because the camps are self-governing, and so remain detached from the life of the town. The encroachment of the Ta'amareh as they gave up a semi-nomadic life and settled in urban areas also came with challenges. Nevertheless, Bethlehem is enriched by this mix, and the town is proud that it has found space for refugees from the Armenian and Syriac diasporas to the Nakba of 1948. Meanwhile, Bethlehem's older families have been granted special status. The PA reaffirmed the tradition that the mayor must be a Christian (as do the mayors of Beit Jala and Beit Sahour).

Bethlehem's Christians have always had opportunities to look for education and work abroad, which has encouraged emigration. Yet as long as their livelihoods have been rooted in tourism and in stone quarrying, the old families have retained a foot in Bethlehem even if their children are scattered around the world. Now, Bethlehem has a population of two hundred and ten thousand, but the Christians, concentrated in the triangle of Bethlehem, Beit Jala, and Beit Sahour, number only around fifty to sixty thousand, less than a quarter of the total. The people may share the anti-elitist streak of all Palestinians, yet they have also enjoyed a sliver of elitism, and I suspect that this has made the occupation bearable. In the past sixteen years, that sliver has melted away, and the bonds that hold the town together have dissolved with it. The wall, the settler bypass, and the constant build-up of pressure in town are close to killing something special.

BOULOS AND I CONTINUE our drive to Wadi Fuqin. Israel makes life difficult in the most isolated villages, and few are more isolated than Wadi

Fuqin. After 1948, the villagers fought through the UN to return to their homes, and they have seen Israel try again to expropriate their land as an "appropriate revenge" for the 2014 murder of the Israeli teenagers. The lack of resources, the lack of jobs, the power and water cuts—these all drive villagers out of the hills and into Bethlehem to look for work and to live with a little more freedom.

The village sits in a valley bottom, overshadowed by an unbroken line of apartment buildings that run along the top of the valley. This is the settlement of Beitar Illit, the largest settlement in the Gush Etzion block. Beitar Illit was established in 1985 by right-wing settlers, but was then identified by the government as a home for ultraorthodox Hasidic Jews. As the Hasidim community expanded, the original settlers moved out: a process that seems to happen a lot in Israel, and especially around Jerusalem. Many of the women work in a call center, which enables them to support their husbands in their lifelong study of the Talmud and Torah. In the shadow of the multistory apartment blocks, Wadi Fuqin is a sad kind of place. There is little to see but a row of polytunnels that stretches along the length of the wadi, and the village of dilapidated concrete houses. Boulos and I find a dog and spend time petting it. When I look up the breed later, I learn it is a Canaan dog. This is the breed domesticated by the sculptor of the Ain Sakhri lovers. It is now also the national dog of Israel.

The rain begins as we climb out of Wadi Fuqin. It is November 4, and this is the first shower in eight months. A long, hot summer has ground a patina of warm rubber and oil into the asphalt, and the rain makes the road surface greasy. On a hairpin turn, I stall as I let a truck pass, then find I have to do a hill start. I remember archaeologist Kay Prag's story about her driving test in Bethlehem: a hill start in her Land Rover. When I try it, the wheels spin furiously while I ride the clutch, which soon gives off an acrid burning smell. Boulos makes a strangled sound. This turns out to be a plea to take over the wheel.

With Boulos driving, we have to avoid the settler roads. We drive through the village of Husan, get lost, and then find a back route into Battir. It turns out to be the most marvelous stroke of luck, because as we enter the valley, the clouds above us billow gray and blue; light appears through the downpour. The steep-sided valley glows with a bright, luminous green. It is an unforgettable display of saturated depth and power. We both get out of the car, standing soaked as we stare in astonishment.

In Battir the rain is so hard that it runs down the steep road in a torrent. There's a small Roman bathhouse set in the valley wall. The rain has overflowed the cistern and is gushing down the terraces. Battir is the site of Bar Kokhba's last stand, the man condemned as the "son of lies" by Talmudic rabbis but now a national hero to Israelis, thanks to Ze'ev Jabotinsky's revival of awareness in him. Jabotinsky wrote a poem for Battir in 1932, an invocation of blood and cruelty that was immediately adopted as the anthem of the Betar Youth Movement.

BETAR (BATTIR)
*From the pit of decay and dust*
*With blood and sweat*
*Shall arise a race*
*Proud, generous and cruel*
*Captured Betar, Yodefet, Masada*
*Shall arise again in all their strength and glory*

We continue our long, circular journey back to Bethlehem through the orchards of al-Makhrour, where Anton Sansour's mother would spend her summers. There's a restaurant in a stone summerhouse, tucked into the folds of the hills. The owners have received notices threatening them with confiscation, but the restaurant is still open.

We return to overcrowded Bethlehem in rush hour. The roads are gridlocked. Boulos has promised to get the car back to Ieva, who has a night class at Bethlehem Bible College where she is training to be a tour guide. We have cut it too fine; we know we won't reach her in time. Hebron Road is choking with gas fumes and the rain-damp dust is leaving red streaks across the car windscreen. The minarets are playing the call-to-prayer too loudly, competing with each other for the newcomers from the villages. It is difficult to know the future, except that Bethlehem will become ever-more crowded, as the countryside empties and the residents move to town. The Israeli-Palestinian conflict has become a cipher for so many other conflicts, not simply triggers like East versus West, or Islam versus Christianity, but genuine political disagreements; the merits of national sovereignty over international law; of universal human rights against the right to self-determination. It is a binary world and most of us have already chosen our camps, so why struggle to see the world differently? In an odd way, we take comfort from the conflict when it really ought to shake us out of our complacency. We ought to adopt positions as stepping-stones to help us reach across the gulfs that divide us, rather than retreat into darkness and silence.

Mustafa, our Ta'amareh taxi driver, once gave Leila advice on the art of negotiations. He told her, in any dispute, you need to send your wise men, your idiots, and your crazies. The wise men are there to strike a deal that keeps everyone happy. The idiots are there to slow things down when one side is playing games and you need time to think. And the crazies are there to remind everyone of the consequences if you don't reach a deal. I am not sure whether this is good advice or not. But I know for sure that you cannot simply send your crazies.

Bethlehem has always been a place caught between worlds: hills and desert, nomads and town-dwellers, east and west, heaven and earth. When there are so many possibilities, there is every reason to hope that one of the possibilities might be a miracle. Bethlehem needs more space, more care, and above all it needs peace. Isn't this the point of the Pardes fable about Rabbi Akiva's visit to the garden? He didn't see that his job was to change what was there, but to understand it. To do that, he only had to enter in peace.

# Acknowledgments

Writing about a town that is so little known, yet the focus of so many deeply held hopes, aspirations, prejudices, and beliefs has not been easy. I have tried to be as clear and accurate as I can, though the results might seem at times to be tongue-tied and clumsy. I am grateful to my agent, Matthew Hamilton, and my editor, Alessandra Bastagli, for their confidence in bringing this work to life. I owe Alessandra a huge debt for her help in giving shape and focus to the story. I am also thankful for the care shown by the team at Nation Books, especially Marco Pavia and Katherine Haigler.

I had help from many historians and archaeologists, and hope I have not forgotten to thank anyone in the course of the text. But I want to express special thanks to Jacob Norris, who was generous in sharing his work on nineteenth and early twentieth century Bethlehem, to Raphael Cohen whose pertinent and challenging questions led to numerous revisions, and also to Felicity Cobbing at the Palestine Exploration Fund. I have been hard on the PEF as an historical institution. But Felicity has been tirelessly kind and helpful. As the PEF prepares for a new start in a new home in Greenwich, I wish it all the very best in the future.

My greatest debt is to the Sansour family. It has been a privilege to be part of the Sansour clan. I owe more than I can say to Leila, and a great deal to her sister and brother, Larissa and Maxim, to Soren Lind and Jacqueline Shoen, and to Carol, Nadira and Vivien Sansour, and to Andre Dabdoub.

I also want to thank Martin Delamere and Daisy Goodwin for reading early drafts, helping to clarify my thoughts and giving me the confidence that I was on the right tracks.

# APPENDIX

# *Settlements*

A list of the settlements that surround Bethlehem, with the date established and the current population, where known. Figures marked with an asterisk are estimates based on the number of families (assuming two parents and 2.5 kids).

## GUSH ETZION WEST

Beitar Illit (1985) population 49,343
Alon Shvut (1970) pop. 3,218
Bat Ayin (1989) pop. 1,226
Carmei Tzur (1984) pop. 1,036
Gevaot (1984) pop. 75*
Elazar (1975) pop. 2,577
Har Gilo (1968) pop. 1,474
Kfar Etzion (1967) pop. 1,071
Migdal Oz (1977) pop. 439
Neve Daniel (1982) pop. 2,275
Rosh Tzurim (1970) pop. 915

## GUSH ETZION WEST OUTPOSTS

Yeshivat Siach-Yitzakh (1995; reestablished as a Yeshiva in 1996) pop. n/a
Giv'at HaTamar (2001) pop. n/a
Sde Bo'az (2002) pop. n/a
Giv'at HaHish (1998) pop. n/a

Bat Ayin West (1999) pop. n/a
Bat Ayin East (2002) pop. n/a
Gavna (2001, as a restaurant) pop. n/a
Derech Ha'avot (2001) pop. n/a
Tzur Shalem (2001) pop. n/a

## GUSH ETZION EAST

Efrata (1983) pop. 8,300
Kedar (1984) pop. 1,490
Kfar Eldad (post-1982) pop. 400*
Ma'ale Amos (1981) pop. 384
Asfar or Metzad (1984). pop. 583
Nokdim (1982) pop. 1,937
Tekoa (1975) pop. 3,500
Herodion, tourist site, pop. n/a

## GUSH ETZION EAST OUTPOSTS

Pnei Kedem (2000) pop. 175*
Ma'ale Rehav'am (2001) pop. n/a
Ibei HaNahal (2000) pop. 100*
Sde Bar (1998, as a farming program for problem youth) pop. n/a
Tekoa B & C (2001) pop. n/a
Tekoa D (2001) pop. n/a

## DEAD SEA AREA

Avnat (2004) pop. 128
Kalya (1968) pop. 300
Mitzpe Shalem (1970), location of an Ahava factory, pop. 173
Mitzpe Dragot (1996, beach and field center) pop. n/a
Ein Feshka (2001, an archaeology/tourist site) pop. n/a

## "JERUSALEM DISTRICT"

Gilo (1970) pop. 40,000
Har Homa (1997) pop. 20,000
Giv'at Hamatos (2016) pop. n/a

# *Notes*

## INTRODUCTION

**4** **The Nabataeans dominated the spice trade for a thousand years; they, along with the Idumaeans (or Edomites), were one of two proto-Arab groups that settled in Palestine before the Persian era.** The role of Arabs (or proto-Arabs, as it is unlikely that they spoke Arabic at this time) such as the Idumeans and Nabataeans is well attested in Palestine from the ninth century BCE. The Bible tells an origins story that opposes the Ishmaelites (Arabs) and the Israelites. The Bible is not a reliable guide to history, but it is true that Arabs are not immigrants in Palestine; they have been there from the dawn of history. See Juan Manuel Tebes, "Assyrian, Judaeans, Pastoral Groups and the Trade Patterns in the Late Iron Age Negev" (2007). See also Taylor, Jane. *Petra and the Lost Kingdom of the Nabataens* (2002): she lists temple / trading bases at Alexandria, Rhodes and Naples in the first century BCE.

**5** **The Jewish faith has ancient roots in a military cult dedicated to a god named *Yehu*.** I chose "Yehu" over "Yahu" or "Yahweh" because it is the least familiar of the three names for the original deity, and so perhaps helps to look at the god with fresh eyes. The story of the journey from the proto-Jewish worship of Yehu to a recognizable Jewish faith is, in part, the story of how the name of this god is downgraded to the name of a patriarchal ancestor, Yehudah or Judah, while the name of God, himself, becomes too holy to utter or write.

**8** **Mentioned by Pliny the Elder in his first-century CE *Natural History*.** Pliny focuses on the ancestor of the lemon. I am indebted to Margaret Visser's *Much Depends on Dinner* (1986) for my knowledge of lemons and, more profoundly, the realization of how human history can be told through food.

16 **There is a short Jewish fable from around the fourth century that illus-trates this.** The *Pardes* fable appears first in the Palestinian Talmud compiled in the fourth or fifth century, c. 375-425 CE, in the maritime city of Cae-sarea. See Palestinian Talmud Hag. 21, revised and expanded in the sixth to seventh century as Babylonian Talmud Hag. 14b. The principle of Pardes exegesis, otherwise known as Kabbalah, is credited to Nahmanides of Gi-rona, Spain, c. 1268. See Bible Exegesis, Jewish Encyclopedia. The connec-tion between the fifth-century fable and the thirteenth-century reading practice is the subject of much argument in Jewish theological circles. See Gershom Scholem, who argues for a strong and continuous tradition. This strikes me as a classic example of retro-engineering, but see more detailed discussions in Ithamar Gruenwald's *Reflections on the Nature and Origins of Jewish Mysticism* (1993).

17 **I came across the idea of Pardes when researching the work of Jacques Derrida.** This is from his memoir *Circumfession*, which Derrida co-wrote with Geoffrey Bennington.

## CHAPTER 1

21 **The discovery brought the pioneering archaeozoologist Dorothea Bate and her colleague Elinor Gardner to Bethlehem**. See Kay Prag's "Bethle-hem: A Site Assessment, 169-181" (2000).

25 **She uncovered a series of letters between Neuville and Breuil.** See Cook Boyd's *A reconsideration of the 'Ain Sakhri' figurine* (1993) pp. 399-405.

26 **The biblical historian Karen Armstrong.** Her model of prehistory based on the movement of nomadic warriors can be found in *Fields of Blood* (2014).

28 **In his powerful account of the way trading networks shaped our world, historian Peter Frankopan.** The observation that supply lines and trade routes are often the same thing appears in *The Silk Roads* (2015).

28 **As Jacques Derrida observed, at some level all history turns out to be the history of writing.** This is from the essay on Rousseau's "Essay on the Ori-gins of Languages" in *Of Grammatology* (1976). History in an academic sense always means "recorded history"; i.e., it must have been something that happened to someone and was noted down, like a tax record, or news-paper report, or eyewitness account, and by extension other cultural marks such as pottery sherds with identifiable, patterned features. For Derrida, this means that history is always the history of recorded stuff ("text" in its broad-est sense meaning "universal database.") This brings in a paradox that history

is the marks of present day, when the present day is gone. These textual marks or "traces" of the "always already past" are Derrida's main interest.

29 **Deleuze speaks of nomad grazers as "Nomadic War Machines."** The key idea, that nomads are the abstract engines of history, occurs in *A Thousand Plateaus* (1987). This is co-written with Felix Guattari, but the underlying theoretical chassis is apparent from Deleuze's earliest works: the student guides on Hume, Kant, and Nietzsche.

32 **A team of Palestinian and Italian archaeologists excavated the subterranean chambers within the hill.** See L. Nigro's "Bethlehem in the Bronze and Iron Ages" (2015).

36 **A city named *Beit Ninurta* had switched allegiances.** See Amarna Letter number 290 in Schroeder 1920.

36 **William F. Albright, the most influential biblical archaeologist of his day, embraced his translation in 1921.** See William F. Albright's "Contributions to the Historical Geography of Palestine" (1921) pp. 1-46. But cf. one of Albright's last books, *Yahweh and the Gods of Canaan: A Historical Analysis of Two Contrasting Faiths* (1968). In this work, written forty years later, Albright changes his mind and identifies Beit Ninurta with Beit Horon—a biblical city that has never been identified. There is a settlement named Beit Horon near the Palestinian city of Ramallah.

36 **That, and the fact that [Albright] hired and trained the generation of Israeli archaeologists.** Such as Benjamin Mazar, patriarch of the Mazar family of archaeologists.

## CHAPTER 2

40 **In July 2004, as the route of the wall was published, the International Court of Justice (ICJ) gave an advisory opinion.** See ICJ advisory opinion, issued 8 July 2004.

40 **Five of the speaheads are inscribed in phonetic script.** The writing might be the very earliest examples yet found of the phonetic script. See Nigro 2015 and Sass-Finkelstein 2013.

40 **The word "alphabet" comes from the Canaanite letters.** The discovery of children's exercises in Lebanon suggests that even the order of the alphabet predates the Greeks' customization of the script. See Willi 2008.

40 **as well as exercises designed to teach children to read and write.** These are often called ABCs, though a better term is *abjads*, because the third letter is "J" not "C."

41 **The inscriptions honor Anat, a goddess worshipped in what is now Syria.** The dedication to Anat suggests that the owners came from Syria (Lorenzo 2015). In conversation, Lorenzo Nigro tells me that Sardinians

would trade local iron ore for copper and tin well into the Iron Age, simply because they liked bronze weapons. Bronze is an alloy of copper and tin and is so expensive because it is rare on our planet.

**43  At different times, they have been confidently identified as Sardinian or Sicilian or some other kind of Italian, as well as Doric and Hittite.** Abulafia (2011) claims they are Greek, which has been challenged by many, for instance by Hitchcock and Maeir. The assumption that they were illiterate and that they are an amalgam of different nationalities originates in the work of Israeli historian Trude Dothan, who nevertheless follows biblical assumptions about the relation between Philistines and Israelites.

**43  There was a group called the *Palastin* among the Syro-Hittites.** Julia Fridman summarized these arguments in a short article entitled "Riddle of the Ages Solved: Where Did the Philistines Come From?" (2015).

**43  In fact, the Philistine settled throughout Palestine.** Philistine-style sarcophagi displayed in the Palestine Museum are credited to finds across what is now Northern Israel. Aside from burial rites, the distribution of Philistine bichromatic pots is also widespread, a fact explored in Gilboa, Cohen-Weinberger, and Goren (2006). The wide distribution is a problem for Bible-based historians, who have to make space for a Canaanite-Israelite culture, separate from Philistine culture (before speculating on its connection to the later Jewish culture).

**46  There are valuable examples of Bethlehem mother of pearl in church museums, including the Vatican, and the Topkapi Palace of Istanbul.** There is a small collection in Bethlehem University, and information is on their website: http://library.bethlehem.edu/e-turathuna/Mother_of_Pearl/.

**46  Held in such high regard that ivory pieces are specifically itemized in a long list of valuables demanded as tribute by the Nineveh-based emperor.** *The Annals of Sennacherib* are written on the stele known as the Taylor Prism.

**47  Taxing the Nabataeans was not a perk or a marginal benefit: entire empires were funded by Nabataean wealth.** Cf. Edens and Bawden, *History of Tayma, and Hejazi Trade During the First Millennium B.C.* (1989).

**47  The Nabataean kingdom with its capital in Petra began to take shape in the sixth century BCE.** See Alessandra Bonazza et al., "Characterization of hydraulic mortars from archaeological complexes in Petra" (2013).

**47  The archaeologist Avraham Negev suggests the word "Nabataean" means "water-finder."** See Avraham Negev's "Masters of the Desert" (1983).

**48  Nabataean chemists found a way to produce quicklime at relatively low temperatures.** All the literature on ancient Middle Eastern hydraulic cement cites Nabataean cement alone, and agrees that this cement is different from Greek and Roman cement. Cf. Bonazza et al. (2013) and De Feo et al. (2013). The underlying assumption is that the Nabataeans had a monopoly on hydraulic cement in the Middle East. One speculative way to account for this unique Nabataean technology is via the work of Joseph Davidovits, the father of geopolymer chemistry: i.e., lime mortars created at relatively low temperatures. *"En 1979, Davidovits a proposé un nouveau nom pour ce matériau : géopolymère. Le terme «polymère» est utilisé parce que ces matériaux ont des structures polymérisées et parce qu'ils durcissent à basse température. Le terme «Géo» parce que ces matériaux sont stables à hautes températures, non inflammables et inorganiques. Nous pouvons retrouver ce type de matrices sous un autre nom de «Alkali-activation slag» qui a été proposé par Purdon (1940) ou comme des «granulosilikaty gruntocementy» nommé par Glukhovski (1959). Mais c'est prof. J. Davidovits qui a rendu ce matériau relativement célèbre."* This appears in Katerina Krausova Rambure's *Vers de nouvelles matrices minerales pour l'immobilisation et la valorisation des dechets ultimes de l'incineration des dechets menagers* (2014). Cf. Davidovits's "From ancient concrete to geopolymers" (1993). Davidovits's work informs the research of Dan Gibson, see "The History of Concrete and the Nabataeans" published online at Nabataea.net. Gibson also cites B. Mason, *Principles of Geochemistry* (1966) and Orchard D. F., *Concrete Technology* (1973). Gibson also draws on original research of fine, naturally occurring lime at Hisma Desert near Wadi Rumm. And lime pits at the Nabataean fort, the Grayn fort, located near Ras al Naqab in Southern Jordan. Both Gibson and Davidovits have unusual hobbyhorses (on Petra and on the Giza pyramids, respectively), yet the work on Nabataean hydraulic mortar is compelling.

48   **In Beit Shemesh, for instance, we see the construction of an entire system of elaborately joined cisterns by the eighth century BCE.** See MacKenzie 1912. The assumption is that the cement lining could only be Nabataean at this time. Cf. De Feo et al., "Historical and Technical Notes on Aqueducts from Prehistoric to Medieval Times" (2013). Nabataean technology is both distinctive and ubiquitous.

49   **Hezekiah is presented in the Bible's Book of Kings as one among a long line of Jerusalem-based rulers that stretch back into a time of myth.** Among the many anachronisms in the bible's account of this king, such as his war with the Philistines, we can add his clamp down on foreign idols. To object to idols would have required knowledge of the laws of Deuteronomy, which appeared only with the rise of the much-later Jerusalem-based religion. As the archaeological record shows, Hezekiah-era Jerusalem was tolerant of other gods.

49   **"While each nation's chief (male) god had a distinctive name ..."** See Stern 2001.

50   **Asherah poles.** See Deuteronomy 16:21. In the King James Bible, the poles are often referred to as "groves."

**52**    **Nothing resembling the Jewish nation of the Bible yet exists.** For a modern reader, the surprise of reading Herodotus and his account of a journey
to Palestine under Persian rule is that he does not mention any Yehu forces
or even the cities where this cult was strongest, such as Samaria and Jerusalem. Herodotus distinguishes Palestine from both Phoenicia and Syria:
showing the contours of these three nations had already emerged. We learn
that both Palestine and Phoenicia supply ships and sailors to the Persian
Navy (the Nabataeans, in contrast, are permitted to trade with the Persians
without being obliged to pay tribute). Herodotus gives us other snippets of
information, noting that Palestinians follow the Egyptian practise of cir-
cumcision, which he claims is an African custom. His book, *The Histories,*
takes culture seriously because the information has political value: it is the
stuff of foreign affairs briefings. Indeed, *The Histories* became a basis of state-
craft for centuries to come.  See The Histories 1:105.

**52**    **The Yehu faith crosses borders of ethnicity and language, but as yet has
no geographic center.** Shlomo Sand's *The Invention of the Jewish People*
(2009) is a thorough discussion of this issue in an Israeli context. Sand notes
that nineteenth century conceptions of nationhood are projected back on to
Bronze Age tribes. I am also struck by how often Israeli formulations of
identity rely upon the work of nineteenth-century German philosophers.
Hegel believes a group becomes a nation when the community acts with the
kind of reflexive self-awareness usually associated with individuals (see
Right). Nietzsche believes the community of the superman does not derive
from an awareness of culture and history but from a primordial "willing"
(see Zarathustra). Nietzsche and Hegel are not usually seen as compatible,
but they mix together quite readily in Israeli discourses. Of course, one result of this is that in order for Palestinians to speak collectively as a "nation"
in Israeli terms, it is necessary they know and embrace nationalistic European philosophy.

**52**    **Alexander conquered Palestine in 332 BCE.** See Antiquities. xi. 8.


## CHAPTER 3

**53**    **William Dalrymple was staying close by in Mar Saba, researching his
first book, *From the Holy Mountain.*** " 'The river? Nowadays it's just sewage from Jerusalem. But on judgment day that's where the river of blood is
going to flow. It's going to be full of Freemasons, whores and heretics: Protestants, Scismatics, Jews, Catholics … More Ouzo?' 'Please.' " Dalrymple,
William. *From the Holy Mountain.* (1997)

**54**    **The Kidron Stream has long been an open sewer.** Sewage data is from 2010.
Plans to build a sewage filtration plant in East Jerusalem recently fell apart

because East Jerusalem is under military occupation and Israel wished the new plant to take sewage from both existing East Jerusalem neighborhoods and also new Jewish settlements, deemed illegal under the Geneva Convention on military occupation. See Hillel Cohen's 2013 article, "Losing Jerusalem Sewage Plant Could Prove Longer Term Win for Palestinians." Available at: http://www.thedailybeast.com/articles/2013/09/13/losing-jerusalem-sewage-treatment-facility-could-be-longer-term-win-for-palestinians.html.

54 **Built with the help of Sanballatian forces who became the city's founding community.** See Josephus. Ant. 8.6.

54 **Alexandria was the city with the world's largest Jewish population.** Philo put the population at one million. Even if this exaggerates the figure by a factor of ten, it is a far larger Jewish population than any other city. Cf. also J. R. Bartlett, *Jews in the Hellenistic World* (1985), especially pp. 20-21.

55 **The Letter of Aristeas.** The seventy-two scribes are said to be drawn from the twelve tribes. The number of Israelite tribes always confuses me, as the Bible states Aaron and Joshua are given their own tribes, which would expand the number past twelve.

55 **The Dead Sea Scrolls are the chief source of non-Greek fragments of Jewish scripture.** The scrolls have almost all been translated, and information is given on the Israeli Antiquities website: http://www.deadseascrolls.org.il/explore-the-archive. While fragments of Dead Sea Deuteronomy texts might date to earlier than 200 BCE, the vast majority have been dated to the late Greek and Roman era; i.e., they are not earlier than the Septuagint. The Dead Sea Scrolls were in the Palestine Museum in 1967, before their removal by Israeli troops.

56 **The lower pool was constructed by combining to original Greek reservoirs in the reign of the Mamluk sultan Khushqadam in the 1460s.** See historian Mujir al-Din's *al-Uns al-Jalil bi-tarikh al-Quds wal-Khalil* ("The glorious history of Jerusalem and Hebron") (c. 1495). I have not read the work, and my knowledge is secondhand.

56 **The water pressure had to be sufficient to raise the water through an inverted siphon to the mouth of the aqueduct.** The Greek-era aqueduct used a terracotta siphon to raise the water to the start point. The later, Herodian-era upper aqueduct was constructed from cut stone blocks but would also have needed an inverted siphon of some kind.

59 **Kay Prag surveyed the work.** It was a pleasure to meet Kay Prag. I would like to thank her as well as Felicity Cobbing of the Palestine Exploration Fund for putting us in touch.

59 **The Bible puts the source of Bethlehem's water at the city gates**. "And the three mighty men broke through the host of the Philistines, and drew water out of the well of Bethlehem, that *was* by the gate" (2 Samuel 23:16).

**60**    **Arculf.** See Adomnan, Bede.

**61**    **Bethlehem figures in three stories, and the town gates feature in two of them.** In the Book of Ruth, Boaz must bargain for Ruth: "Then went Boaz up to the gate, and sat him down there" (Ruth 4:1).

**62**    **The Levite has gone to Bethlehem to buy a sex slave.** "And it came to pass in those days, when *there was* no king in Israel, that there was a certain Levite sojourning on the side of mount Ephraim, who took to him a concubine out of Bethlehemjudah. And his concubine played the whore against him, and went away from him unto her father's house to Bethlehemjudah, and was there four whole months" (Judges 19:1-2).

**62**    **Bethlehem in Greek is Βηθλεεμ, which leaves us no wiser as to whether the name as the locals knew it...** There is no record of the name Bethlehem outside of the Bible until the Christian era—at least, not until very recently. In 2012, Israeli archaeologist Eli Shukron found a bulla—a kind of tax disc— that apparently references Bethlehem. Shukron dates it to eighth or seventh century BCE. This would be the sole reference to Bethlehem outside of the Bible, and several hundred years earlier than its appearance in the Bible. The discovery was met with suspicion. Some of the problems are: it is a sole c. seventh-century BCE reference to Bethlehem, so there is nothing to compare it with, or deduce what it might mean; the bulla is broken, so the text has been reconstructed and competing interpretations are possible; finally, these kinds of bulla are often forged by antiquity dealers in Israel. Even if the seal is read as *bt lhm*, and this is taken to mean House Bread, the absence of any other contemporary references to Bethlehem means it cannot be identified with the town that emerged in the Greek era. The first datable appearance of the name Bethlehem is in Greek, in the Septuagint, and this gives no letter or other diacritic in the second word (i.e., the "leem" in "beth-leem"), which suggests Arabic or Aramaic "meat" or "lamb" over Canaanite/Hebrew "bread."

**64**    **It is notable that the Seleucid shift in policy that sees Jerusalem become independent of Amman receives the approval of Rome.** Rome dominated Alexandria from before 200 BCE because the Nile port city supplied Rome with grain. In 200 BCE, Rome prevented a Seleucid takeover of the city. Rome's early recognition of Jewish demands for autonomy stems from its ascendancy in Alexandria and its interest in limiting Seleucid power. The Jews became a wedge issue for Rome, as Tessa Rajak notes in **"Roman In-tervention in Seleucid Siege of Jerusalem?"** (1980). Rajak makes the wider point that Rome repeatedly used Jewish issues as a way to exercise power over the Seleucids.

**66**    **Most accounts agree that Mary is young, perhaps very young: in the apocryphal writings known as the "Infancy Gospels."** There are Infancy Gospels credited to Thomas, James, a pseudo-Matthew, as well as a Syriac version. In addition, there is a History of St. Joseph and a History of John the Baptist. All date from the second to the sixth century CE.

68 **This puritanical approach had its roots in the philosophy of Plato.** See the discussion of the mimetic function of the arts in *The Republic*.

68 **The Nabataeans worshipped a god so abstract that he could not be represented at all.** See Maximus of Tyre: "The Arabs serve I know not whom, but I saw this statue which was a square stone." Clement of Alexandria also notes that the Nabataeans worship stones. See Joseph Patrich 1990.

70 **Herod funded his grand projects by taxing the spice route, which is why the Gospel of Matthew depicts the Magi arriving with gold, frankincense, and myrrh.** See Matthew 2:11.

73 **The first reference to Christ being born in a cave dates to around the year 145 CE, in a letter written by the Nablus-born Christian, Justin Martyr.** "But when the Child was born in Bethlehem, since Joseph could not find a lodging in that village, he took up his quarters in a certain cave near the village; and while they were there Mary brought forth the Christ and placed Him in a manger, and here the Magi who came from Arabia found Him" (Justin Martyr, Dialogue with Trypho, Chapter 78).

73 **The Gospel of Luke tells us that the Holy Family were visitors in Bethlehem and that the first people to pay their respect were shepherds.** See Luke 2:8.

75 **The global character of the First Jewish War is confirmed by the second, 115-117 CE.** See Sand 2009.

## CHAPTER 4

77 **In 327 CE, a woman in her late seventies stepped down from her sedan chair.** "As soon, then, as she had rendered due reverence to the ground which the Saviour's feet had trodden, according to the prophetic word which says: 'Let us worship at the place whereon his feet have stood,' she immediately bequeathed the fruit of her piety to future generations" (Eusebius, Life of Constantine, XLII).

78 **Constantius was too ambitious to remain married to a commoner and he soon divorced Helena to make a more political alliance.** One of Constantius's early successes was the re-conquest of Britain, which had been independent for a generation. The connection between Constantius and Britain led to a myth that Helena was a British princess, the daughter of Coel Hen, a Welsh King. In the twelfth century, a story linked Coel and Colchester, based purely on the similar sounds of the words. This in turn led to a tradition that Constantius and Helena had met in Essex, rather than in a bar on the Sea of Marmara.

79 **The Talmud shows family farms were disappearing in the Galilee.** Cf. Sperber 1978.

79 **Retired Roman soldiers were invariably poor farmers.** See Beard, Mary. *SPQR* (2015). Beard shows that the practice of paying army pensions as farmland often proved a millstone—the soldiers could not make the land pay.

80 **Antioch was flanked by two semi-independent Arab Christian kingdoms.** These kingdoms had been Christian since the third century CE. Agbar VIII of Edessa converted to Christianity in 200 CE. Palmyra converted at the end of the third century CE. Palmyra gave Jerusalem its first Arab bishop, Mazabanes (251-260 CE), followed shortly afterwards by Zabdas (298-300 CE), who was installed around the time Palmyra formally embraced the faith (Shahid 1988). The neighboring Armenia converted at roughly the same time. By these standards, Antioch was a relative junior Christian city.

80 **Bishop Eusebius became the official chronicler of Helena's journey.** Twenty-five years earlier, in Diocletian's reign, the Bishop of Caesarea had been taken to Antioch in chains and had his tongue ripped out. Helena's quick friendship with Bishop Eusebius reassured the Christian community. See Birley 1990

80 **The salaries of civil servants in Caesarea were said to be higher even than in Antioch.** Cf. Libanius, cited in Stemberger 2000, on the academies in Gaza and Ashkelon, the elite universities of the day.

80 **A carved niche in the shrine held a terracotta and plaster "manger."** Reported by St. Jerome. Homily 88 "On the Nativity of the Lord".

81 **The Roman heiress Poimenia built the Church of the Ascension on the Mount of Olives at the end of the fourth century.** See Kirk 2004.

82 **The bishop, "who must always be in Jerusalem on these days."** See Egeria XXV-12.

85 **The charges against Jerome were secret.** See Kelly 1998.

86 **Jerome claims that he counted fifty thousand monks** See Jerome: Req Pach.

87 **Jerome recorded the short stays of their grand Roman guests.** See Jerome: 107.

87 **Paula's monastery never aimed to be self-sufficient.** See Jerome: Preface to Job. Also see Jerome: 125, 11.

88 **Victorian pilgrims such as Arthur Stanley, Dean of Westminster, took this passage at face value and assumed Paula was hearing the psalms of the scriptures, sung in Biblical Hebrew.** Prothero, 1904.

89 **He always sought to acknowledge the hardships of the sexless path they had chosen.** See Jerome: 22.

90 **Jerome's most tender description of Paula and Eustochium.** See Jerome: 66.

90    **"Like a torrent that carried everything before them."** See Jerome: 126.

90    **This encouraged wide-ranging raids by the Lakhmids, a Christian Arab tribe that worked for Rome's enemy: the Persian Sassanids** .See Irfan V., pp. 22-25.

91    **He would acknowledge some value in Origen.** See Jerome: 62.

91    **In a letter to Rome, he notes that of the three books credited to Solomon.** See Jerome: Preface to Ecclesiastes.

91    **A letter to Roman dowager Principia unpacks Psalm 45.** See Jerome: 65.

93    **The Jewish patriarch in Palestine was recognized by the imperial authorities as a hereditary prince, with a court and a palace in the Galilee.** See Stemberger 2000. Almost all the Roman-era synagogues discovered in the Galilee are dedicated to long-forgotten rabbis in a world before the Talmud.

94    **In his day the Greek words *Hebraois* and *Hebraisti* were used to refer to all Jewish texts, whether written in Greek, Aramaic, or Canaanite.** See Sáenz-Badillos, *A History of the Hebrew* Language (1993).

94    **Jerome's knowledge of Ancient Canaanite/Hebrew has been debunked many times.** See Graves 2007. Later, when Jerome was a more confident linguist, he would use the Latin word *Ibrit* (Hebrew) for "Yehudit," the word used by Jewish scholars to denote the language of Canaan/Phoenicia when used in a Jewish context. Indeed, Jerome might very well have coined the term "Hebrew" (Ibrit) to refer *specifically* to a language.

95    **I picked this up from a mention in an early work by Walter Benjamin.** *The Origin of German Tragic Drama* (1977).

## CHAPTER 5

99    **Netzer proposed that Herodion was a stronghold of the rebels in the Bar Kokhba revolt of the second century CE.** The Bar Kokhba Revolt is a strong theme at the site; indeed, the major attraction from a tourist standpoint. However, Netzer's theories on Herodian's role in the revolt are omitted from the academic literature written after Netzer's death. Cf. Roi Porat et al. 2015.

100    **She adopted Arab Christianity.** See Tsatsos 1977 and Shahid IV.

100    **The successor to Queen Māwiyya's tribe as Rome's foederati were the Salihids, Christians led by a monk king named David/Dawud.** See Shahid IV.

100    **David's scribes invented the flowing Arabic script.** See Shahid IV.

100    **The Romans gave Aspebetos the title *Phylarch*.** Also equal to the civilian Governor of Antioch (the "Count of the East" or *Comites Orientis*). See Shahid V.

**100**    **In 431 CE, Aspebetos attended the Church Council at Ephesus.** See Shahid V.

**101**    **These interminable arguments about the nature of Christ seem distant but at bottom they are actually about freedom and authority.** In his exploration of eastern Christianity, *From the Holy Mountain* (1997), William Dalrymple points out that the issue of Christ's materiality was the great issue that separated the empire's Greek-speaking center from its non-Greek regions.

**101**    **The Salihid king David and his allies Maris and Aspebetos had been weakened fighting the Vandals in North Africa.** See Shahid V.

**105**    **Mar Saba was given agriculture land in the Bethlehem district of Beit Sahour.** See Pringle, Denys. *The Churches of the Crusader Kingdom of Jerusalem: A Corpus*, Vol. 1-4 1993.

**105**    **Maris's monastery became St. Martyrius, after the Patriarch who succeeded Juvenal; Eudocia's hospital became an adjunct of Mar Saba.** It is possible that the laura at Mar Saba predates Saint Sabbas.

**107**    **Julian began his campaign by hosting rebel games in Nablus, tantamount to declaring his own *Imperium Samaritanum* to rival the Imperium of Rome.** See Pummer 1987.

**107**    **The Ghassanids were highly trained horsemen who perfected their skills with obsessive drilling.** See Shahid VI.

**107**    **One by John Malalas, a writer from Antioch who is ultra-loyal to Justininan.** See Pummer 2002.

**108**    **Procopius of Caesarea who is so hostile that he has been identified as a Samaritan.** See Pummer 2002.

**108**    **The families of Bethlehem are divided into clans, and two trace their roots back to Abu Karib and the Ghassanids.** Information comes from the Palestine family website: palestine-family.net. See also the essay by Fayez (Frank) Nasser, "The Nasser-Jaar Genealogic Family Tree with Historical Timelines" (2007), and the research by Dabdoub, Andre at Dabdoub.ps.

**109**    **The tune had been borrowed from a Syriac hymn without ever being credited, or so he said.** God Save the Queen is a galliard, an athletic couples' dance popular in Elizabethan England. The roots of all European couple dances lie in Arabic and Provencal courtly love poetry, and the music that accompanied its performance. A genealogy that traces the tune back to Syriac/Ghassanid roots is more than plausible.

## CHAPTER 6

**111**    **I ordered the largest book in the library on Bethlehem's churches and opened it to the Church of the Nativity.** The portraits are listed in Pringle,

Denys *The Churches of the Crusader Kingdom of Jerusalem: A Corpus*, Vol. 1-4 (1993).

112   **Cathal began his religious life in a monastery at Lismore.** The biography is by Bartolomeo Moroni, but my knowledge comes from Father J. F. Hogan, Saint Cathaldus of Taranto's *Vita e Miracoli di S. Cataldo*.

113   **Travelling on a barque downriver, the fast current would swiftly carry Cathal to Arles.** See *An Historical Geography of France* by X. Planhol and P. Clavel (1994).

113   **With all the love and reverence of a pilgrim.** See J. F. Hogan.

114   **Arculf's account describes the long ridge of Bethlehem.** See Adomnan. *Concerning Sacred Places.* See also Bede, *The Holy Places.*

116   **There was an almost-continuous run of nine Syrian popes from 685 CE until 752 CE.** Often described as a Byzantine Papacy, the term suggests they came from the capital, Constantinople, rather than from Syria. It is a particularly inappropriate term because these Popes drove the secession of Rome from Byzantium: they were anti-Byzantine and anti-Greek. It is impossible to say, now, what tongue these Syrian popes regarded as their mother language, whether Arabic, Syriac or Greek. In any event, they were "Oriental," the contemporary term for Middle Eastern and were seen as such at the time. Cf. Andrew J. Ekonomou's *Byzantine Rome and the Greek Popes: Eastern Influences on Rome and the Papacy from Gregory the Great to Zacharias, A.D. 590-752* (2007).

117   **The contractual term *mukhatarah* entered Italy as a double-exchange contract specifying future payments.** See Heck: Berlin 2006, p. 218.

117   **Amalfi merchants traded first with the Aghlabids...** See Citarella 1967.

117   **The Fatimids gifted the Amalfitans a Ghassanid-era monastery in Jerusalem known as the Hospital, apparently after the Persian word *bimaristan*.** I am struck by the similarity of the name of the monastery's founder, Maris, and the name associated with the institution: bimaristan. I would question why the monastery has a Persian name that refers specifically to medical care. The monastery was a hostel, rather than a medical hospital, though it later developed an association with medical care.

118   **The coin was the Taris, or Quarter dinar.** See Grierson and Travaini 1998.

118   **The Normans were Vikings who had first settled in northwest coastal France. From 999 CE, they came to know Italy as a staging post on their own regular pilgrimages, undertaken in their own ships.** Pilgrimage to Palestine could serve as both punishment and relief for serious crimes, particularly murder. Viking chieftains were obliged to undertake a great many pilgrimages (Runciman 1955).

118   **In 1064–1065, a single pilgrimage saw seven thousand pilgrims walk to the Holy Land led by a party of German bishops.** See Runciman 1955.

120 **It was like calling oneself the Terminator.** The story told in the Book of Job is a Jewish-Arab folktale that tells of man's plight before a single, all-powerful God. In the early Middle Ages, the Book of Job was a best-seller: the extraordinary number of illustrated copies to have survived speaks of its popularity in both Arab Christian and Roman Byzantine circles.

120 **The pilgrimage trade at this time is under-researched, but new work on the distribution of *eulogies* gives a glimpse of the scale of Bethlehem and Jerusalem's pilgrimage industry.** See O'Connor 2016.

121 **The Hospitallers became self-governing, poaching rules from the Augustinians.** The order remains notionally "Augustinian" though autonomous. An order originally created by Ghassanid knights had come full circle, returning by a circuitous route to become a military force of monks embracing chivalric laws dating to the Arab foederati of antiquity.


CHAPTER 7

129 **Bethlehem was becoming increasingly autonomous thanks to the networks provided by the extended family clans.** See palestinefamily.net.

129 **The al-Farahiyeh, in particular, held extensive holdings.** The tax records of families associated with the al-Farahiyeh can be found in Singer 1994. Singer's work is exceptional, yet suffers from a lack of knowledge of Bethlehem. In common with Bernard Lewis, a pioneer of history based on Ottoman records, there is no attempt to refer back to Palestine and place the records in context. Thus, Singer's tax records refer to agriculture alone, at a time when tourism and industry were on the rise, which leads her to underestimate both wealth and population. In addition, Singer does not appear to realize the families named in the tax records all belong to the same clan: al-Farahiyeh. Nor does she seem to appreciate that the records do not refer to modern-day Beit Jala, but to the village of St George (al-Khader). See note, below. Thus, she misses that the families paying tax do not necessarily live on their land: indeed, they are more likely to live in their Bethlehem harat, and to employ peasants to work their land.

129 **As the families trace their roots back to a Ghassanid priest, perhaps their wealth was acquired as the descendants of priests inherited church property.** The tax records discussed in Singer 1994 specify the taxed land is in Beit Jala. The area around St George monastery was known as Beit Jala in the sixteenth century, as contemporary accounts by visiting monks show. See Pringle 2012, Matar 2012. A fourteenth-century Arab pilgrim appears to make a sarcastic joke calling Beit Jala "Beit Zala," or House of Ignorance. If this truly is sarcasm, then it is likely the name "Beit Jala" means the opposite of ignorance. A possibility is "House of the Society" in the sense of a

monastic fraternity of scholars. I may be going out on a limb, but if the name Beit Jala does refer to a society of monks it might explain why this was an original name for the lands associated with the monastery of St George (land that evidently extended over al-Makhrour). In addition it might explain the connection with the priestly al-Farahiyeh clan.

**130**    **I found a passage in a nineteenth-century Baedeker describing a hotelier named Dabdoub as a huge welcoming figure, an image that immediately recalls the gigantic figure of Andre Dabdoub.** The reference does not appear in later editions, and I began to wonder if I imagined this reference. But my notes made in 2009 seem clear, even if I can no longer find the reference. Maybe I saw the reference in the memoirs of a traveler rather than in the Baedeker guide.

**131**    **A high quality product that competed with Marseilles and Venetian.** See Ashtor 1984, p. 208.

**132**    **Elizabethan England was particularly energetic.** English woolen merchants made vast fortunes from Levantine trade. Among these new millionaires was William Shakespeare's family in Stratford (Fallow 2008).

**132**    **The English traded their wool for everything from chemicals to camel hair, but they could not get enough of wine and raisins.** See Epstein 1908.

**132**    **The hills around al-Makhrour, Battir, and Wadi Fuqin, all to the west of Bethlehem, are truly startling, filled with valleys carved into ziggurats that rival any Chinese tea plantation.** Recent work on chemical soil analysis has shown that the large scale terraces that stand relatively remote from population centers date date to the sixteenth century. See Davidovich et al. 2012.

**133**    **The Greek Orthodox Church had changed dramatically.** The Russian Orthodox Church discovered how much the Byzantine Greek Church had changed in the seventeenth century when Tsar Alexei I sought to reunite Russian and Greek churches. Ancient Orthodox rites preserved by the Russian Church were suddenly deemed heretical which led to the historic split in Russian Orthodoxy.

**134**    **The church is mired in property scandals and condemned for its failure to promote Palestinian clerics, and is often seen as an accomplice of the hostile occupation.** In the 1920s, the British forced the Patriarchate to sell off pieces of land to the Yishuv, the pre-state Jewish community in the 1920s. See http://property.co.il/land-ownership-church-land. More recently, Patriarch Irineos was found to have stolen church land and sold it illegally in 2005. It continues to be a hot issue, especially as Palestinian Christians gifted this land to the Greek Orthodox Church in the first place. See http://www.ipsnews.net/2010/01/mideast-sale-of-land-to-israel-threatens-to-split-church/.

134 **From the seventeenth century, the Vatican allowed local Latin Christians to use Arabic liturgy.** See Norris 2013.

136 **Joined by the al-Kwawseh and al-Anatreh, Christian families from the desert borders of Tuqu'.** The al-Anatreh take their name from a lost church named Qasr Antar, identified by Denys Pringle.

137 **The most popular was the epic poem of the Banu Hilal and their chivalrous leader Abu Zeid.** I worked on a translation of a historical/critical essay on the Banu Hilal epic by Muhammad Rajab al-Najjār for the doyenne of Arabic literary studies, Salma Jayyusi. This is the source of my information, but I'm not sure this translation has yet been published. The Banu Hilal furnished the idea of the Qais, or the party of Empire, Unity, and the Ummah. The Yamani, the party of schism, localism, populism, and secularism, opposed it.

137 **These two parties, the *Yamani* and the *Qais*, take their names from a semi-mythical feud between tribes of the Arabian Peninsula, but are "fictive" political identities.** The emergence of both Arab and Palestinian political identities through these romantic, poetic myths of an Arab past has drawn criticism. Bernard Lewis has suggested the Palestinian identity lacks the authenticity of an ancient ancestral identity, mistakenly claiming the term Palestine fell out of use between Roman times and the twentieth century: Lewis, New Yorker, 2001 also cf. Lewis, Atlantic, 1990. (Ironically, the proposition is true of the Latin word Judea, in the sense of Jerusalem and its environs, which was revived by British and German Christians in the nineteenth century). In the *New Yorker* piece as well as the *Atlantic* piece from a decade earlier, Lewis argues that the idealized and heroic fantasy of a "people" actually masks the shame and rage of a disunited mob. Lewis's psychologism has in turn been criticized as "Orientalism"; that is, a continuation of a Victorian tradition that views Middle Eastern culture as weak and ineffective (though often highly seductive and, hence, "feminine"). The Palestinian historian Edward Said coined the term Orientalism, and the study of Middle Eastern history tends to split ideologically into schools that follow either Lewis or Said. Lewis's claim to see into the mind or soul of an entire people deserves criticism; nevertheless, his project has a long, philosophical provenance. It is a legacy of European existential philosophy that sees *all* culturally acquired identities as expressions of shame and weakness, a theme that deeply influenced the works of Leo Strauss, Emmanuel Levinas, Alexandre Kojeve, and Martin Heidegger. These ideas derive ultimately from Friedrich Nietzsche's historiography, which yearns for a more primordial kind of identity than those imposed upon us by our situation: a yearning for a superman that stands outside of cycles of competition and resentment that Nietzsche believes characterize cultural history—in effect,

a demand for a form of identity that stands outside of history entirely. It is hard to see how any historian can usefully employ such an ahistorical analysis. But in the cauldron of Israeli-Palestinian politics, the legacy of European existentialism has encouraged Israeli politicians to talk about "existential dangers" in a quite artificial way. They have also helped sustain the claim that Israeli violence, even at its most regrettable, has a purity because it emerges from an authentic sense of self, while Palestinian violence is only a symptom of "inauthentic" resentment and hatred. More pertinently, it has encouraged Israelis to condemn everything and anything that a Palestinian does as terrorism, from a bomb attack, to a piece of poetry, to an application by the Palestinian Authority to join a UN body, while leaving Israeli commentators often unable to condemn or even discuss the violence of Israelis, whether by contemporary settlers, or by earlier groups in the pre-state Yishuv. One can understand that, in the immediate distress of being a victim of terrorism, one might wish to dismiss one's enemies and opponents via the strongest condemnations, but those using this line should be aware of its roots. The point of this kind of existential critique is to provide a psychological profile of a people one simultaneously disdains to know. Nietzsche's example of a weak and feeble cultural identity, of course, was the European Jews.

138 **Though Napoleon said he would have happily dressed his troops in baggy trousers to escape Palestine and march on Constantinople.** See Andrew Roberts, *Napoleon the Great* (2014). Napoleon is quoted as saying, "Do you not think the subjection of the Asia is worth a turban and baggy trousers?"

139 **Details of the war preparations come from a Greek priest named Neophytus**. See S. N. Spyridon, ed., *Annals of Palestine, 1821-1841: A Manuscript by the Monk Neophytus of Cyprus* (1938).

141 **The photograph is a clue to Beit Jala's prime industry.** This was a city formed by stonemasons. Henry Palmer, an English Orientalist, said a third of the locals were employed as stonemasons in 1895. He is quoted in *Dollar, Dove, and Eagle: One Hundred Years of Palestinian Migration to Honduras* by Nancie L. Solien González (1992). See also *Dilemmas of Attachment: Identity and Belonging among Palestinian Christians* by Bård Kårtvei (2014).

## CHAPTER 8

144 **An Irish doctor named William Wilde.** See *Narrative of a Voyage* (1840).

145 **Another Irish doctor, Richard Robert Madden.** See Madden 1833.

147 **The empire was in a constant process of modernization from the mid-nineteenth century.** See Mazza 2009, p. 17.

148 **The Ottoman Empire's embrace of Free Trade had an enormous impact on Bethlehem.** Jacob Norris explores how Bethlehem families began to develop international trading links in Norris 2013. Norris worked closely with Bethlehem historian Khalil Shokeh, whose own Muslim family was involved in this trade.

148 **Even so, the emigrants would often return, and Bethlehemites became used to moving backward and forward.** See Jacob Norris, "Toxic waters: Ibrahim Hazboun and the struggle for a Dead Sea concession, 1913-1948" (2011).

148 **This remains the case today, as military occupation limits work opportunities, freedom of movement, and as well as freedom to marry.** It is not possible for Palestinian Christians to marry Christians living in cities like Haifa or Nazareth and live in those cities. Moreover, the partner from the Israeli city risks losing their citizenship.

149 **As early as 1841, the English philanthropist Moses Montefiore managed to obtain a leasehold on Rachel's Tomb.** Montefiore, who was born in Livorno, had visited Bethlehem as a young man. He and Lady Montefiore visited in middle age when they knew they would be childless, and their romanticization of Rachel's Tomb seems to have been bound up with their lack of heirs. Lady Montefiore kept a diary of their visits. It is extraordinary that Montefiore seems to have been able to buy a lease. See Glen Bowman, *Sharing and Exclusion: The Case of Rachel's Tomb*.

151 **The Meshullams ran a small hotel in Jerusalem, the first European-owned in the city**. An account of the Meshullams can be found in Naili 2011. See also Blumberg 1980.

152 **The tourists blink and sweat in the full glare of the sun, kept in line by their Israeli tour guides with dire warnings about the town's safety.** There have only been two acts of violence against tourists in the twenty-five years I have known Bethlehem, both widely reported by Palestine news sources. One was a disturbed man in the early 1990s, the other a cited as a "dispute" in Beit Sahour in 2015.

153 **Arthur Stanley, the Dean of Westminster Cathedral.** See *Sinai and Palestine* (1856).

153 **Stanley mocked the fact that Helena had discovered a cave for every aspect of Christ's life.** There were limits to Stanley's criticism. He did not doubt the cave where Christ was born. He had toured local houses like the museum of AWU and seen that their cellars were often caves, which may have been used to stable animals. Stanley thought this was the explanation behind the grotto. His view was immediately influential. In 1910, the surgeon Sir John Treves visited Bethlehem carrying Stanley's *Sinai and Palestine* as his guidebook. Treves was famous for treating the Elephant Man but had

earned his baronetcy for services to the King's appendix. He postulated that houses dating to Christ's time might crumble away to nothing, leaving only the cellars behind, remnants of an older way of life stored in the folk memory. A similar idea can be found in a recent-ish guidebook to the Holy Land, which states: "We should envisage Joseph (then living with his parents) as taking his wife into such a back area in order to give birth away from the confusion of the living room; the cave part of the house would have been used for stabling and storage." The text does not explain why anyone would lead a donkey through their living room to stable it at the very back of the house.

**154** **Most of these shrines were extant in the Victorian era.** But no more. In the 1950s, Israel had a policy of erasing any sign of an Islamic cultural legacy, and bulldozed them despite being fully aware of their archaeological value. See Rapoport, Meron, "History Erased," (2007).

**155** **My former university Professor, Rick Gekoski, amazed me when he announced he had the earliest extant version of the Balfour Declaration.** It was sold as Lot 217 FINE BOOKS AND MANUSCRIPTS INCLUDING AMERICANA on June 16, 2005. It sold for $884,000.

**157** **The Administration may arrange with the Jewish Agency**. See Article II, "Council of the League of Nations Confirmed Text on the Terms of the British Mandate in Palestine 24 July, 1922." Reproduced in Norris 2011.

**158** **Herbert Samuels, an early proponent of establishing a Jewish homeland.** See Aderet 2014.

**158** **The Jewish community was small...** There were around sixty thousand Jews, or eight percent of the population, when the British arrived in Palestine in 1917. The majority of these were not represented in any way by the European Zionist organizations, either because they were indigenous Arab-speaking communities, or because they were religious. Many of them were single men, passing through the country as they studied the Torah, or else elderly men visiting on a charitable grant with a hope of dying in the Holy Land.

**158** **The story of a Bethlehem businessman Ibrahim Hazboun**. For the full gripping story, see Norris 2011.

**159** **It was imperial policy to favor new settlers over the indigenous population, regarding the one group as economic migrants who could help a colony to thrive, and the other as a source of potential nationalism that would challenge the imperial project.** Witness the trafficking of workers, entrepreneurs, and small business owners from India to Eastern and Southern Africa and to the Caribbean. The British saw European Jews in the same light as Indian migrants within the Empire.

**160** **The army sealed the buildings, confiscated records...** The fate of the sporting clubs is covered in Issam Khalidi's histories of sports and football in

Palestine. See also John Bayne for the clampdown on Palestinian organizations in 1936.

160 **Bethlehem had no Jewish population.** See the relevant censuses in McCarthy 1990.

160 **Ben-Gurion regarded them with suspicion**: See Eliot A. Cohen, *Supreme Command: Soldiers, Statesmen, and Leadership in Wartime* (2002).

## CHAPTER 9

162 **Al-Walajeh has a similar story to Malha.** For an overview of the history and legal situation, see Saleh, Ruba. *In the Seam Zone* 2012.

162 **We took a tour of his terraces, which hold the al-Badawi variety of olive.** See Tupper. *Gethsemane Among World's Oldest Olive Trees.* Olive Oil Times. 2012.

164 **In March 1948, Glubb handed field responsibility to a senior intelligence officer, Colonel Norman Lash.** Lash has now been revealed as a security officer, see Hughes, Matthew (2015). The territorial negotiations were carried out between Lash, Golda Meir and Abdullah in April and May. See also Benny Morris, *Road to Jerusalem* (2002).

164 **The Arab Legion entered Jerusalem under the command of a junior Arab officer, Abdullah el-Tell.** See Hart, *Zionism: David Becomes Goliath.* 2009

164 **Despite the apparent superiority of these five Arab forces, there were always more Israeli troops in the field.** By the end of the war, they numbered some one hundred thousand. John Baynes states that Jewish-Israeli forces outnumbered other forces by three to one even at the start of the war. He gives the figures: Israeli troops 60,000; Egypt 10,000; Arab Legion 4,500; Iraq 3,000; Syria 3,000; Lebanon 1,000, making a total of 21,500 (1997, p. 68).

166 **The Israeli cabinet debated launching a second assault on Jerusalem in September. The idea was rejected, and the cited reason was an agreement with Abdullah.** See Morris 1990.

166 **Indeed, Jordan never strayed outside of the original UN plan for the partition of Palestine, outside a few minor exceptions.** See Shlaim 1988.

166 **Kfar Etzion was never evacuated.** Cohen argues that Ben Gurion wanted to buy time to mobilize. Yigdal Yadin, a Haganah military commander, argued against evacuation because of Kfar Etzion's strategic value on the Hebron Road, though I am not clear from sources how he intended to exploit this value.

166 **Israeli accounts also describes mutilations and rapes.** See Morris 1988.

167 **But perhaps Israel's major advantage was the knowledge that Jordan would never press an advantage.** See Shlaim, *Debate about 1948* (1999). Also, Shlaim 1988.

171 **An experience that was a very sad one for all concerned.** Quoted in http://www.jta.org/1982/08/30/archive/west-bank-gaza-village-leagues -termed-as-israeli-collaborators.

172 **The pairing of Che and Leila makes them appear like a sacred couple.** I looked online and found that you can even buy Che and Leila mugs.

## CHAPTER 10

175 **Israel collected Palestinians taxes and tried to claim responsibility for the burst of new schools and universities.** See Sharon. He spends some time making this claim in his biography Warrior 1989.

176 **Begin had entered Palestine in the early 1940s after defecting from General Anders' Polish Army in the Middle East in the Second World War.** Begin wrote two memoirs: *White Nights* (1977) and *The Revolt* (1950). He puts his own gloss on going AWOL from the army, and on leading a terrorist campaign against the Allies while the war against fascism was ongoing.

177 **A Jewish terror group led by an American named Meir Kahane carried out coordinated attacks on three West Bank mayors in May 1980.** See http://www.csmonitor.com/1980/0603/060337.html. The only man convicted of these attacks, Era Rappaport, was serving as an advisor to a government minister at the time. He fled to New York, where he worked for Israeli charities, then returned to face a short prison sentence. He is still active as a settler. See http://myrightword.blogspot.co.uk/2006/11/era-me-and-some-wine.html.

178 **The revolt began in 1987 with a strike by students in Bethlehem.** See Sullivan, "Palestinian Universities in the West Bank and Gaza Strip" (1991).

178 **Prime Minister Begin rejected the suggestion without discussing it with his cabinet or even the US president.** The Israelis dragged the US into the debacle in Lebanon. The American involvement would see the PLO ousted from Beirut, and their relocation to Tunis. The same period also saw the bombing of the American base in Beirut by the then-unknown Hezbollah organization. This was the first terror attack to exceed the death toll of the bombing of the King David Hotel by Menachem Begin in 1946.

178 **It was, he said, "merely the expression of a wish."** See Foundation for Middle East Peace, Report on Israeli Settlements, Vol. 1, no. 5.

178 **He threatened Shamir that the US would withhold guarantees for $10 billion worth of loans. . .** See Friedman in the *New York Times*. Available: http://www.nytimes.com/1992/03/18/world/bush-rejects-israel-loan -guarantees.html.

## CHAPTER 11

**182**  **The conflict flared around issues of corruption by the men from abroad**. See Graham Usher and Tarek Hassan Al-Ahram, "More of the same," *Weekly On-line* 13–19, August 1998, Issue No. 390. Available: http://weekly.ah-ram.org.eg/archive/1998/390/re1.htm.

**183**  **Arafat preferred to appoint businessmen.** See Rubin 1998.

**184**  **Withholding the tax revenues has become a tool Israel uses to exert pressure on Palestine**. The tax was withheld in 2008, 2011, 2012, 2014 and 2015. Each time, this was presented as retaliation for an alleged Palestinian infraction, almost always for appealing to an international institution such as the UN or EU to put pressure on Israel.

**185**  **The party controls the security forces, which provide a police force for Palestinians and offer security guarantees to Israel.** US General Keith Dayton was partly responsible for setting up an elite unit within the security forces. In 2009, he warned: "There is perhaps a two year shelf life on being told that you're setting up a state when you're not." That was eight years ago, so the PA is ever-more reliant on the troops innate loyalty. *Time*, 17 Nov. 2009.

**186**  **In the Israel elections of 2001, Barak went on the offensive by rehashing the negotiations at Camp David. . .** A full discussion in Eran Halperin and Daniel Bar-Tall's "The fall of the peace camp in Israel: The influence of Prime Minister Ehud Barak on Israeli public opinion: July 2000-February 2001" (2007), ends with this conclusion:
"The Palestinian violence during the months of September 2000-February 2001 was of limited scope and not all that different from violent confrontations in the past. Therefore, we suggest that the crucial factors in the psychological earthquake experienced by the Israeli public in the fall of 2000 was the information provided by Ehud Barak, framing the major events of the summer and fall of 2000 in a particular way. That is, we do recognize that the major events of Camp David and beginning of the Intifada had an effect on public opinion. But our point is that the determinative factor in this effect was the interpretation of these events. They do not stand by themselves, but only within the framework in which they were presented to the public. It was the provided information that gave meaning to the events. This major information stated that Barak had offered everything that Arafat had refused to accept the offer, that he intended to eradicate Israel and that he insisted on the right of return of millions of Palestinian refugees to the State of Israel; that he had planned the Intifada and had returned to tactics of terror. This information was accepted by the Israeli establishment and was transmitted massively by most of the media. Eventually the information presented by Ehud Barak was accepted by the great majority of Is-

raeli Jewish society during an early phase of the confrontation, and had a determinative effect on peace politics in Israel and thus on the course of the Israeli-Palestinian conflict. In fact, the provided information has come to serve as a formal hegemonic and popular collective memory among Israeli Jewish society about the Camp David summit and the beginning of the Second Intifada. We suggest that the wide acceptance of Barak's information was a result of a rare coinciding, at a particular point of time, between the social context, a leader (i.e., Ehud Barak), a receptive audience (i.e., most of Israeli Jewish society), information and specific environmental conditions (i.e., violence)."

186     **Clinton . . . backed Barak's story in the hope that this would improve Barak's fortunes at the poll**. There are many accounts of Clinton's intervention citing Arafat as the rejectionist at the Taba talks, though Arafat had in fact agreed on new parameters, and it was Barak who pulled the Taba talks. The key document is the remark President Bill Clinton made to the Israel Policy Forum gala on Sunday, 7 January in New York. He stated that Arafat and Barak had accepted his proposals. See the "Transcript of Clinton's remarks to the Israel Policy Forum gala" (2001), available at http://edition.cnn.com/2001/WORLD/meast/01/08/clinton.transcript/.

186     **Arafat was branded a rejectionist. . .** See "Palestinians Reject Peace Proposal," *The Guardian*, 8 Jan. 2001. This was the story that played in the Israeli elections. Clinton's negotiator, Dennis Ross, also gave interviews during the election campaign to boost Barak. He blamed Arafat's rejectionism. "The way he has defined his bottom line is not compatible with what any Israeli government is able to do." In the same interview, he also blames Sharon for destroying the Peace Process with his visit to the mosque, saying: "I can think of bad ideas, but I can't think of a worst one." See Jane Perlez in the *New York Times*, available at http://www.nytimes.com/2001/01/29/world/us-mideast-envoy-recalls-the-day-pandora-s-box-wouldn-t-shut.html.

189     **Against a backdrop of a UNSC resolution asking Israel to show restraint, and a conference of Arab ministers that produced a widely praised document—The Arab Peace Initiative—offering full recognition to Israel.** The full text is available from news sites such as the BBC: http://news.bbc.co.uk/1/hi/world/middle_east/1844214.stm.

190     **The first Palestinian parliamentary elections following the Israeli invasions only came in 2006 and were a disaster for Fatah.** The *Washington Post* headline for January 27, 2006 is "Hamas Sweeps Palestinian Elections, Complicating Peace Efforts in Mideast." See http://www.washingtonpost.com/wp-dyn/content/article/2006/01/26/AR2006012600372.html. My

brother-in-law, Maxim Sansour, was part of the election committee in Palestine at the time. It was a strange night.

## CHAPTER 12

191 **It was claimed to be an act of memorial and vengeance for the May 1948 deaths at Kfar Etzion.** Al-Dawayima saw somewhere between eighty to two hunrded people killed, over the course of a day with the eyewitness' Israeli accounts detailing the beating to death of children, the rapes of the women, and the immolation of householders. This massacre was carried out by at least some of the same Israeli forces as the earlier Deir Yassin massacre, and is in many ways considerably worse. See Benny Morris 1989 and Illan Pape 2006.

192 **In October 1948 was also justified on the basis of the killings at Kfar Etzion.** See Morris 1988. Also an account online at http://jfjfp.com /?p=80269 We Established a State on the Mass Graves of Others by Jonathan Ofrir with an account of the massacre from the Israeli NGO Zochrot.

192 **The same Betar forces responsible for the Deir Yassin massacre carried out al-Dawayima.** The Israeli intellectual Amos Kenan was one of the Betar/Lehi fighters who participated in both massacres. A biography, written by Kenan's wife, reversed an earlier claim that he had not taken part in Deir Yassin, made to UK journalist Daphna Baram. Gertz, Nurit. *Unrepentant (Al Da'at atzmo: Arbaim pirkei haim shel Amos Kenan)*, Tel Aviv: Am Oved, 2008. I have not read this biography; my information is secondhand from Wikipedia, English and Hebrew.

192 **To live in these settlements, you have already gambled that the whole of Palestine will one day be annexed to a single Jewish state with a permanent Palestinian underclass.** The settlements define Israeli politics, even though the vast majority of Israelis are not settlers. There are six million Jews in Israel, and somewhere over eight hundred thousand living beyond the Green Line, of which half a million would self-identify as settlers. The discrepancy is because the others live in suburbs of Jerusalem that they have forgotten are settlements, or they never regarded them as settlements. See http://www.timesofisrael.com/settler-group-says-421000-israelis-now -living-in-west-bank/.

192 **By 1999, the Bethlehem area had fifty thousand settlers.** The Palestinian figures are from ARIJ/PNA Census of 1997. The organization Peace Now estimated the number of settlers at ninety thousand minus Jerusalem. New figures are also from Palestinian Authority sources, and Peace Now.

194 **French and American donors, including President Donald Trump** See Shuki Sadeh's, "Who Are the Biggest Contributors to Politics in Israel? Many Live in New York and Miami" (2015).

194 **The occupation is unbelievably baroque.** In his book, *Hollow Land* (2007), Israeli architect Eyal Weizman tries to unpick this complexity.

196 **Every member of the UN that has ever been canvassed agrees that Israel is a hostile occupying power.** The US has always been clear that it regards Israel in breach of the Fourth Geneva Convention. However, in 2004, President George W. Bush wrote a letter of understanding to Prime Minister Ariel Sharon stating that Israel should expect to hold on to tracts of the West Bank following a peace deal. It is difficult to imagine an act that more closely resembles Chamberlain's appeasement than Bush's letter.

197 **Elkin's name is prominent in lists of politicians who benefit from donations from real estate developers.** A third Knesset Member, Yuli Edelstein, speaker of the Knesset, lives in Neve Daniel in the western section of Gush Etzion. All three are Russian Israelis, and Edelstein's parents live there. His parents are Christians; his father converted from Judaism and is now a priest.

198 **A government ministry instructed the army to seize 1.54 square miles of land by the Gevaot settlement, privately owned by Bethlehem families.** In February 2016, Bennett sponsored a bill retroactively legalizing the theft of Palestinian private property. There is no clearer illustration of Meron Benvenisti's charge that settlements are a "commercial real estate project that conscripts Zionist rhetoric for profit."

199 **Menachem Froman, was famous for his efforts to speak to Palestinian groups.** Froman wrote, "In school we were taught a formal principle that if a person wants to build his world (as beautiful as it may be) by means of destroying the world of another (as impoverished as it may be), this is 'the sin and its punishment.' The lesson one learns from this is simple: It is forbidden for Jews to build their return to Zion (*shivat Zion*) at the price of the Arabs. It is forbidden for settlers to build their settlements—even if they are beautiful and rooted—in the midst of the destruction of the world of the Palestinians." From Ha'aretz, "The Right To Stand," 1995, quoted in a profile of Froman: *The Tablet*, 4 Aug. 2015.

199 **The idea of "running to seize the hilltops," as Ariel Sharon instructed Israelis to do during the time of the Oslo. Seize the hilltops.** Said to Jewish settlers, 17 Nov. 1998. See https://www.theguardian.com/world/2001/feb/07/israel1.

200 **Enough of this exile mentality.** See Haaretz, 26 Dec. 2016.

**201**   **Presumably, he means as a neighbor from Tekoa.** Palestinian ministers have repeatedly made clear that Jews are welcome to live in Palestine after a peace deal, but they cannot live in illegally built and exclusive settlements. See *Times of Israel*, 27 June 2014.

# CHAPTER 13

**206**   **Betar** For the full poem by Ze'ev Jabotinsky, see http://www.hebrewsongs.com/song-shirbetar.htm.

# Bibliography

Abulafia, David: *The Great Sea: A Human History of the Mediterranean.* London: Penguin, 2012

Adomnan. *Concerning sacred places.* Available online at http://medieval.ucdavis.edu/20B /Arculf.html

Applied Research Institute Jerusalem. *The Status of the Environment in the West Bank.* Bethlehem: ARIJ, 1997

———. An Atlas of Palestine: *The West Bank and Gaza.* Bethlehem: ARIJ, 2000

Albright, William F. *Contributions to the Historical Geography of Palestine.* AASOR 2-3 1921/1922, pp. 24-46.

———. *Yahweh and the Gods of Canaan: A Historical Analysis of Two Contrasting Faiths* Warsaw, Ind.: Eisenbrauns 1990

al-Najjār, Muhammad Rajab. *The Epic in the Arabic Tradition: Structure, Significance, and Function.* Ed. Al-Jayussi, Salma. A personal draft copy.

Arab Educational Institute. *Bethlehem Community Book. Bethlehem.* Bethlehem: Arab Educational Institute, 1999

Armstrong, Karen: *The Bible: The Biography.* London: Atlantic Books, 2007

———. *Fields of Blood: Religion and the History of Violence.* London: Vintage, 2015

Ashtor, Eliyahu. *Levant Trade in the Middle Ages.* Princeton NJ: Princeton University Press, 1984

Baedeker, Karl: *Palestine and Syria, Handbook for Travellers.* Baedeker: Leipzig, 1906

Bartlett, John R. *Jews in the Hellenistic world: Josephus, Aristeas, the Sibylline oracles, Eupolemus.* Cambridge: Cambridge University Press, 1985.

Baynes, John: *For the Love of Justice: The Life of a Quixotic Soldier.* London: Quartet, 1997

Beard, Mary. *SPQR: A History of Ancient Rome.* New York: Norton, 2015

Bede. *The Holy Places.* Available online at en.wikisource.org/wiki/The_Book_of_the _Holy_Places

Begin, Menachem. *White Nights: The Story of a Prisoner in Russia*. New York: Crime Club Doubleday, 1977

Begin Menachem. *The Revolt: Inside Story of the Irgun*. London: Allen, 1951

Benjamin, Walter. *The Origin of German Tragic Drama*. London: Verso, 1977

Benvenisti, Meron: *City of Stone: The Hidden History of Jerusalem*. Berkeley, CA: University of California Press, 1996

Birley, A R. "St. Helena, Discoverer of the True Cross (250-330)" [1990] available online at http://www.brown.edu/

Blumberg, Arnold. *A View from Jerusalem 1849-1858: The Consular Diary of James and Elizabeth Ann Finn*. New Jersey: Associated University Presses, 1980.

Bonazza, Allessandra; Ciantelli, Chiara; Sardella, Alessandro; Pecchioni, Elena; Favoni, Orlando; Irene, Natali and Sabbioni, Cristina. *Characterization of hydraulic mortars from archaeological complexes in Petra*. Periodico Mineralogia 82, 2, 2013. 459-475

Bowman, Glen. *Sharing and Exclusion: The Case of Rachel's Tomb*. Jerusalem Quarterly 58, 2014. 30-49

Boyd, B and Cook J. *A reconsideration of the 'Ain Sakhri' figurine*. Proceeding of the Prehistoric Society 59, 1993. 399-405.

Bronstein, Judith. *The Hospitallers and the Holy Land: Financing the Latin East*. Cambridge: Boydell Press, 2012

Center for Cultural Heritage Preservation. *Bethlehem: A Pictorial Guide*. Bethlehem: CCHP, 2016

Citarella, Armand O. *The relations of Amalfi with the Arab world before the Crusades*. Speculum 42, 2, 1967. 299-312

Cohen, Eliot A. *Supreme Command: Soldiers, Statesmen, and Leadership in Wartime*. London: Anchor, 2003

Dabdoub, Andre. *History of Bethlehem Families*. 2006. Online. Available: dabdoub.ps

Dabdoub Nasser, Christiane. *Anatreh Quarter: An Urban and Architectural Study of a Bethlehem Quarter*. Bethlehem: Centre for Cultural Heritage Preservation, 2005.

Dalrymple, William. From the Holy Mountain: A Journey in the Shadow of Byzantium. London: Flamingo, 1998

Davidovich, Uri; Porat, Naomi; Gadot, Yuval; Avni, Yoav and Lipschits, Oded. *Archaeological investigations and OSL dating of terraces at Ramat Rahel, Israel*. Journal of Field Archaeology 37, 3, 2012. 192-208

Davidovits, J; High performance Roman cement and concrete, high durable building 2006. Available online: geopolymer.org 2006

———. Reworking of "From ancient concrete to geopolymers, published in Art et Métiers Magazine,180, 8-16, 1993." Available online at geoloymer.org

Davidovits, J and Davidovits, F. *Archaeological Analogues (Roman Cements) and long-term stability of geopolymeric materials*. Proceedings of the Geopolymer Institute

1999. Geopolymers, green chemistry and sustainable development solutions. San Quentin, France: Polymer Institute 1999

Davidovits, J; Davidovits, F and Naso, Alessandro. *The Making of Etruscan Ceramic (Bucchero Nero) in VII-VIII Century B.C.* Proceedings of the Geopolymer Institute 1999. Geopolymers, green chemistry and sustainable development solutions. San Quentin, France: Polymer Institute 1999

De Feo, Giovanni; Angelakis, Andreas N; Antoniou, Georgios P; El-Gohary, Fatma; Haut, Benoit; Passchier, Cees W and Zheng, Xiao Yun. *Historical and Technical Notes on Aqueducts from Prehistoric to Medieval Times.* Water 2013, 5 (4), 1996-202

Deleuze, Gilles, Guattari, Felix. *A Thousand Plateaus.* Tr. Massumi, Brian. Minneapolis: University of Minnesota Press,1987

Derrida, Jacques and Bennington, Geoff. *Circumfessions.* Chicago: University of Chicago Press, 1993

Derrida, Jacques. *Of Grammatology* tr. Spivak, Gayatri Chakravorty. Baltimore: John Hopkins University Press, 1976

Derrida, Jacques. *White Mythology: Metaphor in the Text of Philosophy.* Trans. Bass, Alan. Margins of Philosophy. Brighton: The Harvester Press, 1982

Dothan, Trude and Dothan, Moshe. *People of the Sea: The Search for the Philistine.* London: Macmillan 1992

Edens, Christopher and Bawden, Garth. *History of Tayma͗ and Hejazi Trade During the First Millennium B.C.* Journal of the Economic and Social History of the Orient 32, 1 1989. 48-103

Ehrenreich, Ben. *The Way to the Spring: Life and Death in Palestine.* London: Granta, 2016

Ekonomou, Andrew J. *Byzantine Rome and the Greek Popes: Eastern Influences on Rome and the Papacy from Gregory the Great to Zacharias, A.D. 590-752* Lanham, MD: Lexington, 2007

Ephal, Israel. *The Ancient Arabs: Nomads on the Borders of the Fertile Crescent, 9th-5th Centuries B.C.* Leiden: Brill 1982

Epstein, Mordecai. *The Early History of the Levant Company.* London: Routledge 1908

Eusebius, *Life of Constantine.* Oxford: Oxford University Press, 1999

Fallow, David. *Like father like son: Financial practices in the Shakespeare family.* Studies in Theatre and Performance. 28, 3. 2008. 253-263

Foundation for Middle East Peace, *Report on Israeli Settlements.* Vol 1 Number 5. Washington: FMEP, 1991

Frankopan, Peter. *The Silk Roads: A New History of the World.* London: Bloomsbury 2015

Fridman, Julia. *Riddle of the Ages Solved: Where Did the Philistines Come From?* Ha'aretz. 21 Sept. 2015.

Gibson, Dan. *The History of Concrete and the Nabataeans.* Available online at Nabataea .net.

Gilboa, Ayelet; Cohen-Weinberger, Anat and Goren, Yuval. *Philistine Bichrome Pottery: The View from the Northern Canaanite Coast Notes on Provenience and Symbolic Properties*. Published in Maeir, A M. and de Miroschedji, P. eds. *I Will Speak The Riddles Of Ancient Times. Archaeological and Historical Studies in Honor of Amihai Mazar on the Occasion of his Sixtieth Birthday*. 2. 303-334 Winona Lake, IN: Eisenbrauns, 2006.

Graves, Michael. *Jerome's Hebrew Philology: A Study Based on His Commentary on Jeremiah*. Leiden: Brill 2006

Grierson, P and Travaini, L. *Medieval European Coinage. Vol. 14*. Italy III: South *Italy, Sicily, Sardinia*. Cambridge, UK: Fitzwilliam Museum1998.

Gruenwald, Ithamar: *Reflections on the Nature and Origins of Jewish Mysticism*. In Peter Schäfer, Peter and Dan, Joseph: *Gershom Scholem's Major Trends in Jewish Mysticism 50 Years After: Proceedings of the Sixth International Conference on the History of Jewish Mysticism* Tubingen: Mohr 1993

Eran Halperin & Daniel Bar-Tal1. *The fall of the peace camp in Israel: The influence of Prime Minister Ehud Barak on Israeli public opinion: July 2000 – February 2001* Published in *The Peace Journalism Controversy*. conflict & communication online 6, 2, 2007. Available at cco.regener-online.de

Hart, Ian. *Zionism: The Real Enemy of the Jews. Volume II. David Becomes Goliath*. Atlanta, GA: Clarity Press. 2012.

Heck, Gene W. *Charlemagne, Muhammad, and the Arab roots of Capitalism*. Berlin: Walter de Gruyter, 2006

———. *The Islamic Code of Conduct for War and Peace*. Riyad: King Faisal Center for Research and Islamic Studies, 2006.

———. *Islam, Inc*. Riyad: King Faisal Center for Research and Islamic Studies, 2004.

Hegel, G W F. *Philosophy of Right*. Trans. Knox, T M. Oxford: Oxford University Press. 1968

Herodotus. *The Histories*. Marincola, John and de Sélincourt, Aubrey. London: Penguin, 2003

Hitchcock, L. A., and Maeir, A. M. *A Pirates' Life for Me: The Maritime Culture of the Sea People*. Palestine Exploration Quarterly 148, 4. 2016. 1-20

Hogan, J. F., Saint Cathaldus of Taranto. *Vita e Miracoli di S*. Cataldo. Trans. Bartolomeo Moroni. Available: http://catholicsaints.info.

Holland, Tom. *In the Shadow of the Sword: The Battle for Global Empire and the End of the Ancient World*. London: Little Brown, 2012

Hughes, Matthew. *Terror in Galilee: British-Jewish Collaboration and the Special Night Squads in Palestine during the Arab Revolt, 1938–39*. The Journal of Imperial and Commonwealth History, 43:4, 2015. 590-610,

International Court of Justice. *Legal Consequences of the Construction of a Wall in the Occupied Palestinian Territory. ICJ advisory opinion*, issued 8 July 2004.

Irving, Sarah. *Leila Khaled: Icon of Palestinian Liberation*. London: Pluto Press, 2012

Jerome. *The Principle Works of St Jerome*. Eds. Schaff, Philip and Wace, Henry Trans. Fremantle, WH; Lewis, G and Martley, WG. Available. www.ccel.org

Josephus, *The Works of Josephus*. Trans. Whiston, William. Peabody, Mass.: Hendrickson, 1987.

Justin Martyr, *Dialogue Trypho*, Trans. Brown, Henry. Available. www.ccel.org

Kårtvei, Bård. *Dilemmas of Attachment: Identity and Belonging among Palestinian Christians*. Leiden/Boston, 2014

Kelly, JND. *Jerome: His Life, Writings, and Controversies*. Peabody, Mass. Hendrickson, 1998.

Khalidi, Issam. *One Hundred Years of Football in Palestine*. Amman: Sar al-Shorok, 2013

Kimmerling, Baruch, and Migdal, Joel S. *Palestinian People: A History*. Cambridge, MA: Harvard University Press, 1994.

Kirk, Martha Ann. *Women of the Bible Lands: A Pilgrimage to Compassion and Wisdom*. Collegeville: Liturgical Press, 2004.

Kreutz, Barbara M. *Before the Normans: Southern Italy in the Ninth and Tenth Centuries*. Philadelphia, PA: University of Pennsylvania Press, 1996.

Lapin, Hayim, ed. *Religious and Ethnic Communities in Later Roman Palestine*. Bethesda, MD: CDL Press, 1998.

Lewis, Bernard. *The Middle East: 2000 Years of History from the Rise of Christianity to the Present Day*. London, Weidenfeld & Nicolson, 1995

———. *The Revolt of Islam: When did the conflict with the west begin, and how could it end?* The New Yorker, November, 2001.

———. *The Roots of Muslim Rage: Why so many Muslims deeply resent the West, and why their bitterness will not easily be mollified*. The Atlantic, September 1990.

Luckenbill, Daniel David. *The Annals of Sennacherib*. Chicago: Oriental Institute Publications 2, 1924.

MacKenzie, Duncan. "The Excavation of Beit Shemesh November-December 1912." *PEF* 2016 (London, 2016)

Madden, Robert. *Travels in Turkey, Egypt, Nubia and Palestine: In 1824, 1825, 1826, and 1827*. London: Whittaker, Treacher, 1833.

Mason, B. *Principles of Geochemistry*. New York: John Wiley and Sons,1966.

Matar, Nabil. "An Arab Orthodox Account of the Holy Land c. 1590s." *Through the Eyes of the Beholder: The Holy Land, 1517-1713*. Eds. Judy Hayden and Nabil Matar. Leiden/Boston: Brill, 2012.

Maximus of Tyre. *The Dissertations of Maximus Tyrius*. Trans. T. Taylor. London: Evans, 1804.

Mazza, Roberto. *Jerusalem: From the Ottomans to the British*. London: I.B. Taurus, 2009.

McCarthy, Justin. *The Population of Palestine: Population Statistics of the Late Ottoman Period and the Mandate*. New York: Columbia University Press, 1990.

Minns, Denis, and Paul Parvis. "Justin, Philosopher and Martyr: Apologies." *Oxford Early Christian Texts*. Ed. H. Chadwick. Oxford: Oxford University Press, 2009.

Montefiore, Simon Sebag. *Jerusalem: The Biography*. London: Phoenix, 2011.

Moroni, Bartolomeo, trans. *Vita e Miracoli di S. Cataldo*. Naples: A. Migliaccio, 1779.

Morris, Benny. *The Birth of the Palestinian Refugee Problem, 1947-1949*. Cambridge: Cambridge University Press, 1988.

————. *1948 and After: Israel and the Palestinians*. Oxford: Clarendon Press, 1990.

Muhly, James D. "Sources of Tin and the Beginnings of Bronze Metallurgy." *American Journal of Archaeology* 89.2 (1985): 275-291.

Murphy-O'Connor, Jerome. *The Holy Land: An Oxford Archaeological Guide from Earliest Times to 1700*. 3rd Edition. Oxford: Oxford University Press, 1992.

Naili, Falestin. *The Millenarist Settlement in Artas and its support network in Britain and North America, 1845-1878* Jerusalem Quarterly 45, 2011. 43-56

Nasser, Fayez (Frank). "The Nasser-Jaar Genealogic Family Tree with Historical Timelines." 2007. Online. Available: Palestine-family.net.

Norris, Jacob. "Exporting the Holy Land: Artisans and merchant migrants in Ottoman-era Bethlehem." *Journal of Middle East Migration Studies* 2 (2013): 14-40.

————. *Land of Progress: Palestine in the Age of Colonial Development, 1905-1948*. Oxford: Oxford University Press, 2013.

————. "Repression and Rebellion: Britain's Response to the Arab Revolt in Palestine of 1936-39." *Journal of Imperial and Commonwealth History* 36.1 (2008): 25-45.

————. "Toxic Waters: Ibrahim Hazboun and the Struggle for a Dead Sea Concession, 1913-1948." *Jerusalem Quarterly* 45 (2011): 25-42.

Nigro, L. "Bethlehem in the Bronze and Iron Ages, in the light of recent discoveries by the Palestinian MOTA-DACH." *Vicino Oriente* XIX (2015): 1-24.

O'Connor, Lucy. "In Search of the Late Antique Pilgrim Eulogia of Jerusalem." *PEQ* 148.3 (2016): 219-221.

PENGON (Palestine Environmental NGOs Network). *The Wall in Palestine: Facts, Testimonies, Analysis and Call to Action*. Jerusalem: Palestinian Grassroots Anti-apartheid Wall Campaign, 2003.

Pappé, Ilan. *The Idea of Israel: A History of Power and Knowledge*. London: Verso, 2014.

————. *The Ethnic Cleansing of Palestine*. London: Oneworld Publications, 2006.

Patrich, Joseph. *The Formation of Nabataean Art: Prohibition of a Graven Image Among the Nabataeans*. Jerusalem: Magnes Press, 1990.

Philo of Alexandria. *The Complete Works of Philo*. Peabody, MA: Hendrickson, 1993.

Planhol, X., and Paul Clavel. *An Historical Geography of France*. Trans. Janet Lloyd. Cambridge: Cambridge University Press, 1994.

Plato. *The Republic*. Trans. Tom Griffith. Cambridge: Cambridge University Press, 2000.

Pliny the Elder. *Natural History*. Book XII, Ch. 7.3. Trans. John Bostock and T. H. Riley. London: H. G. Bohn, 1855.

Porat, Roi, Rachel Chachy, and Yakov Kalman. *HERODIUM Final Reports of the 1972–2010 Excavations Directed by Ehud Netzer Volume I Herod's Tomb Precinct.* Jerusalem: Israel Exploration Society The Hebrew University of Jerusalem, 2015.

Prag, Kay. "Bethlehem: A Site Assessment, 169-181." *PEF* 132.2 (2000): 169-181.

Pringle, Denys. *Pilgrimage to Jerusalem and the Holy Land, 1187-1291.* London: Routledge, 2012.

———. *The Churches of the Crusader Kingdom of Jerusalem: A Corpus.* Vol. 1-4. Cambridge: Cambridge University Press, 1993.

Prothero, Rowland. *Psalms in Human Life.* London: Nelson, 1904.

Pummer, Reinhardt. *Early Christian Authors on Samaritans and Samaritanism: Texts, Translations and Commentary.* Heidelberg: Mohr Siebeck, 2002.

———. *The Samaritans: A Profile.* Leiden/Boston: Brill, 1987.

Rajak, Tessa. "Roman Intervention in a Seleucid Siege of Jerusalem?" *Greek Roman and Byzantine Studies* 22 (1981): 65–81. Reprinted: Rajak, *The Jewish Dialogue with Greece and Rome: Studies in Cultural and Social Interaction.* Boston: Brill, 2002.

Rapoport, Meron. *History Erased.* Ha'aretz. July 5th 2007. Available online at http://www.haaretz.com/israel-news/history-erased-1.224899

Rebenich, Stefan. *Jerome.* London: Routledge, 2002.

Riley-Smith, Jonathan. *The Feudal Nobility and the Kingdom of Jerusalem, 1174-1277.* London: Palgrave, 1973.

Roberts, Andrew. *Napoleon the Great.* London: Allen Lane, 2014

Rosenthal-Heginbottom, Renate, ed. *Nabataeans in the Negev.* Haifa: Reuben and Edith Hecht Museum, 2003.

Rubin, Barry. "After Arafat: Succession and Stability in Palestinian Politics." *Middle East Review of International Affairs* 2.1 (1998): 1-7.

Runciman, Steven. *A History of the Crusades.* Vol. 1. Cambridge, 1951.

———. "The Pilgrimages to Palestine before 1095." *The Crusades: The First Hundred Years.* Eds. Kenneth Setton and Marshall Baldwin. Philadelphia, PA: University of Pennsylvania Press, 1955.

Sabbagh, Karl. *Britain in Palestine: The Story of British Rule in Palestine 1917-1948.* London: Skyscraper, 2012.

Sáenz-Badillos, Angel. *A History of the Hebrew Language.* Trans. John Elwolde. Cambridge: Cambridge University Press, 1993.

Saleh, Ruba. "In the Seam Zone: Walaja's Fate Between Jerusalem and Nowhere." *Jerusalem Quarterly.* 49. 2012. 49-67

Sand, Shlomo. *The Invention of the Jewish People.* London: Verso, 2009.

———. *The Invention of the Land of Israel.* London: Verso, 2012.

Schlock, Alexander. *Palestine in Transformation, 1856-1882: Studies in Social, Economic and Political Development.* London: Institute for Palestine Studies, 2006.

Schroeder, Otto. *Keilschrifttexte aus Assur verschiedenen Inhalts.* Leipzig: JC Hinrichs, 1920.

Shahid, Irfan. *Rome and the Arabs*. Washington, DC: Dumbarton Oaks, 1988.

———. *Byzantium and the Semitic Orient Before the Rise of Islam*. London: Variorum, 1988.

———. *Byzantium and the Arabs in the Fourth Century*. Washington, DC: Dumbarton Oaks, 1984.

———. *Byzantium and the Arabs in the Fifth Century*. Washington, DC: Dumbarton Oaks, 1989.

———. *Byzantium and the Arabs in the Sixth Century*. Vol. 1. Washington, DC: Dumbarton Oaks, 1995.

———. *Byzantium and the Arabs in the Sixth Century*. Vol. 2.1. Washington, DC: Dumbarton Oaks, 2002.

———. *Byzantium and the Arabs in the Sixth Century*. Vol. 2.2. Washington, DC: Dumbarton Oaks 2010.

Sharon, Ariel, and David Chanoff. *Warrior*. New York: Simon & Schuster, 1989.

Shlaim, Avi. *Collusion Across the Jordan: King Abdullah, the Zionist Movement, and the Partition of Palestine*. New York: Columbia University Press, 1988.

———. "The Debate About 1948." Reprinted in *The Israel/Palestine Question*. Ed. Ilan Pappé. London: Longman, 1999.

———. *The Iron Wall: Israel and the Arab World*. London: Allen Lane, 2000.

Singer, Amy. *Palestinian Peasants and Ottoman Officials: Rural Administration Around Sixteenth-Century Jerusalem*. Cambridge: Cambridge University Press, 1994.

Singer, Isidore, ed. *The Jewish Encyclopedia*. New York: Funk & Wagnalls, 1906.

Sperber, Daniel. *Roman Palestine, 200-400, the land: Crisis and change in agrarian society as reflected in rabbinic sources*. Ramat Gan: Bar-Illan University Press, 1978.

Spyridon, S. N., ed. *Annals of Palestine, 1821-1841: A Manuscript by the Monk Neophytus of Cyprus*. Jerusalem, 1938. 674-683

Stemberger, Gunter. *Jews and Christians in the Holy Land*. London: T & T Clark, 2000.

Stern, Ephraim. "Pagan Yahwism: The Folk Religion of Ancient Israel." *BAS* 27.03 (2001): 21-28.

Strickert, Frederick M. *Rachel Weeping: Jews, Christians, and Muslims at the Fortress Tomb*. Collegeville, MN: Liturgical Press 2007.

Sullivan, Antony T. "Palestinian Universities in the West Bank and Gaza Strip." *Minerva* 29.3 (1991): 249-268.

Taylor, Jane. *Petra and the Lost Kingdom of the Nabataens*. London: I B Taurus, 2002.

Tebes, Juan Manuel. "Assyrian, Judaeans, Pastoral Groups and the Trade Patterns in the Late Iron Age Negev." *History Compass* 5.2 (2007): 619-631.

Tsatsos, Jean. *Empress Athenais-Eudocia: A Fifth Century Byzantine Empress*. Northampton, MA:Holy Cross Orthodox Press, 1977.

Tupper, Naomi. "Gethsemane Among World's Oldest Olive Trees." Olive Oil Times. Oct 30th, 2012.

Visser, Margaret. *Much Depends on Dinner: The Extraordinary History and Mythology, Allure and Obsessions, Perils and Taboos, of an Ordinary Meal.* New York: Grove Press, 1986.

Weizman, Eyal. *Hollow Land: Israel's Architecture of Occupation.* London: Verso, 2007.

Whitcomb, Donald. "Dimitri Baramki, Discovering Qasr Hisham." Reprinted *This Week in Palestine*, Issue 178, February 2013.

Wilde, William. *Narrative of a voyage to Madeira, Tenerife and along the shores of the Mediterranean, including a visit to Algiers, Egypt, Palestine, Tyre, Rhodes, Telmessus, Cyprus and Greece. With observations on the present state and prospects of Egypt and Palestine, and on the climate, natural history, antiquities, etc., of the countries visited.* Dublin: William Curry, 1840.

Wilkinson, John. *Jerusalem Pilgrims Before the Crusades.* Liverpool: Aris & Phillips, 2002.

———. *Egeria's Travels.* Oxford: Oxford University Press, 1999.

Willi, Andreas. "Cows, houses, hooks: The Graeco-Semitic letter names as a chapter in the history of the alphabet." *Classical Quarterly* 58.2 (2008): 401-423.

# Image Credits

Page x: Map design by Mike Morgenfeld, © Avalon Books.
Page 19: The Ain Sakhri lovers figurine. © British Museum, London.
Page 39: Tell el-Yehudiyeh Ware. © Palestine Archaeological Museum.
Page 53: Solomon's Pools. Wadi el-Biyar aqueduct into the upper pool. © American Colony (Jerusalem).
Page 77: Dürer, Albrecht. St Jerome. Woodcut. 1492. © Kunstmuseum, Basel.
Page 97: Church of the Nativity, Bethlehem. 1910. © Robert Smythe Hichens.
Page 111: Page from Notebook with details of artwork in the Church of the Nativity, Bethlehem. No. 4: St. George. 1946. © C. N. Johns, Mandate Department of Antiquities of Palestine.
Page 127: Workers in Mother-of-Pearl, Bethlehem. © American Colony (Jerusalem).
Page 143: Soldiers (Australian) Church of the Nativity, Bethlehem. © the G. Eric and Edith Matson Photograph Collection.
Page 161: Landscape and trainline between Jerusalem and Jaffa. © Die Gartenlaube Magazine, 1893, Published Ernst Keil, Leipzig.
Page 173: Mitzpe Shalem settlement, and the Ahava factory. © Wiki Air in Israel.
Page 181: Bethlehem wall with graffiti depicting Leila Khaled. © Bluewind (Photographer).
Page 191: Tunnel Road, seen from Gilo settlement looking towards Beit Jala. © David King (Photographer).
Page 203: Nation Estate © Nation Estate—Poster, Paper Print, 100x150cm, Larissa Sansour, 2012.

# Index

LEILA SANSOUR

**Nicholas Blincoe** is a bestselling, award-winning novelist, playwright, and screenwriter. Married to the Bethlehem filmmaker Leila Sansour, he co-produced two feature-length documentaries on the Palestine-Israel conflict, *Jeremy Hardy vs. the Israeli Army* and *Open Bethlehem*. Nicholas has long divided his time between London and Bethlehem.